Bill Barn...
Spring 75

THE HUMAN FACE OF GOD

Books by John A. T. Robinson
Published by The Westminster Press

The Human Face of God
The Difference in Being a Christian Today
Christian Freedom in a Permissive Society
The New Reformation?
Christian Morals Today
Liturgy Coming to Life
Honest to God
On Being the Church in the World

THE HUMAN FACE OF GOD

by
John A. T. Robinson

THE WESTMINSTER PRESS
Philadelphia

© SCM PRESS LTD 1973

Unless stated otherwise, biblical quotations
are from the New English Bible

Published by The Westminster Press
Philadelphia, Pennsylvania ®

PRINTED IN THE UNITED STATES OF AMERICA

Library of Congress Cataloging in Publication Data

Robinson, John Arthur Thomas, Bp., 1919–
The human face of God.

1. Jesus Christ—Person and offices. I. Title.
BT202.R59   232   73–78
ISBN 0–664–20970–X

CONTENTS

PREFACE

For ten years now I have promised myself that my next book would be on Christology, or the person of Christ. Of all the ground broken up in *Honest to God* it was in the area covered by the chapter 'The Man for Others'[1] that I most wanted to dig deeper. As early as *The Honest to God Debate* I said, 'I am deliberately not touching in this essay on questions relating to the person and work of Christ, as I should like, when time allows, to follow these up in a separate book'.[2] But there always seemed to be other aspects of faith or practice that demanded more immediate attention: Christian morals, the church and its mission, its ministry and liturgy, etc. In the preface to *Exploration into God* I wrote: 'My original intention had been to devote the lectures to the subject of Christology. But it became increasingly clear that, before one could develop the theme "God was in Christ"... one must try to explore further the meaning of God.'[3] As the 'death of God' controversy subsided, I ventured to predict in a lecture at Princeton in 1968 that 'Christology will be the next focus of debate'.[4] So when the invitation came from Cambridge University to give the Hulsean Lectures for 1970 I knew I must take the opportunity which they offered. I was also able to develop the material further in the Owen Evans Memorial Lectures in Aberystwyth and the Nelson Lectures at Lancaster University in 1971. For the stimuli these provided and for the many kindnesses that went with them I am most grateful.

[1] John A. T. Robinson, *Honest to God*, SCM Press 1963, pp.64–83.
[2] John A. T. Robinson and David L. Edwards (eds.), *The Honest to God Debate*, SCM Press 1963, p.266.
[3] John A. T. Robinson, *Exploration into God*, SCM Press 1967, p.9.
[4] John A. T. Robinson, 'The Next Frontiers for Theology and the Church', in *Christian Freedom in a Permissive Society*, SCM Press 1970, p.135.

Revising and expanding them for publication has presented me with a number of dilemmas.

The first was one of timing. F. J. A. Hort, who delivered one of the most famous series of Hulsean Lectures just a century earlier, in 1871, spent twenty-one years revising two of them, and then died before they were published.[5] The elegance and polish he achieved makes them to our ears perhaps too smooth, and some of the most striking material is in my judgment to be found in the notes and illustrations that he never incorporated.[6] But even if one had the patience to work at that pace, anything one had to say would in these days be long since out of date. Indeed, as I indicate at the beginning of the first chapter, the scene has already changed quite markedly since I first delivered the lectures. I am not so sure now that in any traditional sense Christology will be the next focus of theological debate. We appear to be in a particularly volatile situation, and this book could already come too late for some and too soon for others.

This reflects the second dilemma for anyone writing on Christology today – the audience one is hoping to address. I was aware of the difference of mood, for instance, at Cambridge and at Lancaster. In the former, at any rate in the Divinity Schools, the questions were still fundamentally Christian questions, and the answers were being tested by these presuppositions. In Lancaster one had the healthy experience of 'playing away'. One sensed that what one was saying should somehow be starting from some-where else. And I am fully prepared to expect that I shall satisfy no one, and share the fate of the 'white liberal' in politics.

Churchmen and professional theologians who know what they are looking for will be ready with their stickers to label my position 'reductionist', 'adoptionist', 'humanist' and the rest. I believe in fact that they will be wrong and that it is none of these things. For I fully share their concerns – yet doubt if these can be matched by the old orthodoxies.

On the other side there will be incredulity that serious men can still spend their time grubbing around the old holes. The question

[5] F. J. A. Hort, *The Way, the Truth, the Life*, Cambridge University Press 1893.
[6] Hort, op. cit., Appendix, pp.169–219.

is not so much, *How* do we speak today of 'the humanity and divinity of Christ',[7] or his historicity, his sinlessness, his uniqueness, his finality, or his 'full, perfect and sufficient sacrifice, oblation and satisfaction for the sins of the whole world'?, as *Why*? Who would think to begin there with the world perhaps a generation from disaster? Genocide rather than parthenogenesis, Auschwitz rather than the empty tomb, look more relevant foci of enquiry for those who would really know 'what is in man'.[8]

As I indicate at the end, I am very sympathetic to this approach, if Christ is ever to become 'the man for all'. Perhaps one should have started all over again, laying aside the traditional questions of Christian theology. But I have not done this, partly no doubt because my own rootage is too deep, but partly because Christians must, as I see it, be prepared to work through and out the other side of the traditional questions, if they are to be liberated to contribute *Christologically* to the secular debate – if they are not, that is, to be hung up with quite inadequate Christ-answers to the great human questions of our day. For if they are so hung up, they will not be able to be more than humanists or theists who insist on 'bringing in Jesus', rather than men who see *all* things, political, aesthetic, scientific and the rest, in Christ and through Christ.

A good deal of what follows will be taken up with clearing the undergrowth, with prolegomena to a contemporary Christology, that is, to discerning the human face of God today. To some, perhaps most, it will seem too bogged down in the past, to others an inadequate and lightweight response to it.

And that raises the third dilemma. At what level should one seek to write? Academic? Popular? Hardback? Paperback? I faced the same question in the preface to *Exploration into God* – which compromised by appearing in Britain as a paperback, in America as a hardback, and probably fell between both stools. For, however much one may have a popular concern, this is a site where if one wants to dig or to build there is a formidable amount of

---

[7] To take the title of one of the best recent books on Christology: John Knox, *The Humanity and Divinity of Christ*, Cambridge University Press, 1967.

[8] See John 2.25.

previous workings to be taken into account. Indeed it was on this
subject that it was said back at the beginning that if all were told,
'I suppose the whole world could not hold the books that would
be written'.[9] The burden of proof lies heavily on anyone offering
another. Yet the Christ has over again to become the contemporary of each succeeding generation. And for the 'Christ today'
the 'Christ yesterday'[10] cannot be written off. I am not a historian
of doctrine, unlike the last Hulsean Lecturer (in 1936) to devote
the series to Christology, J. M. Creed, whose wise and mature
little book *The Divinity of Jesus Christ* carried the sub-title *A Study
in the History of Christian Doctrine since Kant*. I can make no claim
to original work in this area. Yet the deposit of faith from which
we start is so conditioned by the questions by which the answers
have been shaped that if we are genuinely to ask *our* questions we
have to examine and re-examine the assumptions of our predecessors. This is particularly true of the formative, not to say fixative,
period leading up to and from the Definition of the Council of
Chalcedon in AD 451.[11] But still more must any distinctively
Christian assessment constantly be prepared to go freshly, and
deeply, into the New Testament witness, if we are to get beneath
the presuppositions with which over the centuries we have come
to read it.

In both of these areas, therefore, there are sections, especially
in chapters 4 and 5, that I fear may be heavy going for the general
reader. They can, however, be skimmed or skipped. I have trans-
literated and translated any Greek that seemed to be necessary, and
tried to keep the detailed workings to what one of my daughters
calls the 'foot-prints' – which explains the number of them. As in
my other writings, I have unashamedly included a good many
quotations from and references to the mass of books in the field, so
that if anyone does see a door or window opened for him he will
know where to look further. The references are to English translations and to British editions whenever available.

---

[9] John 21.25.   [10] Heb. 13.8.
[11] This is reprinted in many of the books on the subject, but is perhaps most easily
available in H. Bettenson (ed.), *Documents of the Christian Church*, Oxford University Press 1943 (reprinted many times), p.73.

But when all is said, this book makes no attempt to be a balanced survey of the doctrine or a New Testament study for its own sake. There are areas, in a subject that for Christian theology is so central as to touch upon almost every other, that I have deliberately not gone into, if the book was to be kept within bounds. In particular, I have not followed up the implications for the closely connected doctrines of the Trinity and the Atonement.[12] Moreover, there are great writers and thinkers in the field to whose position as a whole I am well aware that I have not been just. I have used, or abused, what they have said for my own purposes. For ultimately, if this book has any value, it will be for its faithfulness not to others' answers but to our questions. It is more concerned to be an honest trail of exploration than a balanced construction carefully compacted against all heresies. Chalcedon has done the latter better than we shall ever do it. But the former constantly beckons and lures us afresh.

Finally, an exploration presupposes that the reality is there to explore. As the Quaker quotation has it that I set at the beginning of *Exploration into God*, 'We do not "seek" the Atlantic, we explore it'. It is the same with Christ, or what Teilhard de Chardin called the Christosphere. We begin, if we are Christians, from within a given, gracious reality. I am not here concerned to prove it or to justify it. I shall not be arguing the case for why I am a Christian, or why anyone else should be. I shall be presupposing it in myself – though not necessarily in others. But I shall not be assuming it dogmatically, uncritically or narrowly. Indeed, my concern – and it is an existential and not just an academic concern – is to a large extent with self-questioning – with *how today* one can truthfully and meaningfully say (in the words of the earliest and shortest Christian confession), 'Jesus is Lord'.[13] I shall be writing as one who *wants* to make that confession. 'For,' as Paul said of himself, to those who have known it 'the love of Christ leaves us no choice.'[14] I cannot step out of my skin. For 'to me life is Christ.'[15] Yet to presuppose is not to prescribe. The centre is

---

[12] I touched very briefly on my approach to the former in *The Honest to God Debate*, pp.254–6, and I refer to the latter again very briefly on pp. 231-3 below.
[13] I Cor. 12.3.   [14] II Cor. 5.14.   [15] Phil. 1.21.

thankfully given – but the edges and the ends are teasingly and liberatingly open.

Finally, I should like to express a very special word of gratitude to my long-suffering secretary, Mrs Stella Haughton, who has struggled with my palimpsistic scripts and 'miles and miles of recorded tape'; and also to my pupil Chip Coakley for meticulous help in the tedious task of checking references and correcting proofs.

ACKNOWLEDGMENT

Sydney Carter's poem 'Anonymous', on pp. 242f., is quoted by permission of Galliard Ltd. © 1970 Sydney Carter.

ONE

OUR MAN

Where we start

'What think ye of Christ?' That is a Christian question expecting a Christian answer. Indeed, until the day before yesterday it was *the* preacher's question, which no one in our culture, it was claimed, could avoid or evade. The person of Christ demanded that one made up one's mind one way or the other. It was a natural title for a book on Christology by a great preacher of the last generation.[1] But as originally put by Jesus himself,[2] it was a Jewish question expecting a Jewish answer: 'What is your opinion about the Messiah?', as the New English Bible correctly renders it. And far from compelling a response, it led to what another great preacher, my colleague at Trinity, Mr. F. A. Simpson, has called Jesus' 'enviable reputation', that 'no one dared ask him another question'. Yet the questions went on – from Caiaphas[3] and Pilate[4] – as they go on today: 'Do you think you're what they say you are?'[5] And still the reply might come back to the contemporary lyric writer, 'Is that your own idea or have others suggested it to you?' – and with it the counter-question, 'Am I a Jew – or indeed a Christian?'

I begin this way to indicate that the state of the 'Christological question' is fluid – more fluid perhaps than it has been since the earliest Christian debates with Judaism. In fact the very word

---

[1] C. E. Raven, *What Think Ye of Christ?*, Macmillan 1916.
[2] According to Matt. 22.41–46.
[3] Mark 14.61 par.
[4] Mark 15.2 par.; John 18.33–5.
[5] Andrew Lloyd Webber and Tim Rice, *Jesus Christ Superstar*.

'Christology' cannot be taken as understood. 'Is that something to do with crystals?' was the response even of one academic's wife. And the level of interest is difficult to gauge. As I write, with 'the box-office Christ' bidding fair to top the bills on stage and screen and charts and with the 'Jesus people' stealing the scene from the hippies, one could be forgiven for considering that no theological question could be hotter. Yet it is hard not to believe that, as after the first Hosannas, the cult-hero will soon be different. Moreover, the Jesus movement is basically fundamentalist and individualistic, and if it makes a contribution to any '-ology' (which is doubtful), it would be to a Jesuology. In fact the backlash from it is more than likely to discredit serious attempts to focus theological reflection and social concern in the meaning of Christ for us today. And the mood of the poem 'Anonymous' by Sydney Carter which I quote at the end[6] could well reflect a growing dissociation of the great human questions not only from 'God' language but from 'Jesus' language. For, underneath, the issues that engage the young do not naturally find their focus in a Jesus figure. What these are, or will be, is probably faithfully reflected in a report on the interests of fifteen-year-old pupils in Sweden:

> Questions which might be termed existential were regarded as important, while questions expressed in traditional Christian terminology were regarded as unimportant. Important were questions about life and death (how life is created, the moral right to take life, life after death), about race and social equality, about war and peace, about suffering and evil, about solitude and companionship, about sex and family, about faith and reason. Unimportant were questions about Jesus and salvation, about church and confession, about prayer and sacrament.[7]

Of course, within the church and around its wide and nostalgic penumbra in modern society the question of Jesus retains its importance and fascination. Yet even here it is not the centre-

[6] See pp. 242f. below.
[7] *Religious Education in Secondary Schools*, Schools Council Working Paper, London 1971, p.46.

point or the starting-point that one might expect. So far from the question 'What think ye of Christ?' being the one about which everyone must have some view, even Christians seem to get by on an extraordinarily residual Christology. And at a more serious theological level, one of the things one discovers is that this is evidently not a layman's subject. Unlike the doctrines of God and the church, the storm-centres of recent debate, where laymen have been well prepared to have a go, Christology has been a preserve of professional ministers and academic theologians. And it is surely a sign that something is wrong somewhere if there is no lay participation, particularly on an issue so central to Christianity as the person and work of Christ.

There have been two main exceptions to this. The first is in the field of the Jesus of history (T. R. Glover's book of that title[8] was, I suppose, the English best-seller of the century in Christology), where laymen have written many of the lives of Jesus and most of the worst. The second is in novels about the Christ-figure, incognito or otherwise, in our world, and some of them have been very good. But between the form of Jesus in Palestine and the shape of Christ in modern life there has been a blank. Or rather, the gap has been filled with the decaying deposit of religious images superimposed on each other through Sunday school, sermons and stained glass. These have purveyed two main pictures: of a Christ who was God in disguise and of Jesus the perfect man. Both have removed him from 'the likes of us' and therefore from much relevance to ordinary folk. Yet these are the pictures which, it is firmly held, Christians are 'meant' to believe; and it is when either expectation is apparently contradicted, especially by newsworthy spokesmen of the church, that popular interest in Christology momentarily flares up.

But the base of this interest is too narrow for a sustained, intelligent lay theology. Shock at the knocking of supposedly orthodox pictures of Christ (which theologians have questioned for ages anyhow), though still played up by the press, has given way, I suspect, to a diffused resignation about the possibility, and

---

[8] T. R. Glover, *The Jesus of History*, Student Christian Movement 1917. It carried a foreword by the Archbishop of Canterbury, Randall Davidson.

indeed the necessity, of saying very much about Jesus at all. A Christian life-style does not seem to many of the younger generation to depend too much on what is made of him historically or theologically. In any case, if Christology is simply about Jesus and who he was, interest in it is increasingly confined to a contracting circle of Christians. I do not detect among the kind of people most concerned for the mystical quest or the political revolution any great patience with the traditional problems of Christology. The questions that have agitated churchmen in the past about the person and work of Christ seem singularly irrelevant to the burning human issues of our day. Why waste time on them?

Briefly, my answer would be twofold.

1. I believe the need to think through intelligently and contemporaneously – in answer to *our* questions – what is to be made of Jesus Christ is as central as it ever has been to a dynamic Christianity. If there is dead wood *here*, then the faith deserves to lose its living impact. So I shall in fact be devoting most of this book – more than I should choose if there were not so much to thin out – to the man Jesus and how we can think of him today.

2. But, secondly, I believe we must insist that Christology is not simply about Jesus. Its questions are of far wider concern even than to Christians. If we are interested in Christology it should be *because* of the burning human issues of our day, not despite them. For if we are concerned about God with a human face, if we are concerned about a world with a human face, then we are concerned, or should be concerned, with Christology. One of the clearest expressions of this that I know is by the Brazilian Christian, Rubem Alves, whose book *A Theology of Human Hope* is passionately concerned for the politics of engagement in the Third World.[9] His recurring question is, 'What does it take to make and to keep life human in the world?', and he writes: 'To speak about

9 Rubem Alves, *A Theology of Human Hope*, Corpus Books, Washington 1969. It is sad that this book, with a foreword by Harvey Cox, has so far found no British publisher and that the American one has gone out of business. As its title indicates, in contrast with Jürgen Moltmann's *Theology of Hope*, SCM Press 1965, it is an attempt to make *human* hope the subject of *theological* reflection in a profoundly Christological manner.

God is to speak about the historical events that made and make man free.'[10] And that is to speak about Christology.[11]

The heart of the mystery

At this point a definition is clearly called for. The word 'Christology' means *logos* about *Christos*, just as 'theology' means *logos* about *theos*. So let us begin by drawing out the similarity and the difference between these two.

Tillich used to define theology as taking rational trouble (*logos*) about a mystery (*theos*). The mystery of *theos* is the mystery of what lies ultimately at the heart of being. In Lao Tzu's famous analogy, it indicates the hole at the centre of the wheel on which all the spokes converge but which must be preserved even though it cannot be filled in or defined. It points to the ultimate, incommunicable, ineffable mystery of reality – the divine Name of Judaism, the Tao that cannot be spoken, the Brahman of Hinduism, the *Ungrund* of Jacob Boehme, the Eternal Thou of Martin Buber. It is that which cannot be expressed yet which cannot be eliminated or translated without remainder into anything else. It is the Beyond in the midst, the Ground of all being.

'Theology' is taking rational trouble about this mystery, trying to speak about it lest by silence, as Augustine said, you appear to be denying it – yet also erecting 'keep off' notices to guard its character as mystery. 'Come no nearer; take off your sandals; the place where you are standing is holy ground.'[12] Keep silence – even from good words. Yet some *logos* is indispensable, if one is to communicate at all – words, pictures, images, maps, 'God-talk', which is what literally theo-logy means.

And recently, as everyone knows, this *logos* has been giving a good deal of trouble. The meaningfulness of 'God' language, the helpfulness of old images, the value of traditional maps, have been under question. The accepted projection of Western theism (corresponding to Mercator's projection in the school atlas) has had

[10] Alves, op. cit., p.99.
[11] For the same connection between Christology and 'humanness' cf. David E. Jenkins, *The Glory of Man*, SCM Press 1967.
[12] Exod. 3.5.

for many a displacement effect, banishing God, like the poles, to the edge of the map, making the mystery peripheral, remote, unreal. The exercise of my book *Exploration into God* was concerned with looking for a projection which might enable us to speak of the 'Thou' at the heart and centre of things without too much distortion or displacement. Yet many would go further and say that 'God' or 'God' language is, at any rate for the time being, dead. '*Theos*', they would say, is not a natural way of speaking about transcendence for Hindus, Buddhists, Taoists or modern secular man – or even for modern religious man represented in the new cult of 'inner space'. If we are to keep the verbal coinage of *theos*, we must be aware of its limited area of convertibility and exchange.

And even more is all this true when we move to Christology.

Christology is *logos* about the mystery of *Christos*. And *Christos* is the mystery of *theos* incarnate, of Immanuel, God with us, the primal mystery as it is earthed, expressed, embodied in the processes of nature and history, reaching its fullest articulation (so far) in the meaning and destiny of man. It is 'the Word' of the Johannine prologue – the divine-human clue to the universe as personal. For the mystery of *Christos* contains by its very nature reference *both* to God *and* to man and the cosmos. As Jung puts it in psychological terms,[13] the Christ-figure corresponds to the archetype of the self, the God-image in us. Hence its numinosity: for it is 'consubstantial' both with God, the ground of our being, and with our own existence. Inescapably, therefore, Christology finds itself viewing the mystery under two aspects, two languages, two 'natures'. It is significant that two recent studies in the subject should have been called *The Humanity of God*[14] and *The Glory of Man*:[15] either way in is equally possible and equally valid. And this is true even for the most radical 'death of God' theologian:

> Christ is the Christian name of the God who is totally for us and with us . . . at the centre of flesh and consciousness. Thus

---

[13] C. G. Jung, *Aion*, Collected Works IX 2, Routledge and Kegan Paul 1959 pp.37–9.
[14] Karl Barth, *The Humanity of God*, Collins 1961.
[15] See note 11 above.

Christ is also the Christian name for the fullness of life and the world, for the total expansion of consciousness and experience. . . . The Christian confesses the Christ who is present wherever life and experience are most active and real.[16]

It is this universality of the Christ figure, standing for the 'ultimate' dimensions of human existence, which explains the perennial power and fascination of 'Gnostic' ways of thinking in this field. For Gnosticism, ancient and modern, is basically the understanding of 'theology *as* self-awareness'.[17] It appeals to the deepest springs of unity between the self and God (figures which for Jung and for many of the mystics, Eastern and Western, almost coalesce). Hence Christology, from the Epistle to the Colossians onwards, was *the* point where Gnostic influence penetrated Christianity and where it fed and burgeoned. For, with all its threat to the once-and-for-all in space and time, Gnosticism spoke of something universal in man, and was indeed the first factor in lifting 'the Christ' out of the narrow confines of Jewish messianism. The origins of Gnosticism are still obscure and will be debated for a long time to come.[18] But it is becoming clearer that, so far from simply being the 'acute Hellenization of Christianity' that Harnack supposed, it has roots deep in Judaism and Jewish Christianity. And the fact that it sprang from a culture 'expecting a Messiah'[19] is far from accidental. For the Christ figure is in some form the matter of its 'ultimate' concern – represented in the myth of the God–Man or Heavenly Man. Yet Judaism alone could not have triggered it off or explained its hold over the imagination of a much wider world. As a recent assessment has recognized,

Behind the 'material' of Gnostic doctrines and traditions,

---

[16] T. J. J. Altizer, *The Descent into Hell*, Lippincott, Philadelphia 1970, p.38.

[17] I adapt this phrase from the title of H. A. Williams' essay 'Theology *and* Self-awareness' in A. R. Vidler (ed.), *Soundings*, Cambridge University Press 1962, pp. 67–101 – which is very different.

[18] See among recent writings in English: H. Jonas, *The Gnostic Religion*, Beacon Press, Boston 1958; R. McL. Wilson, *The Gnostic Problem*, Mowbrays 1958; R. M. Grant, *Gnosticism and Early Christianity*, Columbia University Press, New York [2]1966; and Aloys Grillmeier, *Christ in Christian Tradition*, Mowbrays 1965, pp.94–101, and the bibliography there cited.

[19] Cf. Reinhold Niebuhr, *The Nature and Destiny of Man* II, Nisbet 1943, ch.1.

which were often to longer understood in their original sense, and behind the elaborate myth of redeeming Gnosis, there stood a new experience of God, man and the world which had not emerged in antiquity hitherto. This experience stirred the world of the time more and more, pagans and Christians alike.[20]

If, as Sartre has claimed, 'existentialism is a humanism',[21] Gnosticism was both, and a mysticism and a theosophy as well – or better, perhaps, anthroposophy. For, in Gnosticism, 'man occupies the central position' – yet man's nature derives from the world above.[22] Hence its affinity with, and its challenge to, Christianity – and its continuing force to our day.[23]

Because of this universality sensed by Gnosticism, Christology is no more confined than is theology to one tradition: it is as broad as man and the cosmos. In the words of that great Christian humanist, Nikos Kazantzakis:

> Every man partakes of the divine nature in both his spirit and his flesh. That is why the mystery of Christ is not simply a mystery for a particular creed: it is universal.[24]

Yet the *word* 'Christ' or Messiah from which it takes its name is still more severely conditioned historically and geographically than *theos*. It is Jewish, and late Jewish at that: it does not even occur as a title in the Old Testament, and probably was not in common use until shortly before the time of Jesus. Technically it relates to one religious tradition only, the Judaeo-Christian – and Paul was to

[20] Grillmeier, op. cit., p.95.
[21] J-P. Sartre, *L'existentialisme est un humanisme*, Paris 1946. The English title is *Existentialism and Humanism*, Methuen 1948.
[22] Grillmeier, op. cit., p.96.
[23] E.g. Maurice Nicoll, *The New Man: An Interpretation of Some Parables and Miracles of Christ*, Stuart and Richards 1950; and Preston Harold (a pseudonym – a recurring mark of Gnosticism), *The Shining Stranger*, Dodd Mead, New York 1967 (with an introduction by Gerald Heard), which characteristically claims to reinterpret Jesus in terms of the 'symbol of God subjectified in one's being' (p.391), the 'God-seed' in every man (p.393).
[24] Nikos Kazantzakis, *The Last Temptation*, Cassirer 1961, p.7; cf. pp.354f.: 'Man is a frontier, the place where earth stops and heaven begins. But this frontier never ceases to transport itself and advance towards heaven. With it the commandments of God also transport themselves and advance.'

testify to its foolishness outside that.[25] Indeed the word 'Christ' has taken on currency outside Judaism only by ceasing to be a title and becoming a proper name – as it already is in the earliest New Testament writings, the Pauline Epistles.[26] Ironically, since it was attached to him like a surname, it was an appellation with which, as far as we can judge from the evidence, Jesus himself felt unhappy. Even if he accepted it from others, he immediately went on to speak of himself in terms of the Son of Man.[27] As a historical designation, it was just one of a number used by Judaism to focus its hopes, and not even the controlling one it became for Christianity. As a theological category, to bear the weight and meaning the church saw in Jesus, 'Messiah', with its political and eschatological overtones, was soon superseded by others like 'Lord' and 'Son of God' and 'the Word'. 'Christ' survived as a name, interchangeable for most purposes with 'Jesus'.

Today Messianism is dead, except for the sectarian fringe. Practically no one expresses his deepest convictions or hopes about the universe in these categories – not even in modern Judaism, where it has been said,

> The message of the *one* man, the Messiah, more and more takes second place to the message of the one time, of the days of the Messiah . . . of the kingdom of God.[28]

No one seriously looks for a Messiah who will be the single solution to all the world's problems, spiritually or politically. Yet, oddly enough, the Christ-figure remains in our culture as an indispensable symbol for a phenomenon that constantly recurs in modern literature. If we wish to designate the role of the central character, for instance, in Pasolini's film *Theorem*, or the fat lady in Salinger's novel *Franny and Zooey*, it is almost impossible to do

[25] I Cor. 1.23.
[26] But this significantly is not true of the Fourth Gospel, where it remains a title, except in 1.17 and 17.3, which may reflect subsequent additions by the hand of the author (or another). For by the time of the Johannine Epistles, which I believe to be by the same hand appreciably later, the position is reversed.
[27] Mark 8.29–31; 14.61f.; cf. John 12.34.
[28] Leo Baeck, *Das Wesen des Judentums*, Frankfurt 1932, quoted (without page reference) by Dorothee Sölle, *Christ the Representative*, SCM Press 1967, p.108.

so except in terms of some sort of Christ-figure.[29] It is a way, like the word 'God', of pointing to the mystery, of saying, This is *it*: here is a universal figure who gives significance to all the rest. The concept of the Christ-figure is wider than that of Jesus. Of course, it would never have been so styled had it not been for what Christians have seen in Jesus, and there are usually echoes of this identification to be detected. But it is important to insist that the two are not to be equated.

The fundamental affirmation of Christianity is that in Jesus is to be seen the *clue* to the mystery of *Christos* – of what the divine process is about and the meaning of human existence is. For those who call themselves Christians, this piece of history, continuing into present participation, is decisive for interpreting the Christ. Yet the Christ is bigger than Jesus – and certainly than the thirty-year event to which 'the Incarnation' tends in popular parlance to get narrowed down. Of course it has always been recognized in Christian theology that there are elements in 'the Christ' not included in the historical Jesus – the eternally pre-existent and post-existent Logos, the corporate Christ of his body the church, the Christ who is to come. Yet more than this needs to be said. The early Christian message was that Jesus is the Christ – not that the Christ, or the Logos, the meaning of the mystery of life, is exclusively or exhaustively to be found in Jesus, so that the two are simply interchangeable.

There is an instructive parallel in the doctrine of the church. Until recently the Roman Catholic church was held by its theologians to *be* the 'one, holy, catholic and apostolic church' of the Creed, and *vice versa*. They were conjoined by a simple 'is'. But in the Decree on the Church of Vatican II the relationship was more carefully stated. The holy catholic church, it was said, 'subsists in' the Roman Catholic church.[30] Certainly the Roman Catholic church is the holy catholic church, but the holy catholic church is not simply or exclusively the Roman Catholic church.

[29] The latter has even been made the subject of a Christological thesis, by Mary V. Ferguson, *The Parable of the Fat Lady: Salinger's Syncretic Salvation* (presented to the Department of English, University of Puerto Rico 1971).

[30] *De Ecclesia*, 1964, 1.8. Contrast the encyclical *Mystici Corporis Christi* of Pius XII, 1943.

Similarly, we should be more careful in stating the relationship between Jesus and the Christ than Christians in their period of 'triumphalism' (that is, when Christian theology had it to itself) have cared or needed to be. Fundamentally the Christian claim is that the Christ subsists in Jesus. For those who would call themselves Christians the truth of the mystery is seen through Jesus, focussed in Jesus and is not to be grasped apart from Jesus. He is the clue to the mystery of the Christ in the same way that the Christ is the clue to the mystery of God. Here, for them, is the centre wherever the circumference, the master key whatever other keys fit, the essential clue however complex the final solution.

I am not arguing that this is the case, but stating what I think would be agreed to be the irreducible minimum of the distinctively Christian affirmation. In the words of J. M. Creed,

> Christian theology need not claim that the christian religion contains within itself all truth, or even all truth that is of religious value, but if it loses the conviction that in Christ it has found the deepest truth of God, it has lost itself.[31]

In that quotation 'Christ' is simply assumed (as in common usage) to be identical with 'Jesus as the Christ'. I believe we must discriminate further and say that 'Christian theology need not claim that Jesus contains within him all truth, or even all truth that is of religious value, but if it loses the conviction that in him it has found the deepest truth of the mystery of Christ, it has lost itself'. But to this theme of the finality of Christ we must return at the end. I introduce it here to indicate that if, inevitably, I shall be focussing the discussion of Christology on the person of Jesus, this is the centre rather than the circumference of the subject and of my interest in it.

The frame of reference

Meanwhile we must move on to the second half of the word 'Christology'. The *logos* about *Christos* concerns how we speak

---

[31] J. M. Creed, *The Divinity of Jesus Christ*, Cambridge University Press 1938; Fontana edition 1964 (to which all references are made), p.113.

about, describe, picture and correlate with the rest of our knowledge, this mystery (whether it is seen wholly or partly or not at
all in Jesus). How do we put it on the map of our thought-
world?

We have observed the crisis in theism at this point. How do we
speak about *theos* in a way which does not make it remote or
unreal – and therefore no longer, by definition, *God*, the *ens
realissimum* (or most real thing in the world)? Similarly, there are
ways of speaking about the Christ, or of Jesus as the Christ, which
today are unreal or remote – or merely not ours – so that they
cease to convey the mystery. The same expressions may have the
effect, for instance, for us, as opposed to those for whom they were
first formulated, of throwing doubt on his humanity or rendering
his divinity bizarre. But even if they do not make the gospel story
incredible, they can certainly succeed in muffling it as gospel, as
good news. No resonance is set up. They do not immediately
evoke the response, Yes, that is *it*. As Altizer has said, 'Christ
cannot appear as God at a time in which God is dead'[32] – nor, one
might add, as Messiah, Logos, Son of God, Saviour, apocalyptic
Restorer, or even as the last word about man. I recall a conversation I once had with a make-up girl in a television studio. 'What
do you mean,' she said, 'by saying that Christ is the first man?'
Even when one had disentangled Adam and Christ, it would not
have helped much to say, 'No, we say he is the last man.' Nor if I
had said 'the complete man' or 'the perfect man' would this, I
suspect, have got us much further. For people today, I believe, are
as 'blocked' by this model man as they are by God or the church. I
was once invited to speak to a large conference of high-school
children, under the title, 'Does God get in the way?' – and the
question would not have been framed like that unless he did. And
one can equally hear the question, 'Does Christ get in the way?'

[32] T. J. J. Altizer and W. Hamilton, *Radical Theology and the Death of God*,
Penguin Books 1968, p.138. Altizer has subsequently said, *The Descent into Hell*,
p.34: 'One of the bitterest truths which we have been forced to learn is that . . . no
longer is it possible to believe that a sacred, a revealed, or a biblical language
stands autonomously on its own ground, being in no need of a human or a historical expression. Therefore we also no longer believe that any language whatso-
ever, including the symbolic language of faith, can contain any genuine meaning
which cannot be given a human expression.'

To many, to keep harping on Jesus seems like getting stuck in a groove. Can this man really have had everything? Does he not impose a ceiling on the human potential? Can he seriously serve as a focus for 'the next development in man'[33] – or even for present humanity? There is a hang-up here we cannot ignore. When indeed I put the question 'Does Christ get in the way?' to a very varied group of Christians and non-Christians, one woman, a Roman Catholic, replied, 'No, but he gets in my daughter's way'; and she went on (in her native Californian): 'How can I speak of what gets me without turning them off?' To 'them' there appear other, less restrictive ways of exploring what it means fully to be human. Dragging in Jesus is embarrassing. It empties the hotel lounge as rapidly even as Dennis Potter's very earthy television play *Son of Man*, which I had the interesting experience of seeing repeated in these circumstances.

Dietrich Bonhoeffer spoke for many when he wrote from prison now more than a quarter of a century ago: 'What is bothering me incessantly is the question . . . who Christ really is, for us today.'[34] Yet even to ask this question is to invite two closely related objections which it will be well to clear out of the way at the beginning.

First, it may appear to spring from a desire to accommodate him, to make him 'our man' in the sense of a Christ we can find acceptable and accessible. But a Christ who is really a Christ (like a God who is really a God) is never going to be at home in this world. We cannot domesticate him without destroying him. As Schweitzer concluded:

> The historical Jesus will be to our time a stranger and an enigma. . . He does not stay; He passes by our time and returns to His own,[35]

though Jeremias rightly adds:

[33] L. L. Whyte, *The Next Development in Man*, Cresset Press 1944.
[34] Dietrich Bonhoeffer, *Letters and Papers from Prison*, The Enlarged Edition, ed. Eberhard Bethge, SCM Press 1971 (from which all quotations are taken), p.279.
[35] Albert Schweitzer, *The Quest of the Historical Jesus*, A. and C. Black 1910, p.397.

Jesus did not stay in his own time, but he also passed beyond his own time. He did not remain [as Schweitzer depicted him] the rabbi of Nazareth, the prophet of Late Judaism.[36]

No age, not even his own, can accommodate him to itself.

But that is not what we are wanting to do. To seek a Christology for our day is not to look for one that is popular or palatable (a Christianity truly centred on the cross can never be that). The aim of a contemporary Christology is not to sweeten the pill but to hinder hindrances, to remove obstacles in order that the real 'offence', of Christ and him crucified, can be exposed rather than overlaid. This cannot be stressed too much, as I find that, whatever one says, people suppose that the motive of much modern theology is to reduce and to accommodate. It is nothing of the sort. It is not to reduce but to locate: to enable 'the beyond', in Bonhoeffer's phrase, to be met '*in the midst*', where people are, to allow it to come as the answer to *their* questions.

But, secondly, it is said, to see Christ as 'our man' is merely to subjectivize him, so that he becomes (in Tyrrell's famous image) the reflection of our own faces in the bottom of a well.[37] Schweitzer's survey of nineteenth-century portraits serves as a monument to this persistent peril. I was recently asked to write a new introduction to one that he did not mention – Sir John Seeley's *Ecce Homo*.[38] It struck one reading it today as incurably Victorian. Indeed even a contemporary (and sympathetic) pamphleteer[39] recognized that its success stemmed largely from the psychological needs it met in middle-class nineteenth-century England: 'Much of the *popularity* of this book is, I think, owing to the fact that it

[36] J. Jeremias, *The Problem of the Historical Jesus*, Fortress Press, Philadelphia 1964, p.19; included in H. K. McArthur (ed.), *In Search of the Historical Jesus*, SPCK 1970, p.128.

[37] G. Tyrrell, *Christianity at the Crossroads*, Longmans 1909, p.44: 'The Christ he [Harnack] sees looking back through nineteen centuries of Catholic darkness is only the reflection of a Liberal Protestant face, seen at the bottom of a deep well.'

[38] Sir John Seeley, *Ecce Homo*, London 1865; Everyman Library, revised ed. 1970 (from which all quotations are taken). I have used here some material from my Introduction, pp.v–ix.

[39] Anon., *The Credentials of Conscience: A Few Reasons for the Popularity of 'Ecce Homo'*, Longmans, Green 1868. The author is recorded in the British Museum catalogue as Marie Sibree.

meets in a most acceptable manner some of the special wants and tendencies of our day.'[40]

This, I think, is a percipient recognition. The real achievement of the book lay in the fact that it enabled Jesus to come as the answer to some of the great inarticulate human questions of the 1860s. I recognize the same process at work in the reception of *Honest to God* in the 1960s, and the reviews, both abusive and effusive, have a strange familiarity. The danger, of course, is that each generation simply sees its own Christ. This cannot indeed be totally avoided, or Jesus would not be the Christ for us, our man. The safeguard lies in the rigour of our historical criticism, so that we do not 'modernize Jesus'[41] at the cost of taking him out of his age. From this test the author of *Ecce Homo*, later Professor of Modern History at Cambridge, does not emerge too well ('one of the least "scientific" books ever written on a historical subject' was how a holder of the same chair, G. M. Trevelyan, later described it).[42] There is a real difference between making Christ in our own image and allowing the best, critically controlled scholarly picture to speak to our century.

The demand that the Christ be 'our man' is asking not that there be a mere reflection (that does not help us at all) but that there be what Tillich called a correlation[43] – so that the answers can be seen to come as the answers to our questions, the fulfilment of our needs, hopes and expectations – however much they may *also* judge them, as Jesus judged the Messianic hopes of first-century Judaism. We remember that Jesus is recorded as deliberately inviting the questions: 'Who do men say I am?',[44] 'Who do you say I am?',[45] 'What is your opinion about the Messiah?'[46] This is not theology by Gallup poll. It is not because the answers in themselves are significant contributions – even Peter's reply,

---

[40] These the writer discerned as the demand for Utility, the cry for Authority, the claim for Rationality, the desire for Unity and the demand for Morality. It would be an interesting exercise to compare and contrast these with the 'wants and tendencies' of our own day.

[41] Cf. H. J. Cadbury, *The Peril of Modernizing Jesus*, SPCK 1962.

[42] G. M. Trevelyan, *An Autobiography and Other Essays*, Longmans 1949, p.17.

[43] Paul Tillich, *Systematic Theology* I, Nisbet 1953, pp.67–73. The pagination in the original American edition is always slightly different.

[44] Mark 8.27.   [45] Mark 8.29.   [46] Matt. 22.42.

according to our earliest record, gets pretty short shrift[47] – but because no answer that did not come from the inside, that was merely given from above or without, was worth anything. For the question 'Who is Christ for us today?' (or at any time) is the corollary of another question Bonhoeffer asked himself, 'Who am I?'[48] The mystery of the Christ is primarily a matter of *recognition* – not, Can you believe this individual to be the Son of God?, but, Can you see the truth of your humanity given its definition and vindication in him?

'The Messiah' must correspond to certain expectations, or it is a meaningless category. I once saw scribbled on a church notice-board proclaiming 'Christ is the answer', 'Yes, but what is the question?' What are the questions to which he would be *that* answer today? Leonard Hodgson formulated the question with regard to the biblical writers: 'What must the truth have been and be if men who thought and spoke as they did put it like that?'[49] The complementary question is: 'What must we say for it to be what they meant when they said things like that of Christ?', or, 'What must we say if the same truth is to come as the answer to our questions?' And we must recognize that the answers may have to be different for the truth to be the same. For Jesus Christ to be 'the same yesterday, today and for ever'[50] he has to be a contemporary of every generation, and therefore different for the men of every generation. He must be *their* Christ.

But the critical question is, What is the relation of the 'Christ for us today' to the Christ for other ages – whether of the first century or the fifth or the fifteenth or the nineteenth? The test is still that formulated in I John 4.1–3 and II John 7 – that of 'confessing' Jesus Christ as come and coming in the flesh. But the word used, *homologein*, implies much more than parrot-like repetition. As its root indicates (and that of its Latin equivalent *con-fiteor*), it means speaking in concurrence or congruity. And this is not the same as *autologein*, giving the identical answer. To

[47] Mark 8.30–33, where the word *epitimao*, rebuke, occurs three times in four verses. Contrast Matt. 16.17.
[48] Bonhoeffer, op. cit., p.347.
[49] Leonard Hodgson, *For Faith and Freedom* II, SCM Press ²1968, pp.15f.
[50] Heb. 13.8.

mean what the New Testament writers or the Fathers *intended* to say of Jesus' humanity or divinity we may well have to say different things.[51] And we should constantly be aware of the danger of closing the gap too easily. As a radical American writer has put it:

> One mistake the liberal tradition has made has been to wish too fervently that the biblical writers might say exactly what needs to be said today. It is the same error in reverse of the traditionalists who wish too fervently that the biblical message might be the exact word we ought to pronounce now. It is the hermeneutical mistake of expecting simple correspondence between the biblical good news and good news for today.[52]

Yet our *first* preoccupation cannot be to ask, Are we saying the same thing? It must be, Are we saying our own thing? Are we really attending to *our* authentic questions? If not, the answers may have orthodoxy but they will not have integrity. They will be empty shells, echoing the 'fear, deep in all of us' of which Sebastian Moore has spoken, 'that there *may* be nothing human inside the great dogmatic assertion of the divinity of Christ'.[53] It is only after testing for reality that it is worth going on to test whether our answers are idiosyncratic or even idiotic. This is a different point of departure from that of beginning with the biblical text or doctrinal formulation and asking how we may interpret it in our own categories. That, of course, is a perfectly legitimate and necessary approach – as every good sermon shows. But there is need also to start from our, twentieth-century questions. This is a more perilous approach to the truth as it is in Jesus, and there is no guarantee in advance of congruence or

[51] Cf. M. F. Wiles, *The Making of Christian Doctrine*, Cambridge University Press 1967, p.181: 'I believe that we are more likely to prove loyal to the past, in the important sense of the word "loyal", if we think not so much in terms of the translation of old formulae into new sets of words as in terms of the continuation of the same task of interpreting the Church's Scriptures, her worship and her experience of salvation.'
[52] N. Q. Hamilton, *Jesus for a No-God World*, Westminster Press, Philadelphia 1969, p.292.
[53] Sebastian Moore, 'The Search for the Beginning', in: S. W. Sykes and J. P. Clayton (eds.), *Christ, Faith and History: Cambridge Studies in Christology*, Cambridge University Press 1972, p.89.

correspondence – let alone simple identity. And there is every danger that when we do come to the texts or the formulae we shall merely read them through our own spectacles or see our own reflections in them.

Yet I refuse to believe that this approach is impossible or hopeless. As I shall be insisting later, it is the function of scientific and historical criticism to deliver us from mere subjectivism and help us check our vision. That does not mean that we can ever be wholly objective, let alone that our science or history can be 'without presuppositions'. Far from it. The more we are dealing with personal truth, the more the existential factor is involved. What we see in Jesus will be relevant according as it comes as some sort of answer to our questions. And this will profoundly affect what it is even possible for us to see. It will be conditioned truth – not for all time or all people. Yet it is *truth* precisely as it is not just created or projected by us, but heard and followed in obedience.

If Jesus Christ is to become our man, as Kierkegaard would have put it, in 'subjectivity' rather than subjectivism,[54] then considerable freedom, and corresponding risk, is required. If there is to be *both* consonance *and* resonance – and each without the other produces in doctrine what has been called a 'tinkling cymbal – it may be necessary to sit light to many of the answers given in the course of Christian history, many of the categories even in the New Testament and on the lips of Jesus himself. For Christian faith is the capacity to 'see' in Jesus the clue and the key to all reality: it is not to 'see', in the sense of understand the point of, concepts (such as messiahship or pre-existence or the 'impersonal humanity' of Christ) which may now mean nothing, whatever they may have said to another age or consciousness. For, as John A. Phillips has put it, 'Faith and discipleship do not and cannot require one to become less than a man of one's own time'.[55] The categories that are meaningful constantly change. We shall have to return to consider what are hopeless and what

[54] Cf. his *Concluding Unscientific Postscript*, Oxford University Press 1941, particularly the chapter headed 'Truth is Subjectivity', pp.169–224.

[55] John A. Phillips, 'Radical Christology: Jesus and the Death of God', *Cross Currents* XIX, 1969, p.292.

are hopeful today, what are ways in and what are merely road-blocks. But let us acknowledge the fact and the speed of change. As Phillips says again in the same article, 'Christology has always been the most dynamic area of Christian thought, and it is in this area that the most profound changes have occurred since the first century'.[56] This was recognized, too, by Creed:

> To each age its own problems. . . . Now we find ourselves round a headland with a new prospect ahead of us. To affirm the doctrine of Christ's divinity today cannot mean the same to us that it did to Coleridge or to Liddon or to Sir John Seeley or to Bishop Gore.[57]

Yet there has probably been a greater change in the third of a century since those words were spoken than in the entire previous century – and the rate of acceleration is increasing.

But, above all, it is a matter of understanding what *sort* of change has occurred.

Four fundamental shifts

It is not simply that the questions have altered once again, so that the old answers seem strangely unreal. I believe something more fundamental has happened. It is that the whole framework – the *logos* about *Christos* by which response to the mystery *in whatever terms* has been given its objectivity, its place in the scheme of things, its relatedness to what is real and true – has been shaken, if not shattered. The result is that the best belief now appears to be reduced, tentative, private and subjective. The conviction existentially may remain as compelling as ever, but with nothing solid and agreed to give it anchorage it is difficult to have the confidence of the Victorians (and even Tennyson found himself writing of Christ: 'Thou seemest human and divine').[58] Traditionally, language about the mystery of Christ has been attached to, secured within, a certain frame, which has afforded it relatedness and objectivity. But the spider's web of truth, as it were, has

---

[56] Phillips, op. cit., p.294.   [57] Creed, op. cit., pp.99, 104.
[58] *In Memoriam*, Prologue, stanza 4.

become loosened and detached. Though the mystery may still be there at the centre, the *logos* which has given it a coordinated place within reality as a whole has been fatally weakened. And this has been happening, over a period, at four critical points.

(1.) The first and perhaps the most fundamental of these is *myth.* For men today, myth is equated with *un*reality. The mythical is the fictional. But in fact myth relates to what is deepest in human experience, to something much more primal and archetypal and potent than the intellect. Psychologically and sociologically myth has been the binding force holding individuals and societies together. The loosening of it has had the disintegrative effect on our culture of the kind that Shakespeare envisaged following the loss of belief in 'degree'.[59] Until relatively recently myth was taken quite realistically (which is *not* to say literally) as the framework of all life. Within the Christian scheme of things (to which Milton is a classic witness), Adam's fall caused things to happen: it explained why labour was painful for women and work oppressive for men. The myths of the beginning and end described what set things in motion (as objectively as 'the big bang' today) and what will bring them to an end. The Incarnation – God's sending his Son from heaven to redeem man – was seen as having changed the human condition by a divine transaction as real as any event in the physical order. And this has supplied the self-authenticating, 'revealed' framework of all Christian liturgies, hymns and popular theology (as reflected in the church's year). To be a Christian has meant believing in a series of events of salvation history, all stated as if they were objectively true in the same kind of way. Thus the Apostles' Creed says of God's only Son, our Lord, Jesus Christ, that he was:

conceived by the Holy Ghost,
born of the Virgin Mary,
suffered under Pontius Pilate,
was crucified, dead, and buried;
he descended into hell;
he rose again from the dead,
he ascended into heaven,

[59] *Troilus and Cressida,* I, iii, 74–137.

and sitteth on the right hand of God the Father Almighty;
from thence he shall come to judge the quick and the dead.

All these statements are presented quite realistically as parallel descriptions of what happened, and no need was felt to distinguish what is to be taken as history, what as myth, and what as a mixture of both.

Yet today myth cannot be taken as a description of how things did, do or will happen. For us it is an expression of significance, not an explanation for anything.[60] By now we all recognize this of the Fall – and it is none the less profoundly true for that. Bultmann has forced the same questions of the Christ who 'reversed' the Fall.[61] To say that the Fall is a way of giving theological expression to our existential condition rather than a once-and-for-all 'event' appears at first sight to be a sell-out to subjectivism, and one can still sympathize with the nineteenth-century conservatives who believed they could preserve the truth of Christianity only by retaining the Fall as an objective occurrence. One can sympathize even more with those who feel that to 'demythologize' Christ is to reduce him. And there is of course a historicity to Jesus, which the myth *interprets*, that does not simply make him parallel with Adam. Yet it is impossible to go on doing theology or using the language of myth as though nothing had happened. The self-authenticating objectivity of certain supernatural events or acts of God which for our fathers explained the course of nature and history has been irrecoverably shattered.[62] Myth has become part of the web rather than one of the fixed points to which the web was fastened. In fact, merely to try to think of it as describing an order of events by which physical phenomena are in any way 'caused' is today psychologically impossible.

2. Much the same is true, secondly, of *metaphysics.* What myth is to the imagination, metaphysics is to the intellect. It is the way of

[60] Cf. Gordon D. Kaufman, *Systematic Theology: A Historicist Perspective*, Scribner, New York 1968, p.203.
[61] See especially his 'New Testament and Mythology', in: H. W. Bartsch (ed.), *Kerygma and Myth*, SPCK 1952, pp.1–44, and the succeeding debate in that and subsequent volumes.
[62] Cf. A. O. Dyson, *Who is Jesus Christ?*, SCM Press 1969, ch.1.

trying to state what is most real, most true, ultimate. One cannot, I believe, get away from metaphysics any more than from myth.[63] It is concerned with how things are. Yet the meaningfulness of metaphysical statements in our day is equally problematic. Above all, confidence has gone in the type of supranaturalistic ontology to which Christian theology in its classical presentations has been attached. According to this, what is 'really real' (*to on*) is located in another realm, above, beyond or behind phenomena (the latter belonging to the world of appearance rather than reality). To affirm Christ's divinity or finality has meant seeing him from all eternity as part of that realm of being – however much he might also enter, temporarily, the world of becoming. Hence the importance of his pre-existence, of his uncreated reality as the second person of the Trinity, and his eternal generation as the Son of God. Essentially, in his being or *ousia*, he belongs to what Tillich called, in this way of thinking, the ' "superworld" of divine objects'.[64] And to say that he is alive now has meant affirming that he is *there*, for ever, where time cannot touch him.

Today this language has almost the opposite effect. A child of a friend of mine was heard saying in his prayers, 'I'm sorry for you, God, up there while I am in the real world down here'. For we most naturally locate reality, not in another realm, but as the profoundest truth of this one. God and God-language (theology) thus seem to belong to 'another world' – remote and shadowy. So far from making things more real, pre-existence is a most un-natural way of stating our conviction about the cosmic significance of Christ in an evolutionary universe. No one could have stressed the latter more powerfully than Teilhard de Chardin, but it is significant that 'pre-existence' does not even feature in the index of the major study of his Christology.[65] Equally, people find considerable difficulty today even in understanding what has been indicated by Christ's post-existence. In what sense – or realm – is Christ living now? The old confidence that he belongs securely to the invisible order 'in the power of an endless life' has yielded to

[63] Cf. P. R. Baelz, *Christian Theology and Metaphysics*, Epworth Press 1968.
[64] Paul Tillich, *Systematic Theology* II, Nisbet 1957, p.8.
[65] C. F. Mooney, *Teilhard de Chardin and the Mystery of Christ*, Collins 1966.

the vague affirmation that in spirit he is somewhere around or that he lives on in his followers. However sweeping his dismissals, Neill Hamilton no doubt speaks for many when he writes:

> There is no way for the convictional structure in which we are working now to *conceive* of a way or a place for Jesus to continue to live literally after having died.

He goes on at once to say:

> This does not mean that Jesus is not alive. Indeed, Jesus is very much alive for the person who believes that he is the last word on the destiny of man. But he is alive in the only way this secular view of reality permits persons of past history to be alive – in the lively remembrance of history.[66]

I have quoted this, not because I believe his answer to be satisfactory, but because it shows vividly how the bottom can drop out of belief merely because of a change in the framework or 'convictional structure'.

We cannot, as I said, dispense with metaphysics.[67] The mystery of *Christos* is the clue to the profoundest reality of how things are or it is nothing. But the *logos* is lacking with which to give it anchorage in what for our generation lies 'beyond the physical' – and it is a generation which is very far from saying that there is nothing beyond the physical. This lack has had a profound effect on the objective statement of Christian truth. For the ontic beam to which the web of classical theology has been fastened appears to have got the worm. It is hardly surprising that in the newer constructions men miss 'the grand certainties'.

3. Thirdly, and closely connected with the last, is the demise of the language of the *absolute*. The classic way of expressing ultimate

---

[66] N. Q. Hamilton, op. cit., p.182.
[67] I would therefore want to dissociate myself from the kind of view propounded by Robert Kysar in his 'Christology without Jesusolatry', *The Christian Century*, 2 September 1970, that the Christ figure is simply 'a sort of ethical model which functions to incite Christian values in men' and 'must not be assigned transcendent status or mysterious presence'. But his protest is valid against the use of Christology as a *substitute* for the loss of a transcendent God. Cf. T. W. Ogletree, *The 'Death of God' Controversy*, SCM Press 1966, p.36.

reality has been to use the vocabulary of uniqueness, of finality, of once-and-for-allness, of timeless perfection, of difference not merely of degree but of kind. Truth has been seen as unitary, rising like a Gothic arch and meeting in the One who is the answer to all possible questions. And it is not difficult to see how important a part this has played in Christian theology. Jesus Christ has been presented as *the* Son of God and Son of Man, the Alpha and Omega, in whom all lines meet, unique, perfect and final.

Yet we live in a world of what Paul van Buren has called 'the dissolution of the absolute'.[68] The monistic model has lost its power over our thinking, whether about space or time. Ours is a relativistic, pluralistic world in which we are compelled to be more modest about our claims.

> The question may fairly be asked whether theology and faith can survive this shift of focus: whether Christianity, for example, which has for so long proclaimed a monistic view of the universe, a single and unique point of reference as the only valid one, with a single and unique revelation of this truth, can learn to live in a world from which the Absolute has been dissolved.[69]

Supremely is this a question for Christology, which is where the crunch really comes. To go on saying the same thing in the old terms is to be in danger of rendering Christ invulnerable but meaningless – unquestionably the answer because he corresponds to no questions. Above all, any kind of exclusive uniqueness or finality in relation to other truth or other religions strikes men as incredible. Christ may be *a* centre, or even *the* centre for me, but to say that he is *the* centre absolutely seems as naïve today as thinking of Delphi as the navel of the earth. For, in the words of the prospectus of one of the most successful centres of spiritual exploration in America,[70] we are 'committed to diversity'. The model for our age is not so much the Gothic arch as the mobile.

[68] Paul van Buren, 'The Dissolution of the Absolute', *Theological Explorations*, SCM Press 1968, pp.29–42.
[69] Van Buren, op. cit., p.42.   [70] The Esalen Institute.

As changeless Absolute, the Christ cannot come as good news. Yet to present Christ as other than absolute, as different in degree but not kind, as not final or unique or perfect in the old sense, inevitably appears reductionist. *How*, today, supposing we want to, do we say that for us there is 'one Lord, Jesus Christ'[71] in whom 'all things are held together'?[72] If this is still the heart of the mystery, what is now the *logos* for expressing it?

There is an understandable tendency to paralysis at this point. Christians feel that the centre can hold only if they cling securely to the things that cannot be shaken. Yet in fact this static model is largely the imposition of an alien culture. The Bible is much more at home with the God who moves on, who confronts men in and requires their obedience through the unrecurring particularities of the here and now. He is characteristically to be found on the shifting frontiers of social change, in the relativities of events rather than in a timeless absolute above or beyond it all.

Again, it is a question not of reduction but of re-locating 'the beyond' '*in the midst*'. This does not mean in any way denying 'the beyond', the dimension of transcendence, of unconditionality. But it does mean starting from where it has some chance of being heard and encountered by 'pluralistic man'. It means beginning from the many, from the 'thusness' of things (to use the Buddhist term), and *in* their surd-like contingency (without seeking to impose any premature uniformity) responding to what *you* must take seriously without reserve.

In this process the claims of honesty and integrity, of justice and freedom, of solidarity with the suffering body of humanity, may be every bit as searching and as 'absolute' as ever they were. One may not see how it all adds up, one may not discern any final truths or laws which never shall be broken, nor 'plumb lines hanging from a fixed metaphysical ceiling'.[73] But in the particular, concrete situation one knows that one has to be there, that there are sticking-points where one may not sell out, that fidelity to the quality of relationship is the deepest test, that *persons matter* more than any precepts or sabbaths. In such a style of life the sensitivity,

---

[71] I Cor. 8.6.   [72] Col. 1.17.
[73] Colin W. Williams, *What in the World?*, Epworth Press 1965, p.57.

the openness is all. One cannot hope to complete the arch, yet these multiple broken columns are shafts of transcendence thrusting beyond themselves, meeting-points of secular mysticism, where the unconditional is made flesh, and afterwards one may say, like Jacob, 'The Lord is in this place, and I did not know it'.[74] The mobile may be equally good for catching the moment of truth – though it does not allow one to fix it or freeze it.

In this cultural milieu the place of theology, that is of Christians doing their thinking, is in the servants' quarters, not, as in the period of Christendom, on the throne. Its style will be more modest, more broken. And yet at its centre will be a figure, as the author of the Hebrews insists he always is, who 'fits our condition'[75] and whom in all his humiliation Christians still do right to call 'Master' and 'Lord'.[76]

Christianity, said Whitehead, is a religion 'seeking a metaphysic'.[77] It does not presuppose a metaphysic. The dissolution of the absolute is not the crumbling of its foundations. It can start from what a black American writing on the mood of modern literature calls 'the broken center'.[78] Yet it also *makes* for wholeness, reconciliation, in the faith (though not the sight) that ultimately all things *do* cohere and hold together in Christ. It cannot give up its claim to make one *out of* the many. Yet much depends on how that is understood. And the difference has not, I think, been put better than by William Temple in a prophetic pamphlet published just before he died. Previously, he wrote:

> Theologians could undertake the task of showing that Christianity enables us to 'make sense' of the world with the meaning 'show that it *is* sense'. . . . I was still talking like that when Hitler became Chancellor of the German Reich. All that seems remote today. We must still claim that Christianity enables us to 'make sense' of the world, not meaning that we can show that it *is* sense, but with a more literal and radical

---

✓ [74] Gen. 28.16.   [75] Heb. 7.26.   [76] John 13.13.
[77] A. N. Whitehead, *Religion in the Making*, Cambridge University Press 1926, p.50. He sets it in contrast to Buddhism as 'a metaphysic generating a religion'.
[78] Nathan A. Scott, *The Broken Center: Studies in the Theological Horizon of Modern Literature*, Yale University Press, New Haven 1966.

meaning of making into sense what, till it is transformed, is largely nonsense.[79]

The *logos* for such a Christology remains a task for our generation. The fact that the codes and dogmas shaped by the quests and questions of a monistic age seem uninviting should neither surprise nor deter. All may look lost when the categories of what Schleiermacher called 'absolute ideality' are apparently surrendered. Yet I believe that a gospel – and a theology – is capable of being reborn out of 'the end of the stable state',[80] and that it will centre in the liberating discovery, vindicated in the witness of many a contemporary Christian and secular saint, that uncompromising stands are not tied to unchanging standards, that wholeness is a function not of uniformity but of integrity, that the dissolution of the absolute is not the end – but a condition of resurrection.

4. But there is yet a fourth fixed point to which the web of Christian truth has hitherto been secured, and this is *history*. One of the most fundamental and distinctive claims of the Christian preaching is that the Incarnation of God in Christ (as opposed, for instance, to the *avatars* or incarnations of Hinduism) was rooted in history. 'That which was from the beginning' not only has its objectivity in the unshakable world of metaphysics: it is something 'which we have seen with our eyes, which we have looked upon and touched with our hands'.[81] Whatever the element of myth in the gospel story, there has been the surety of sheer happenedness 'under Pontius Pilate'. As Creed pointed out, it became customary in the nineteenth century to fall back from talking of Christianity as 'the Revealed Religion', when that certainty became suspect, to speaking of it as 'the Historic Faith'.[82] And traditional Christology has had a large and fairly crude stake in historicity. From the start much of the classical construction – particularly the doctrine of the two natures – has depended on being able to regard even

[79] William Temple, *What Christians Stand for in the Secular World*, SCM Press 1944, pp.5f.
[80] For further development of this I would refer to my book, *The Difference in being a Christian Today*, Collins 1972.
[81] I John 1.1–3.   [82] Creed, op. cit., p.106.

the Fourth Gospel as preserving the *ipsissima verba* of Jesus – a belief that could still be held by Bishop Westcott. And the resurrection, equated with the empty tomb as brute historical fact, has been seen as the hinge of the Christian faith.

Again, we cannot escape the question of historicity any more than that of metaphysics. Yet the change that has come over the scene is so familiar as not to need describing. There is no absolute certainty that Jesus did or said any one of the things attributed to him. Even his very existence is a matter of probability, however high; and almost everything we can know about him is to be derived from documents designed to present the Christ of the church's faith, not 'how it actually happened'. Of all the four challenges I have mentioned, this is the least new. But its popular impact has greatly increased. The question has got through to the man in the street, and particularly to the younger generation: Can we know *anything* of what the Jesus of history was really like, and *does it matter anyhow*? Once again, the confident objectivity, still expected in the 'reassuring' sermon, has been whittled away. The most familiar landmark of all, locating Jesus securely as part of our world, appears to have been submerged. It is not surprising that Christology is adrift.

Having said this, it is only right, at the risk of a little digression, to say that I believe that this particular change, however funda-mental, can be greatly exaggerated. The time is over-ripe for counter-attack against some of the absurdities that are allowed to pass for critical conclusions. We are dealing here with a much fought-over battlefield, and to get bogged down in it at this point would seriously distort the balance of the argument.[83] There are two closely connected questions, What *can* we know of the historical Jesus?, and, What, for Christian faith, do we *need* to know? To the latter I shall be returning later. But when every-thing has been said that can – and must – be said about the uncer-

[83] The following recent surveys contain reference to the most important con-tributions: Heinz Zahrnt, *The Historical Jesus*, Collins 1963; James Peter, *Finding the Historical Jesus*, Collins 1965; Carl E. Braaten, *History and Hermeneutics*, Lutter-worth 1966; Van A. Harvey, *The Historian and the Believer*, SCM Press 1967; Otto Betz, *What Do We Know About Jesus?*, SCM Press 1967; D. E. Nineham, 'Jesus in the Gospels', in Norman Pittenger (ed.), *Christ for Us Today*, SCM Press 1968, pp.45–65; H. K. McArthur (ed.), *In Search of the Historical Jesus*.

tainty of any of our knowledge about Jesus, I believe that what is corrosive of Christology is as much a popular impression (and none the less potent for that) as any established results.

This may be illustrated at the lay level by the way in which periodic books about Jesus or Christian origins are treated by otherwise responsible historians and scientists with a lack of critical discrimination that in any other field would be inconceivable. Two passing instances will make the point. In 1971 a professor of German literature, G. A. Wells, produced a book called *The Jesus of the Early Christians*.[84] It was among those indefatigable attempts which appear from time to time to show that Jesus never lived or that in all essentials he was a mythical construction of the early church.[85] Despite a considerable parade of learning, its scholarship was not impressive. Being asked to discuss it on television, I thought I would take six leading British New Testament scholars and see what he made of them. Not one of them was mentioned. His chief resource seemed to be the *Encyclopaedia Biblica*, published in 1903 (and even then hardly the most balanced statement of biblical scholarship). Yet the book was certainly no worse than anything I should produce had I the temerity to venture into the history of German literature. What was astonishing was that it carried an enthusiastic commendation by Hugh Trevor-Roper, the Professor of Modern History at Oxford, who wrote in *The Spectator* a correspondingly sweeping denunciation of C. H. Dodd's *The Founder of Christianity* which appeared about the same time.[86] Between the scholarship of the two (though in the latter case the learning was not paraded) there could be no comparison. But in this field apparently all the usual critical criteria go out of the window.

For my second illustration I take the popular apologist John Wren-Lewis, for whom I have a good regard and who is well used to sifting scientific evidence. In his book *What Shall We Tell the Children?*,[87] he asserts that what Jesus actually stood for is

[84] G. A. Wells, *The Jesus of the Early Christians*, Pemberton Books 1971.
[85] Cf. the review of earlier essays in this field by H. G. Wood, *Did Christ Really Live?*, SCM Press 1938.
[86] C. H. Dodd, *The Founder of Christianity*, Collins 1971.
[87] John Wren-Lewis, *What Shall We Tell the Children?*, Constable 1971. For a

now so hidden in the mists that no one has the right to say, 'I
believe in the values of Jesus', but only 'I believe in the values of
the Roman Catholic Church', or, 'The Evangelical Christian
Tradition', or 'British Public School Christianity', or whatever.
But it is just not true to say that one is shut up either to a self-
chosen private picture of Jesus or to handing oneself over to some
authoritarian tradition. The value of the empirical method here,
as everywhere else, is precisely to deliver from such a sterile choice.
To say of the gospels,

> I do not think it is possible for us to know anything now
> about the historical basis for their assertion, since there is little
> doubt that the story of Jesus has been enormously elaborated
> with quotations and allusions to the Hebrew scriptures and
> possibly other religious writings,[88]

represents the abdication of the critical method, not its conclusion.
Of course, the traditions must be sifted rigorously, and the
scientists in the subject have been doing that for two centuries.
Naturally their conclusions will not coincide, any more than those
of the psychologists. But to claim that there is no possibility of
objective control or, as he does, that preference for another view
of Jesus over Allegro's theory of the sacred mushroom[89] is 'only
speculation on my part'[90] is to throw up the scientific sponge.

I have given these ephemeral examples because they illustrate
the extent to which the erosion of historical confidence is a matter
of popular mood. But clearly it is more than this. Don Cupitt's
engaging essay, 'One Jesus, Many Christs?',[90] reflects the considered conclusion that there are as many ways of seeing Christ as
there are people. 'The image of Jesus,' he says, 'is perplexingly
vague and blurred', and 'close study of the New Testament has
only made matters worse'.[92] One can sympathize with a philoso-

judgment on the book as a whole cf. my review in *Faith and Freedom* XXV,
Spring 1972, pp.159–62, from which some sentences are here taken.
    [88] Wren-Lewis, op. cit., p.191.
    [89] John Allegro, *The Sacred Mushroom and the Cross*, Hodder and Stoughton
1970.
    [90] Wren-Lewis, op. cit., p.194.
    [91] In Sykes and Clayton (eds.), *Christ, Faith and History*, pp.131–44.
    [92] Cupitt, op. cit., p.135.

pher receiving this impression, but still want to dispute it. There is indeed a very wide spectrum of conclusions in current New Testament scholarship, which shows no immediate sign of narrowing. But I have every confidence that continued study does not 'make matters worse', and I believe that new methods,[93] so far from reducing the historical content of the gospels to vanishing point as is often supposed, enable one to strip off the layers of church tradition to reveal more of what lies beneath them.[94] In fact I am increasingly convinced that there is a lot of very good history in the gospels – not least in the Fourth Gospel.[95] I cannot stop to substantiate this, and some of it must be allowed to come out in the working as we proceed. I mention it here merely to keep the discussion in balance.

The old securities in history on which Christology was based may indeed have been undermined beyond repair, but I do not believe that this need lead to scepticism or cynicism – or to a flight from the Jesus of history as unattainable or unnecessary. Indeed, I would echo the concluding words of a recent survey:

If God truly entrusted himself to the changes and chances of

[93] Particularly so-called redaction criticism (an extension of form criticism), which tends to see the history in the gospels primarily as the history of the early-church situations for which the tradition was edited. Enthusiastic and, I believe, grossly overblown claims are made for this method in Norman Perrin's *What is Redaction Criticism?*, SPCK 1970. Typical of his presuppositions is a comment in his annotated bibliography: 'A strange book in that the author combines redaction criticism with the assumption "that Mark believes that the incidents he uses actually happened"!' The exclamation mark is his, and further comment is really unnecessary. There would appear no reason why the gospels should not provide valuable evidence *both* about the communities which created them *and* about the events which were firmly believed to have created the communities. For a balanced assessment, cf. R. S. Barbour, *Traditio-Historical Criticism of the Gospels*, SPCK 1972.

[94] For a discussion of the criteria available, cf. H. K. McArthur (ed.), *In Search of the Historical Jesus*, especially chs.14 and 15 by N. A. Dahl and H. K. McArthur. For a working model, even where one disagrees with his conclusions, see Joachim Jeremias, *The Parables of Jesus*, SCM Press ³1972, and id., *New Testament Theology* I, SCM Press 1971.

[95] Cf. C. H. Dodd, *Historical Tradition in the Fourth Gospel*, Cambridge University Press 1963; A. M. Hunter, *According to John*, SCM Press 1968; and John A. T. Robinson, *Twelve New Testament Studies*, SCM Press 1962, especially chs.2, 4 and 7; id., 'The Place of the Fourth Gospel', in P. Gardner-Smith (ed.), *The Roads Converge*, Edward Arnold 1963; id., 'The Use of the Fourth Gospel for Christology Today', in B. Lindars and S. S. Smalley (eds.), *Christ and Spirit in the New Testament: Studies in Honour of C. F. D. Moule*, Cambridge University Press 1973.

the historical process (and most Christians do not really believe that he did) we can do the same. If we do, *and only if we do*, are we likely to encounter him afresh.[96]

Yet we cannot set predetermined limits to what 'afresh' may mean. For each of the four respects in which the scene has shifted must, I believe, prepare us for a radical new look at the *logos* by which to say the same things about *Christos* today – quite apart from any new or different things we may wish or need to say.

Revolutions in reality

Perhaps, to sum up the change of perspective, I could draw a parallel from another area of Christian thinking – again, the doctrine of the church. Richard McBrien, the American Roman Catholic, in his book *Do We Need the Church?*,[97] has spoken of two revolutions with which contemporary theology must come to terms at one and the same time: what he describes as the 'Copernican' and the 'Einsteinian'. In Christology the former relates especially to the first two changes I have noticed, the latter to the second two.

In regard to mythology and to metaphysics the centre has shifted – the earth, as it were, is now seen to go round the sun, rather than *vice versa*. Thus, the war in heaven between Michael and his angels and the Devil and his angels, or the procession of the Spirit from the Father and the Son, are no longer thought of as representing the real, essential events of which occurrences in the contingent, existential order are the reflection or consequence. Rather, it is the other way round. These mythical or metaphysical 'events' are ways of speaking (and to us fairly strange ways of speaking) about the profoundest realities of *this* historical order. The real world ('where we are down here') is the starting-point: the rest is interpretation, in terms of the imagination or the intellect. This means that we have to start any Christology today from this end – from the worldly rather than the heavenly, the

[96] Barbour, op. cit., p.47. Italics mine.
[97] R. P. McBrien, *Do We Need the Church?*, Collins 1969.

human rather than the divine. To *begin* by asking Anselm's question, *Cur deus homo?* – why (or how) did God become man? – is to move from the unknown to the known rather than *vice versa*.

Secondly, we must learn to live also with an Einsteinian revolution. Finality and uniqueness, both in relation to absolute significance and in relation to historical process, will have to be decisively reinterpreted. The first century or even the sixteenth may have had no difficulty with 'one oblation once offered' as a 'full, perfect and sufficient sacrifice for the sins of the whole world'. We have. And this, I believe, is not simply because we are not the Christians our fathers were. If we want to say anything like the same thing we have to say it differently.

To borrow a short-hand classification of the Dutch philosopher Cornelis van Peursen,[98] which I have used before[99] and shall return to later, man has moved in the ways in which he has sought to represent reality from a mythological way of thinking to an ontological, and is moving from an ontological to a functional. The first transition is reflected in Christology in the shift from Jewish categories to Greek. The former viewed finality in terms of the eschatological act of God in history, embodied in the sending of his Messiah as saviour and judge of everything in heaven and earth and under the earth. The latter saw ultimate reality not in terms of final act but of timeless being, in the categories of substance rather than will. Now, as Gregory Dix pointed out in his book *Jew and Greek*,[100] it appears to *us* (schooled through the history of Christian doctrine and Western culture in ontological ways of thinking) that the replacement of the mythological categories by the ontological *in itself* involved a heightening of Christology – from the Lord's Messiah to the second person of the Trinity, from the Son of God to God the Son. There is, of course, no denying that development did take place, as the implications of the Christ event were pondered. But, as Dix

[98] 'Man and Reality – The History of Human Thought,' *The Student World* LVI, 1963, pp.13–21; reprinted in John Bowden and James Richmond (eds), *A Reader in Contemporary Theology*, SCM Press ²1971, pp.115–26.

[99] For a summary of his position, cf. my *Exploration into God*, SCM Press 1967, p.40; Stanford University Press 1967, p.34.

[100] Gregory Dix, *Jew and Greek*, A. and C. Black 1953, pp.79f.

insisted, there could be nothing more exalted for the Jew than to designate someone the agent of God's final act in history. Yet the Greek categories seem to us to be saying something higher and more 'substantial'. In the same way, later in Christian history, the Antiochene school of theology, operating with the more biblical and historical categories of grace and moral union, *appear* to have a lower doctrine of the Christ than the Alexandrians who, with their insistence on being and substance, largely dictated the terms of the debate and on those terms won out.

Conversely, we must be on our guard against a similar prejudice attending the shift from ontological to functional ways of thinking. We have to recognize that *any* contemporary Christology is bound to *appear* reductionist compared with that done in the more 'full-blooded' (but actually rather bloodless) categories of classical ontology. To say that Jesus *was* God in the most literal sense of substantial identity (as still in the majestic certainty of Liddon's title *The Divinity of our Lord and Saviour Jesus Christ*)[101] appears to be saying more than anything that can possibly be asserted if one starts from the end of *this man*, a genuine product of the evolutionary process with all its random mutations, and then asks how he 'functions' as a clue to the whole. Wherever one ends up, the other side appears to be holding the higher ground.

Indeed, within the terms of traditional theology, whether Catholic, Evangelical or merely conservative, any answer which begins from this end *will be* reductionist, just as any answer about the truth of Adam and Eve which began from the presuppositions of Darwin and Huxley could not but be reductionist to Bishop Wilberforce and the conservatives a century ago. But that does not mean to say that it was reductionist, in the sense of diminishing the significance of the Genesis story. On the contrary, it freed it to carry much greater significance than ever it could if confined to the individual history of our most distant ancestor. Similarly today, to speak of Jesus in the ontological categories of divine consubstantiality or 'impersonal' humanity may appear to be defending the faith against those who would sell it short. But we must have the courage to ask our own questions in terms of what

[101] H. P. Liddon's Bampton Lectures for 1866, London 1867.

is most real for us, and not be put off by the presumption, for instance, that what is sometimes rather sneeringly called a 'degree Christology' is somehow lower-class or less respectable than one which asserts that Jesus was different *in kind* from all other men. Or we may end by finding that he has ceased to be one of us at all and cannot therefore be 'our man'. The *logos* may have safe-guarded the *Christos* at the expense of killing the mystery.

All this will have to be explored and expanded as we proceed. It is enough for now to have insisted – as theology has always had to re-insist – on the *Christus pro nobis*, the Christ for us. This means being prepared for the charges of cultural relativism and psycho-logical subjectivism which this has constantly brought in Christian history. But it is a risk which any genuinely *incarnational* theology must be ready to run. For the truth with which Christology wrestles is essentially of the absolute *made relative* – 'the mystery', as Paul put it to his converts, of 'Christ *in you*'.[102]

[102] Col. 1.27.

TWO

A MAN

A man among men

If Jesus as the Christ is to be our man, he must be one of us: '*totus in nostris*', completely part of our world, to use a phrase from the so-called *Tome* of Leo which was endorsed as orthodox by the Council of Chalcedon;[1] in other words, a man in every sense of the word.

This is so obvious that it is astonishing that anyone should ever have had to say it, and it is an indictment of the language Christians have used that it should have had to be insisted on again and again in the history of doctrine (often in vain) and that we should need to spend a whole chapter on it now. It is indeed a constant astonishment that the *first* serious heresy that the church had to face was that of docetism (from the Greek word *dokein*, to seem), that is to say, that Jesus merely *appeared* to be human. Whatever else one would have expected men to doubt, one would have not expected them to doubt the evidence of their own eyes and the memory of one who, whatever *more* he was, was so obviously one of themselves, a man among men. Indeed the New Testament shows quite clearly that the early Christians began with a view of Christ which left this memory uncomplicated and unthreatened. They certainly did not see him to be of *merely* human significance: he spoke of what God had done in their midst. But that he was *not* in their

<hr>

[1] *Tome* 3. Translation in T. H. Bindley, *The Oecumenical Documents of the Faith*, ed. F. W. Green, Methuen [4]1950, pp.168–80. The *Tome* was a letter (Ep. 28) written by Leo, Bishop of Rome, to Flavian, Archbishop of Constantinople, in 449.

memory a man in every sense of the word is incredible in the
light of Peter's speech on the day of Pentecost (which, whenever
it was written, clearly represents a very primitive, not to say
simplistic, Christology):

> Men of Israel, listen to me: I speak of Jesus of Nazareth, a
> man singled out by God and made known to you through
> miracles, portents, and signs ʾhich God worked among you
> through him, as you well know. When he had been given up to
> you, by the deliberate will and plan of God, you used heathen
> men to crucify and kill him. But God raised him to life again.[2]

John Knox, in his beautiful little study, *The Humanity and
Divinity of Christ*, has made the point that as long as this primitive, 'adoptionist' Christology prevailed,

> the simple actuality of the humanity was in no sense or degree
> compromised. Not only could it be whole and intact, but it
> was also subject to no theological or mythological pressure of
> any kind.[3]

But the pressure began (and I agree with him in thinking that it
began very early – within a decade or two), when the fore-
ordination of God became translated as the pre-existence of
Christ. As soon as Jesus Christ was, or could be, represented as a
pre-existent being who had come down from heaven,[4] then the
genuineness of his humanity while he was on earth was open to
question. This does not mean that it was questioned. The memory
was far too strong. And from the beginning of theological reflection on his significance there was the weightiest possible reason for
insisting on his total solidarity with 'us men and our salvation'.
Otherwise all his relevance for us would be undercut. Nevertheless, the threat was there, precisely because of the story which was
told about him to bring out the *significance* of his humanity. And
the more the story was elaborated, the greater the pressure became
to defend the humanity which it threatened.

[2] Acts 2.22–24.   [3] Knox, op. cit., pp.6f.
[4] I return to the whole question of what the New Testament writers actually
intended by pre-existence in ch.5.

The intention of the church in insisting to the limit on the indispensability of Christ's humanity has never been in doubt. In view of what follows, this should be fully acknowledged. And it constitutes a vital difference, for instance, between Christianity and Buddhism. There may be docetic tendencies in the pictures both of the Christ and the Buddha, but it is only in the former that they have been viewed or condemned as destructive.[5] In a Christmas sermon, the same Pope Leo said for his time what Christians have wanted to say in every age:

> It is as dangerous an evil to deny the truth of the human nature in Christ as to refuse to believe that his glory is equal to that of the Father.[6]

Yet it is equally true that:

> Traditionally an over-emphasis on the humanity has always tended to lead to positions that the church labelled as eccentric; an over-emphasis on the divinity has led to positions which were comfortably accommodated within orthodoxy.[7]

But today the slightest suggestion that he was not, in the words of the Chalcedonian Definition, 'completely human (*teleion en anthrōpotēti*) . . . of one substance with us (*homoousion hēmin*) as regards his manhood' is in fact much more destructive of the gospel than doubts about his divinity. For this is to undermine it from the start. It cannot even begin to be good news – let alone where it ends. In the words of an ancient writer:

> If Christ's being flesh is found to be a lie, then everything which was done by it was done falsely. . . . God's entire work . . . is subverted.[8]

---

[5] Cf. E. G. Parrinder, *Avatar and Incarnation*, Faber 1970, pp.244–6, 264. This applies even more strongly to the incarnations of Hinduism, where the historical foundation is still less important.

[6] *Serm.* 27.1; J. P. Migne, *Patrologia Latina* (=PL), Paris 1844–55, vol. 54, 216.

[7] Erik Routley, *The Man for Others*, Peter Smith 1964, p. ix.

[8] Tertullian, *adv. Marcion*.3.8. The same principle underlies the famous maxim (summarizing teaching in Irenaeus, Tertullian and Origen) of Gregory of Nazianzen (*Ep.*101.7) that 'the unassumed is the unhealed'. For the use of this principle today, cf. the article of that title by M. F. Wiles, *Religious Studies* IV, 1969, pp. 47–56.

Or a modern:

> Unless it be agreed that he was 'truly man', it does not greatly
> matter what else can be said of him.[9]

To say that Jesus was not God but like God at least says something,
and something important. To say that he was not man but like
man is to condemn his entire life as a charade.

But what does it mean today to insist that Jesus was a completely
human being – *post* Darwin, Marx, Freud and the cracking of the
genetic code? The intention of the Fathers, as I said, was not in
doubt. They thought they were meeting the requirements. But
their expression of what it meant for Jesus to be human, even at
its best, is hopelessly unsatisfactory for us.

To say, as they did, that Jesus was truly man but not a man is
simply to invite blank incomprehension in a modern listener.
The orthodox doctrine of Christ's 'impersonal humanity' (of
anhypostasia or *enhypostasia*),[10] according to which the individual
personality of the man Jesus was supplied by, or included in, the
hypostasis or substance of the second person of the Trinity, so that
what was human was the *nature* this superhuman person assumed,
strikes us as threatening the very core of his manhood. What
made him *him* was something alien to the human condition. As
Bonhoeffer put it, in this view 'Christ the God is substance, Jesus
the man is accident'.[11] The extremes represented by Apollinarius
and Eutyches may have been condemned as heretical, but for us a
docetic streak runs through and discredits almost the whole of
Alexandrian Christology.[12] Hilary was canonized for views which

---

[9] John Knox, *The Death of Christ*, Collins 1959, p.70.
[10] For a fuller discussion of this see below, pp.105-9.
[11] Dietrich Bonhoeffer, *Christology*, Collins 1966; Fontana edition 1971 (to
which all references are made), p.81.
[12] The following statements are representative:
Clement of Alexandria: It would be ridiculous to imagine that the body of the
Redeemer, in order to exist, had the usual needs of man. He only took food and
ate it in order that we should not teach about him in a docetic fashion (*Strom.*
6.9; cf.3.7, where he takes over from the Gnostic Valentinus the view that no true
digestion or elimination of food took place in the Lord).
Athanasius: The Word disguised himself by appearing in a body. . . . By the
works he did in the body [he] showed himself to be, not man, but God the
Word. But . . . having become man, it was proper for these things [eating, etc.]

can only cause us the acutest embarrassment,[13] and later Thomas Aquinas, the angelic doctor of Catholic orthodoxy, defends the same position.[14]

But there is no need to stress all this. It has been said again and again, most notably by Donald Baillie in his great book *God was in Christ*:

> It is . . . nonsense to say that He is 'Man' unless we mean that He is a man.[15]

to be predicated of him as man, to show him to have a body in truth, and not in seeming (*De Incarn.* 16.18. For a further selection of passages from Athanasius and other Fathers, cf. J. H. Newman, *Select Treatises of St Athanasius in Controversy with the Arians* II, Longmans 1881, pp.161–72, 295–303).

Cyril of Alexandria: He permitted his own flesh to weep a little, although it was in its nature tearless and incapable of grief (*Comm. in Joh.* 7). Seeing it was in a sense necessary that he should adapt himself to the custom of our nature, lest he should be reckoned something strange as man by those who saw him, while his body gradually advanced in growth he concealed himself, and appeared daily wiser to those who saw and heard him (*Thesaur. assertio* 28, p.251). Although he knows everything he does not blush to attribute to himself the ignorance proper to manhood (*Resp. ad Tib.* 4. For a catena of passages in Cyril relating to Christ's knowledge, cf. A. B. Bruce, *The Humiliation of Christ*, T. and T. Clark ²1881, pp.366–72).

Such teaching did not go without vigorous protest from the Antiochenes; e.g. *Theodoret:* If he knew the day and, wishing to conceal it, said he was ignorant, see what blasphemy is the result. Truth tells a lie (cited in Cyril, *Apol. contra Theodoret.*, anath. 4).

[13] E.g.: When he ate and drank, it was a concession, not to his own necessities, but to our habits (*De Trin.* 10.24). He felt pain for us, but not with our senses; he was found in fashion as a man, with a body which could feel pain, but his nature could not feel pain; for, though his fashion was that of a man, his origin was not human (10.47). His soul could suffer only because by divine miracle the Logos permitted it (10.23f.).

The 'natural' condition of Christ's body and soul was complete freedom from the usual human needs: the miracle was that he *did* feel weary. Cf. Bruce, op. cit., pp.237–48; J. K. Mozley, *The Impassibility of God*, Cambridge University Press 1926, pp.102–4.

[14] Aquinas supports Hilary in saying that, to show the reality of his human nature, he voluntarily assumed fear, even as sorrow (*Summa Theologica* III.15.7 ad 2). The whole of Aquinas' treatment of what he calls the 'defects' of body and soul 'assumed' by Christ (*Summa* III.14 and 15), though much more sophisticated than Hilary's, presents a Christ who is extraordinarily unreal, retaining perfect beatitude of soul while 'by the consent of the divine will . . . the flesh was allowed to suffer what belonged to it' (III.14.1 ad 2). His fundamental position is that 'Christ assumed all the fullness of wisdom and knowledge absolutely. But he assumed our defects economically (*dispensative*), in order to satisfy for our sin, and not that they belonged to him of himself' (III.14.4 ad 2. I quote the edition published by Burns Oates 1913–14; the new edition by Thomas Gilby is unfortunately not yet complete for Aquinas' Christology).

[15] D. M. Baillie, *God was in Christ*, Faber 1948, p.87.

No more docetism! . . . That is the first factor in the distinctive situation of Christology today.[16]

Indeed, our greatest difficulty is even to *understand* what the
Fathers could have been meaning by such language. And the
modern phrase 'impersonal humanity' does not help. For what
they were disputing was not Jesus' personality in our sense.
Indeed, it is inconceivable that they really did not think he was a
man. As we shall see, the heart of what they were denying is that
he was a man apart from, independently of, God's indwelling of
him. He was constituted and brought into being solely by God's
action in himself becoming man: he would not have existed
otherwise.

But it is the negative corollary of this – that he had no independent solidarity with the rest of us *qua* man – that is disturbing and
undermining. And the reason why we are disturbed and the
Fathers were not is well brought out by Paul van Buren, whose
positive appreciation of patristic Christology is one of the best
and most neglected aspects of his book *The Secular Meaning of the
Gospel*.[17] He points out the presuppositions behind the second-
century Christology of Justin Martyr. According to Justin, Jesus
was fully a man,

> because he had the body and soul and spirit of a man. Justin's
> Christ is like a specimen on the anatomist's dissecting table. It is
> opened to see that all the parts are there. All the parts are found,
> and the specimen is judged to be a fair representative of the
> species in question.[18]

But this is to ignore completely what for us is a *sine qua non* of
personal existence, namely, the nexus of biological, historical
and social relationships with our fellow-men and with the
universe as a whole. If that is not there, then Jesus may have
entered completely into the place where we were – but only as a
visitor. He was like one of us, but he was not one of us.

[16] Baillie, op. cit., p.20.
[17] Paul van Buren, *The Secular Meaning of the Gospel*, SCM Press 1963. He also
tells me that it is one of the few parts of it that he would now wish to stand by.
[18] Van Buren, op. cit., pp.38f.

A product of the process

This insistence on Jesus being a genuine product of the process, with all the pre-history of man in his genes, is, I believe, one of the distinctive presuppositions of a twentieth-century Christology. Previous ages have found it difficult enough to assert that he was genuinely subject to *environmental* influences when he got here – that he really was *shaped* by these, instead of just passing through them. Schleiermacher, for instance, is a fascinating and instructive example of this from the nineteenth century. In many ways he was the first of the 'moderns', and no one criticizing him can do so without first sitting under the encomium of Karl Barth (who differed from him far more radically than I should wish to do – mainly for presuming to attempt what Tillich was to call an 'answering theology', which is bound to be culturally conditioned).[19] Like Tillich,[20] too, Schleiermacher tried to find a position between naturalism and supernaturalism, insisting that the Christ could neither be solely the product of the natural order nor be absolutely unrelated to it nor unassimilable by it.[21] Yet he produced what Barth was to call 'a tolerably modernized Christology',[22] which is in fact fatally compromised. He thought he was saying all that was necessary by requiring that in Christ the supernatural, though inserted from without, had become completely naturalized:

Since we can never understand the beginnings of life, full

[19] Karl Barth, *Protestant Theology in the Nineteenth Century*, SCM Press 1972, p.427: 'We have to do with a hero, the like of which is but seldom bestowed upon theology. Anyone who has never noticed anything of the splendour this figure radiated and still does – I am almost tempted to say, who has never succumbed to it – may honourably pass on to other and possibly better ways, but let him never raise so much as a finger against Schleiermacher. Anyone who has never loved here, and is not in a position to love again and again, may not hate here either.' For an assessment of Schleiermacher's contribution to Christology, cf. J. A. Dorner, *History of the Development of the Doctrine of the Person of Christ* III, T. and T. Clark 1863, pp.174–213; also Creed, op. cit., ch. 2.

[20] Paul Tillich, *Systematic Theology* II, pp.6–9.

[21] Cf. Richard R. Niebuhr, *Schleiermacher on Christ and Religion*, SCM Press 1965, pp.165–8; 226–7.

[22] Barth, op. cit., p.461. Nevertheless, he had the courage to discard the time-honoured doctrine of the 'two natures' of Christ, subjecting it to criticism from which it has never really recovered.

justice is done to the demand for the perfect historicity of this perfect ideal, if, from then on, he developed in the same way as all others.[23]

But even Jesus' environmental conditioning was for Schleiermacher limited to the manner of his life-style. His inner 'unchangeable entity' was not really affected by his experiences. His humanity had the kind of impassibility (in the fundamental sense of not being acted upon) which was ascribed by the Fathers to his divinity. Nothing he was was genuinely the product of his environment. Martin Kähler, who followed Schleiermacher closely, was able to write as late as 1892 on the difference between Paul and Jesus:

> On the one hand we see the true Jew, so profoundly and indelibly influenced by the cultural forces of his people and epoch; on the other hand we see the Son of Man, whose person and work convey the impression of one who lived, as it were, in the timeless age of the patriarchs.[24]

In the light of all that was known even then of Jesus' background in the Judaism of his day, it is an incredible judgment.

Yet the influence not only of his environment but of his heredity must be pressed to the full. Schleiermacher's concept of a perfect humanity introduced like a cuckoo into the human nest[25] can no longer find refuge in the 'God of the gaps', by appeal to our ignorance of 'the beginnings of life'. We know enough at any rate to say that to be a member of the species *homo sapiens* includes having genes and chromosomes shaped and transmitted by millions of years of evolution. No one can just *become* a man out of the blue: a genuine man (as opposed to a replica) can only come out of the process, not into it.

[23] F. D. E. Schleiermacher, *The Christian Faith* (ed. H. R. Mackintosh and J. S. Stewart), T. and T. Clark 1928, p.381.

[24] Martin Kähler, *The So-Called Historical Jesus and the Historic, Biblical Christ*, Fortress Press, Philadelphia 1964, p.54.

[25] He rightly sees that the *manner* of his insertion is irrelevant. It makes no fundamental difference whether or not we think of him as born to the foster-mother by virginal conception—a miracle in fact which he rejects.

Since this point is, I believe, of crucial importance, I should like
to reiterate it in the crystal-clear words of John Knox:

> An affirmation of Jesus' manhood is an assertion that he was
> born out of, and into, humanity in the same sense every man is;
> that he was a son of Abraham, just as every man participates in
> his own race or nation or culture; and, more important, that he
> was a son of Adam, as all men are, regardless of what their
> culture, nation or race may be. There is no other conceivable
> way of being a man. Not only is it impossible, by definition,
> that God should become a man, it is also impossible, by
> definition, that he should 'make' one. A true human being
> could not be freshly created. Such a creation might look like a
> man and even speak like a man. He might be given flesh like a
> man's and a man's faculties, but he would not *be* a man. He
> would not be a man because he would not belong to the
> organic human process, to the actually existing concrete entity
> in nature and history, which is, and alone is, *man*.[26]

Now this concern for Jesus' solidarity with the rest of creation is
not only modern but very biblical. For writers like Justin,
brought up in a Greek way of thinking, to say that 'the Word
became flesh and dwelt among us' was quite compatible with the
idea of insertion from without, as long as the human was not
displaced or denied by the divine. But for the biblical writers,
'flesh' stood for man bound up indissolubly in the bundle of life
not only with his fellow men but with 'rocks and stones and
trees'.[27] Man did not simply have flesh, he was flesh; and to assert
incarnation was to assert solidarity with the entire order of nature
and history.

This is why 'according to the flesh', in so far as his humanity
is concerned, the biblical writers see Jesus not as isolated, 'without
genealogy' like Melchizedek[28] (with whom at the human level
this parallel significantly is *not* drawn – 'for it is very evident that
our Lord is sprung from Judah'),[29] but 'of the seed of David'.[30]

---

[26] John Knox, *The Humanity and Divinity of Christ*, pp.67f. Italics his.
[27] W. Wordsworth, 'A Slumber did my Spirit Steal'. Cf. my book *The Body*,
SCM Press 1952, ch. 1.   [28] Heb. 7.3.   [29] Heb. 7.14.
[30] Rom. 1.4; Luke 2.4; Acts 13.23; II Tim. 2.8.

This, of course, is emphasized to bring out his Messianic significance.[31] But not all were Messiahs who were 'sprung from Judah',
a lineage indeed that was a theological liability for the writer to
the Hebrews, for from this tribe no priest could come. The point
which he, like the others, regarded as indispensable was that 'the
children of a family share the same flesh and blood; and so he too
shared ours'.[32] For 'a consecrating priest and those whom he
consecrates' must be 'all of one stock; and that is why the Son
does not shrink from calling men his brothers'.[33] Indeed it must
be possible to say of Jesus, as he says of Levi, that he was in the
loins of Abraham his ancestor.[34] For, unless he were, he could not
have been, in Paul's phrase, the 'seed' (*sperma*) to which the
promise was made.[35] As Karl Rahner has put it:

> Christ had not only to be 'like us in nature' so as to be our
> Redeemer, but with us had to spring 'from one' (Heb. 2.11),
> our brother according to the flesh. For he could only possess this
> flesh, which was to be redeemed, if he who was 'born of
> woman' *shared our origin as well as our nature*.[36]

It is not for nothing that the New Testament begins with 'a
table of the descent of Jesus Christ'.[37] Indeed I am convinced by
Krister Stendahl that the whole of Matthew's first chapter is
focussed not on the birth of Jesus but on his origin, the word
genesis having the meaning 'lineage' in 1.18 as in 1.1.[38] The fact
that this lineage is necessarily (for a Jew) traced through the male
line places the genealogy for us in glaring contradiction to the
accompanying narrative which claims that Joseph was not
genetically the father – and Luke, or his scribe, is evidently
conscious of the difficulty.[39] The solidarities of 'the flesh' in

---

[31] Cf. John 7.42.   [32] Heb. 2.14.   [33] Heb. 2.11.   [34] Heb. 7.10.
[35] Gal. 3.16.
[36] Karl Rahner, 'Current Problems in Christology', *Theological Investigations* I,
Darton, Longman and Todd, 1961, pp.196f. Italics mine.
[37] Matt. 1.1.
[38] See his important article 'Quis et Unde?', in W. Eltester (ed.), *Judentum,
Urchristentum, Kirche: Festschrift für Joachim Jeremias, Zeitschrift für die neutestament-
liche Wissenschaft*, Beiheft XXVI, 1960, pp.94–105.
[39] Luke 3.23: 'The son, *as people thought*, of Joseph.' The textual variants at this
point may indicate a later gloss. It is also possible that this qualifying phrase was
added to bring the Lukan genealogy into line with the subsequent addition of a

Hebrew thinking were not so confined to or dependent upon the biological nexus as they are for us.[40] Yet clearly the men of the first century did not intend the genealogies to be set *against* the assertion of Jesus's heavenly conception, or *vice versa*. They were affirming *both* in the closest juxtaposition, just as the early formula had conjoined the statements that 'on the human level he was born of David's stock, but on the level of the spirit – the Holy Spirit – he was . . . Son of God'.[41] In other words, each is true – at its own level. The purpose of the nativity story is not to deny something at the level of flesh asserted in the genealogy, but to affirm something at the level of spirit – namely, the initiative of God in and through it all. The significance of Jesus is not to be understood solely from the point of view of heredity and environment. Yet these solidarities are not abrogated – any more than they are for Christians who, *as children of God*, insists John in his parallel prologue, are 'not born of any human stock, or by the fleshly desire of a human father, but [are] the offspring of God himself'.[42] But this is not, of course, to deny that *at the level of nature* they are so born. The one truth does not contradict the other.

Subsequently, the New Testament does not seem in the least embarrassed by Jesus' natural connection with the rest of his fellows: 'Is not this the carpenter, the son of Mary, the brother of James and Joseph and Judas and Simon? And are not his sisters here with us?'[43] The existence (and acceptance) of Jesus' brothers is attested not only by Mark,[44] our earliest gospel, but by

birth narrative. Whereas in Matthew the two are closely integrated, the first draft of Luke's gospel may well have begun with the elaborate dating of 3.1. In this case the original purpose of the genealogy will have been to explain how Jesus could be 'son of God', the title in which it culminates (3.38), which has been introduced at the baptism (3.22) and is to be expounded in the temptations (4.3,9). Later combination of it with a story denying Joseph's paternity required the modification. Matthew, as we shall see, has another (and I believe profounder) way of holding them together.

[40] Cf. M. D. Johnson, *The Purpose of the Biblical Genealogies*, Cambridge University Press 1969.

[41] Rom. 1.4.

[42] John 1.13. I do not see either dependence on or, as some have asserted, polemic against the synoptists at this point.

[43] Mark 6.3 par.

[44] See also Mark 3.31f. par.

I Corinthians[45] and Galatians,[46] two of our earliest epistles, as well as by John[47] and Acts[48] – a combination of witnesses as strong as for any incidental fact about Jesus and, of course, far stronger than for the virgin birth story, which itself, on any natural reading of the words that Joseph 'had no intercourse with her *until* her son was born',[49] implies rather than rules out subsequent relations. It asserts that Jesus was Mary's first-born son (*prōtotokos*),[50] not her only son (*monogenēs*), a word which is never used of Christ's human descent.

The need for a break

The later theory that Jesus' siblings were half-brothers or cousins reflects the resistance felt in the church to a real continuum between his humanity and ours. Even Thomas Aquinas' customary coolness deserts him at this point:

> Without any hesitation we must abhor the error of Helvidius, who dared to assert that Christ's Mother, after his birth, was carnally known by Joseph, and bore other children. This error is an insult to the Holy Ghost, whose shrine was the virginal womb, wherein he had formed the flesh of Christ: wherefore it was unbecoming that it should be desecrated by intercourse with man.[51]

Why this heated language? It is, I believe, healthy that we should examine this resistance and have a good look at it. And if this is painful, it merely confirms the reluctance. For I think we

[45] I Cor. 9.5.   [46] Gal. 1.19.   [47] John 2.12; 7.3,5,10.
[48] Acts 1.14.
[49] Matt. 1.25. The Jerusalem Bible still disingenuously translates this as 'though he had not had intercourse with her, she gave birth to a son'. It appends a note to say: 'The text is not concerned with the period that followed, and taken by itself, does not assert Mary's perpetual virginity, which, however, the gospels elsewhere suppose and which the Tradition of the Church affirms.' On the contrary, it clearly *does* refer to the period after Jesus' birth and implicitly denies subsequent virginity, which is nowhere supposed by the gospels. Honesty would suggest a revised translation.
[50] Luke 2.7. When Luke wishes to indicate an only child he does so quite specifically (7.12; 8.42).
[51] *Summa* III.28.3.

have to recognize among Christians (in all of us if we are honest)
a psychological necessity to set a break between Jesus' humanity
and our own. We cannot stand the identity of the same flesh and
blood, the continuity of genes and sperm and plasm. We want
solidarity with us, but from the outside: identification rather than
identity.

The language that even Knox finds himself having to use to
emphasize Jesus' obvious humanity is symptomatic:

> For all his goodness and greatness, the ·wonder of his man-
> hood, the qualities of mind and spirit which lift him so far
> above us, he was still a human being like ourselves. Not only
> should we not *want* it otherwise; we *ought* not to be able to *bear*
> it otherwise. Jesus was a man like ourselves; Jesus' nature was
> our common human nature. To say this is not to make a
> *grudging concession* to secular reason; it is to make a vital affirma-
> tion of Christian faith.[52]

The words I have italicized betray the resistance he feels required
to counter.

This need to set, as it were, a *cordon sanitaire* between the manhood of Jesus and what the Fathers called 'common' humanity
comes out very clearly in the use made of the virgin birth story.
I stress 'use made' because this interpretation is not implied in the
biblical story itself. This, like the prologue to the Fourth Gospel, is
concerned fundamentally to ask the question, Who is this man?,
and to see the answer not simply in the immediate accidents of
history and geography but in the plan and purpose of God.
Clearly it is intended to affirm the divine initiative and to declare
that God is doing a new thing, but the question is *how* this is
understood.

One can mark the difference by noting the two Greek words
in the New Testament for 'new' – *neos* and *kainos*. Basically *neos*
refers to novelty, *kainos* to renewal. With the odd variation for
stylistic effect,[53] one can say that all the theologically significant

[52] Knox, *The Death of Christ*, p.125.
[53] E.g. Col. 3.10, *endusamenoi ton neon (anthrōpon) ton anakainoumenon*, compared with Eph. 4.23f., *ananeousthai . . . kai endusasthai ton kainon anthrōpon*.

phrases, like 'the new man', 'the new covenant', 'the new commandment', 'the new Jerusalem', are *kainos* rather than *neos*. The difference is well brought out in the new (or fresh) wine which is not to be put into old skins[54] and the wine which is to be drunk 'new' (or transformed) in the kingdom of God.[55] The 'new thing' that God is doing is always concerned with the re-creation of the old rather than with its scrapping and supersession. He takes up the continuities to remake them.

This fundamental distinction is illustrated in the question Irenaeus raised as to why, in order to create the new Adam, God did not take fresh dust from the ground but formed him from Mary. It was, he answered,

> that what was formed should not be different, nor what was [to be] saved be different, but that he himself [the original Adam][56] should be recapitulated [or restored], with the likeness preserved.[57]

This is highly relevant to the presuppositions with which the scriptural story is meant to be read. As I said earlier, it is not intended to make negative statements about the continuities of the flesh (which are regarded as theologically important). Whatever the 'new creation' may mean it does not mean making a start *ab initio* with totally different material: it means, as Jeremiah was told to learn from the potter's workshop,[58] remoulding the same lump of clay to incalculable new possibilities. It is the Spirit of the Lord at work once again, as in the fashioning of the first heaven and earth,[59] 'overshadowing' the process. And it is for this reason, not because his 'matter' will be different, that Mary is told that the child to be born to her will be called 'Son of God'.[60]

---

[54] Mark 2.22.   [55] Mark 14.25.
[56] Or, following the Latin text, 'the very same formation'.
[57] *Adv. haer.* III.21.10. I owe this reference to C. F. D. Moule, who gives the original versions in his essay 'The Manhood of Jesus in the New Testament', in Sykes and Clayton (eds.), *Christ, Faith and History*, p.104. I have made my own paraphrase.
[58] Jer. 18.1–11.
[59] Gen. 1.2; cf. C. K. Barrett, *The Holy Spirit and the Gospel Tradition*, SPCK 1947, pp.18–24.
[60] Luke 1.35.

It is, I think, important to recognize that if today with our knowledge we take the virgin birth literally we are almost bound to distort it. For the ancients there was no suggestion that it involved the making of new matter – except in the sense that *every* child was a fresh gift from the Lord's hand. In the Lukan story indeed there is no necessity to see the promise to Mary to mean more than that her son when he comes would be 'great', like Elizabeth's,[61] and would bear the title 'Son of the Most High' because the Holy Spirit would be at work in his conception as he had already been in that of his cousin John.[62] In fact,

> the natural way for Mary to take the announcement from Gabriel was to suppose that she was destined, when married to Joseph, to bear the wonderful son . . . prophesied for her.[63]

Human intercourse is no more ruled out than it was in her cousin's miraculous pregnancy – equally the result of the Word of God, with whom nothing is impossible.[64] In neither case is it mentioned (though it is implied of Zechariah),[65] but there is no statement, as there is in Matthew,[66] that Joseph refrained from it.

But even assuming, as Luke himself probably did,[67] that the male contributed nothing, the interpretation of the ancients, as reflected subsequently in the Fathers, would have been that Christ took the *substance* of his humanity complete from Mary his mother, which in this case was activated by the breath of the divine Spirit rather than by what John calls the 'impulse of a man'.[68] As Aquinas was still to state it centuries later (following Aristotle), 'the law of nature is that in the generation of an animal the female supplies the matter, while the male is the active principle of generation'.[69] We now know that genetics works differently,

---

[61] Cf. Luke 1.15 and 32.   [62] Luke 1.30–38.

[63] A. R. C. Leaney, 'Mary and the Virgin Birth', to be published in *The Christ of the Synoptic Gospels*, London 1973; cf. T. Walker, *Is Not This the Son of Joseph?*, James Clarke 1937, pp.24f., who argues that the virgin birth story is developed from the Jewish notion that God or his *Shekinah* is the third partner in the procreation of any holy child.

[64] Luke 1.36–38.   [65] Luke 1.23f.   [66] Matt. 1.25.   [67] Cf. Luke 3.23.

[68] John 1.13 (my translation).

[69] *Summa* III.31.5; cf. III.28.1 ad 3: 'In conception the seed of the male is not by way of matter, but by way of agent: and the female alone supplies the matter.' The matter was understood to be blood ('which is flesh potentially'), whose

and that even if human parthenogenesis were biologically possible, Jesus would have been female. Mary could not have supplied what alone could have made him male – and no one in fact is attributing *this* miracle to her.[70] Therefore fresh matter – the male genes – must have been created and introduced by God. And if Jesus was genuinely an individual, if, as the Fathers insisted, his flesh was his 'own and sole',[71] then it must have been as unrepeatable in its genetic composition as that of any other human being. On the male side, as much as on its female, it must have focussed the entire history of the human race in one particular unique combination. But on its male side the vital difference was that it was not part of what Sir Alister Hardy has called 'the living stream'[72] at all, but created to look like one, and presumably, unless Jesus was sterile, to function like one and continue the stream *as if* there had been no break at all. And built into the genetic code in his case, as in every other, must have been the peculiar hereditary elements, physical and psychic, which made his contemporaries judge that he 'took after' some one rather than another – whereas actually, of course, he was related on his male side to no one.

By the time we reach this point we are bound to ask whether anything different is being asserted than was asserted by the defenders of conservative orthodoxy in the last century when they said that God created rocks with fossils in them to look as though evolution were true. The appearances may have been saved, but the position was fundamentally untenable. This, of course, is not to say that 'science' has disproved the virgin birth or that physical miracles of this sort are impossible. That would be totally unwarranted dogmatism. But it is to raise the question whether the credibility gap has not been so stretched that it becomes reasonable to ask whether this kind of gap, this sort of special creation, is not only not *necessary* as a condition of believing

emission in the Virgin's case was uninfected by 'concupiscence' (III.31.5).
[70] Aquinas specifically denies to her the exercise of any active power in Christ's conception (III.32.4).
[71] Andrew of Samosata, cited in Cyril, *Apol. adv. orient.* 11.
[72] The title of the first volume of his Gifford lectures: Sir Alister Hardy, *The Living Stream*, Collins 1965.

in the Incarnation but may be so counter-productive of belief as to require us to say that it is something the Christian faith does *not* involve (any more than it involves artificial fossils). Indeed, it seems to me questionable whether today belief in a physical virgin birth can be stated in a way that does not throw doubt on the genuineness of Jesus' humanity. Originally it was told by the evangelists not to question that humanity or its place in the biological process but to enhance it. But can it now have any other effect?

Yet the notion that the divine initiative requires (even if only symbolically) the kind of break and fresh creation which the virgin birth has been interpreted to involve is deeply ingrained in Christian thinking. Teilhard de Chardin wrote of the similar psychological need to represent the appearance of the first man as a special, discontinuous act of creation:

> Many people suppose that the superiority of spirit would be 'jeopardized' if its first manifestation were not accompanied by some interruption of the normal advance of the world. One ought rather to say that precisely because it is spirit its appearance must take the form of a crowning achievement, or a blossoming.[73]

The same applies to the appearance of the Christ which, the New Testament writers stress, comes in the fullness of time, the fruit of a purpose growing out of the past, not cutting across it: the 'recapitulation', as Irenaeus was to delight in calling it, of all that went before.

This supposition that God needed for his purpose new flesh rather than common flesh has been connected with the extraordinary notion that in Christ he assumed 'unfallen' human nature. I call it 'extraordinary', not because it is exceptional or eccentric in Christian theology (indeed until recently it has scarcely been challenged),[74] but because it apparently flies in the

[73] Included in the collection of *pensées* in Pierre Teilhard de Chardin, *Hymn of the Universe*, Collins 1965, p.100.

[74] See the survey in Barth, *Church Dogmatics* (=CD), T. and T. Clark 1936–69, I 2, pp.155f.; and cf. Bruce, op. cit., pp.248–57; Baillie, op. cit., pp.16f.; W. Pannenberg, *Jesus: God and Man*, SCM Press 1968, p.362. I suspect, though I have

face of all the biblical evidence. The account which the Epistle to the Hebrews gives of Jesus as a man who 'has been tested every way' as we are,[75] who was 'beset by weakness'[76] and who 'in the days of his earthly life . . . offered up prayers and petitions, with loud cries and tears' and 'because of his humble submission . . . was heard',[77] clearly points to a man of common clay with ourselves. And for Paul, too, the solidarity of Christ with our present human condition is of fundamental theological importance. Without questioning the sinlessness of Christ, Paul makes it clear that this has significance only if he really did share our fallen lot. God sent his Son 'in a form like that of our own sinful nature'[78] and 'made him one with the sinfulness of men'.[79] For our sake he came under the curse and custody of the law[80] and in bearing the human likeness he assumed the position of a slave to the powers of evil and of death.[81] Barth sums up the inescapable picture by saying:

He was not a sinful man. But inwardly and outwardly His situation was that of a sinful man. He did nothing that Adam did. But He lived life in the form it must take on the basis and assumption of Adam's act. . . . Freely He entered into solidarity and necessary association with our lost existence. Only in this way 'could' God's revelation to us, our reconciliation with Him, manifestly become an event in Him and by Him.[82]

not the learning to document this, that there is here much less of an unbroken tradition than has been assumed. Thus Nestorius wrote of Christ: Because in fact he took this [likeness] in order to abolish the guilt of the first man and in order to give his nature the former image which he had lost through his guilt, rightly he took that which had proved itself guilty and had been made captive and had been subjected to servitude, with all the bonds of scorn and contempt (G. R. Driver and L. Hodgson (eds.), *The Bazaar of Heracleides*, Oxford University Press 1925, p.62).

Mark Santer has drawn my attention to a remarkable exception in Julian of Norwich, which probably shows that (as with the doctrine of the impassibility of God) popular piety was all along instinctively closer to scripture than the official theology of the church: Our foul mortal flesh that God's Son took upon himself, which was Adam's old kirtle, strait, threadbear and short, then by our Saviour was made fair, new white and bright, of endless cleanness, large and ample: fairer and richer than was the clothing which I saw on the Father (*Revelations of Divine Love*, 51; ed. J. Walsh, Burns Oates 1961, pp.142f.).

[75] Heb. 4.15.   [76] Heb. 5.2.   [77] Heb. 5.7.   [78] Rom. 8.3.
[79] II Cor. 5.21.   [80] Gal. 3.13,23; 4.4f.
[81] Phil. 2.7f.; cf. Gal. 4.3,8. Cf. my *The Body*, pp.37–40.
[82] Barth, CD I 2, p.152.

In the light of this it is indeed astonishing that the Council of Chalcedon should have endorsed such a statement as that of Cyril that Christ's flesh was not 'the flesh of a man like one of ourselves'[83] or the gloss by Leo that 'complete in what belonged to us' meant 'what the Creator put in us from the beginning', i.e., unfallen human nature, in contrast with 'what the Deceiver brought upon us'.[84] Indeed, the gulf in presupposition comes out strikingly in what Leo thought *totus in nostris* implied. For us, to belong in every respect to the human race, Jesus must have been linked through his biological tissue to the origin of life on this planet and behind that to the whole inorganic process reaching back to the star dust and the hydrogen atom – as much part of 'the seamless robe of nature'[85] as any other living thing. This is the one kind of pre-existence of which we can be sure – though not, needless to say, of the individual as such. And theologically this has indeed always been asserted by saying that the Incarnation was prepared from the foundation of the world. Yet there has been an extraordinary reluctance (despite the New Testament genealogies, and particularly the Lukan one, tracing Christ back to Adam) to admit the physical basis of this spiritual judgment.

The need, psychologically and theologically, to set a break between our human nature and the immaculate flesh of the Redeemer has also been fed by views of original sin as a physically

---

[83] *Ep. Nest* III. This statement is made in a eucharistic context, but is based on the fact that the flesh of Christ's incarnate body was life-giving because 'unfallen'. Even Luther, who at times gets very near to saying that Christ took our fallen humanity, insists that his flesh, though real, is to be distinguished from all other flesh: 'By nature he is Mary's child, yet he has spiritual flesh, a true divine, spiritual body, in which there dwells the Holy Spirit who begot him and permeates his flesh with spirit' (WA 33.262.34. WA = *Weimarer Ausgabe*, the Weimar critical edition of Luther's works, Weimar, 1883-, 90 vols; cf. WA 23.203.32; 39/II 28.7); quoted by I. D. K. Siggins, *Martin Luther's Doctrine of Christ*, Yale University Press 1970, p.215.   [84] *Tome* 3; cf. n.1 above.

[85] Barry Wood, *The Magnificent Frolic*, Westminster Press, Philadelphia 1970, ch. 2; cf. Nels F. S. Ferré, *Christ and the Christian*, Collins 1958, p.97: 'His biological tissue, with its strains and stresses, went back to before the Ice Age. His mental make-up and mental environment came from human history as such, and from his specific history in Palestine as well. Before any child is born it repeats the history of the race in the womb, and after birth it repeats the history of its people as it is relevant to the child. In no way was Jesus different with regard to his humanity from any normally born child. Only by being fully and normally human could Jesus enter entirely and organically into our human predicament.'

transmitted taint. For how could Christ be free of sin and therefore able to cure it if the infected stream were not cut? But this is a
thoroughly sub-personal (and unscriptural)[86] conception of sin.
If it is rejected, the need for a biological break disappears. As
Norman Pittenger puts it:

> If 'original sin' means, not the quasi-biological 'inheritance of
> Adam', but the straightforward fact that our situation and state
> is conditioned by the 'solidarity of the race' in accumulated
> wrong-doing and wrong-thinking and hence 'wrong-being',
> we can also see that One who did not consent to this fact but
> rather *gave himself without reserve* to the will of God, as he saw it,
> responding in full love and dedication to the God who moved
> in and through him, was in fact without that 'original sin' save
> in so far as its results affected him. He need not be regarded as
> having been preserved from the 'taint' of man's inheritance by
> some utterly miraculous and entirely unique action.[87]

This, needless to say, does not explain how such unreserved
obedience was possible, if it was, but it enables us to think of it
without severing the connection with the only kind of obedience
open to those who *do* consent to their conditioning.

The use once more of the virgin birth story in later Christian
theology (though not in the New Testament) to set a *cordon
sanitaire* to break the entail of sin was, of course, also bound up
with the Fathers' views of the sexual act itself as evil. And the
break worked, the transmission of Adam's taint was interrupted,
because they were able to see the latter as carried solely by the
male seed, the woman supplying merely the soil or breeding-
ground of evil. Thus Aquinas could say that Christ was related to
Adam and the patriarchs only in 'bodily substance' (derived from
Mary) and not by 'seminal virtue' 'by which original sin is
transmitted'.[88] But, as the subsequent doctrine of the Immaculate

[86] It depends on taking Rom. 5.12 to mean 'in whom [Adam] all sinned',
which is possible (as Augustine disastrously found) with the Vulgate's *in quo* but
impossible in the original Greek (*eph' hō(i)*), which must mean 'inasmuch as all
have sinned'.
[87] Norman Pittenger, *The Word Incarnate*, Nisbet 1959, p.213.
[88] *Summa* III.31.8.

Conception has shown, for a perfect upbringing it is necessary also to presuppose from the start a perfect mother – which we should now see as even more important for sinless development – and indeed a perfect society. By this time, of course, the whole exercise becomes self-defeating. Indeed, Aquinas repudiated the doctrine of the immaculate conception of Mary (whom he goes so far as to describe as 'wholly conceived in original sin')[89] precisely on the ground that if she had been 'sanctified before animation' 'she would not have needed redemption'.[90] For by this route one becomes involved in an infinite regress of immaculate conceptions.

Testing for reality

But rather than pursue this unprofitable line, let us use the subject of sexuality as a good, because sensitive, spot of *our* testing for reality in this matter of the full humanity of Jesus. In all this, of course, the issue is not what historical statements we can confidently make about Jesus of Nazareth. The answer is quite clearly, None. We do not know for certain anything about his sex-life. As Dennis Nineham has reminded us, the gospels 'do not even think to tell us definitely whether or not he was married!',[91] though a book has recently appeared with the title *Was Jesus Married?*,[92] which is not in fact as mad as it sounds. The gospels do not exist to provide answers to these questions. But what we can do is to use these questions to test *our* presumptions about what is implied by asserting of Jesus that he was completely human. Are we *free* to say certain things of him? Or do we find,

---

[89] *Summa* III.31.7.   [90] *Summa* III.27.2.
[91] D. E. Nineham, *St Mark*, Penguin Books 1963, p. 35.
[92] William A. Phipps, *Was Jesus Married?*, Harper and Row, New York 1970. It contains a useful study of Christian sexuality. But it is over-motivated and over-argued. The decisive argument against Jesus' being married (at any rate during the time of his public ministry) is not the silence of the gospels (nor the subsequent anti-erotic bias of the church), but I Cor. 9.5: 'Have I no right to take a Christian wife about with me, like the rest of the apostles and the Lord's brothers, and Cephas?' If Jesus, like his brothers, had been known to have been married, it is inconceivable that Paul would not have appealed to the fact. This very early evidence must outweigh that of second-century Gnostic documents like the Gospel of Philip.

psychologically, that we *have* to deny them – and if so on what evidence? I am probing again for the resistance to wanting him 'too human', a resistance which I believe causes many today to dismiss him as not one of themselves at all. And by 'too human' I do *not* mean brought down to their level by sin – a subject which I should like to postpone till the next chapter, when we come to ask in what sense Jesus was a perfect man, as opposed to perfect man.

Since we have been starting at the beginning, how do we view alternatives to virginal conception, if we do not take this as a physical account of Jesus's birth? This is a question, I find, that is strangely ignored by those who are relieved to think they have left behind their difficulties by taking the story symbolically.

There are three possibilities: (*a*) conception and birth in wedlock; (*b*) conception by Joseph outside wedlock, subsequently legitimized; (*c*) conception outside wedlock by an unknown party, subsequently condoned by Joseph. (*a*) is the only alternative for which there is no evidence at all. (*b*) could explain some of the Lukan evidence, but is specifically denied by Matthew.[93] (*c*) is obviously the most embarrassing alternative for the church and one that Christians would naturally have been most concerned to repudiate. There may indeed be such a charge already behind Jesus' own countrymen's description of him as 'son of Mary'[94] (which Matthew has carefully altered – despite his own infancy narrative – and where Luke and John have 'son of Joseph'),[95] and perhaps behind the remark of the Jews of Jerusalem: '*We* are not base-born.'[96] We know that subsequently scandalous (and historically worthless) allegations were made on this count by the Jews.[97] Of greatest interest, however, is the line of defence adopted by Matthew.

[93] Matt. 1.18f.
[94] Mark 6.3. So E. Stauffer, *Jesus and His Story*, SCM Press 1960, p.24. He also sees the same imputation concealed in the charge of Matt. 11.19 = Luke 7.34 of being a glutton and a drinker (pp. 23f., 165). But the evidence for this is very thin.
[95] Matt. 13.55, 'Is he not the carpenter's son? Is not his mother called Mary?'; Luke 4.22; John 6.42.
[96] John 8.41.
[97] See Stauffer, op. cit., pp. 24f., who cites a Jewish genealogical table dating, he claims, from the period before 70 where Jesus is listed as 'the bastard of a

There are a number of instances in Matthew's gospel where his material is clearly adapted to the purposes of anti-Jewish apologetic. The story of Joseph's dream in 1.19–25 is evidently intended to represent him as a Jew of strict principle, while at the same time a man of humanity desirous of protecting his seemingly faithless fiancée from public exposure – and theoretically indeed from death by stoning, which the law required of 'a virgin pledged in marriage', on the ground that in principle she was already 'another man's wife'.[98] Later in the gospel we have such additions as the defence of Jesus' baptism by John,[99] Pilate's wife's dream[100] and his hand-washing,[101] and above all the story of the guard at the tomb specifically to counter Jewish rumours that the disciples had stolen the body of Jesus.[102] In this last instance the evangelist dismisses the charge as baseless fabrication. But in the case of Jesus' *genesis* or origin his tactic is strangely different, and surprisingly bold.

As in Luke, the lineage of Jesus as the Messiah is traced through Joseph, described as 'the husband of Mary',[103] which indeed by the time of the child's birth he legally was for Matthew[104] – though not for Luke.[105] Matthew is not apparently disturbed by

wedded wife' (*Yebamoth* 4.13); and H. Laible, *Jesus Christ in the Talmud* (tr. and ed. A. W. Streane, Cambridge University Press 1893), pp.7–39, who quotes *Shabbath* 104b: 'He was not the son of Stada, but he was the son of Pandera. Rab. Chisda said: The husband of Jesus' mother was Stada, but her lover was Pandera. Another said: Her husband was surely Paphos ben Jehudah; on the contrary Stada was his mother; or, according to others, his mother was Miriam [Mary], the women's hairdresser.' Cf. also *Sanh.* 47a; *Pesiqta rabb.* 100b; *Tos. Hul.* 2.24; and Origen, *Contra Celsum* I.32: 'Let us return . . . to the words put into the mouth of the Jew, where the mother of Jesus is described as having been turned out by the carpenter who was betrothed to her, as she had been convicted of adultery and had a child by a certain soldier named Panthera' (tr. and ed. H. Chadwick, Cambridge University Press 1953, with his note *ad loc.*), and I.28,29 and 33.

[98] Deut. 22.23f. The provision was doubtless not strictly enforced (and is not even hinted at by Matthew), though John 8.2–11 shows that in a similar situation, knowledge of the penalty was live enough, if only for the polemical purpose of testing Jesus' faithfulness to the law.   [99] Matt. 3.14f.

[100] Matt. 27.19.   [101] Matt. 27.24.

[102] Matt. 27.62–66; 28.11–15.   [103] Matt. 1.16.

[104] Matt. 1.24f. Cf. Stauffer, op. cit., p. 25: 'It was part of the consummation of the marriage that the bride should be fetched to the house of the bridegroom. When the husband named the new-born infant, he recognized it as his child biologically, or at least legally, and admitted it into his family with all the rights appertaining thereto.'

[105] Luke 2.5 – unless we should here read 'his wife', regarding the received text

the difficulty involved if Joseph was not genetically the father. On the contrary, instead of trying to cover up the irregularity of the union, his line seems to be to emphasize it and to make the point that this makes no difference to God's Spirit being at work in and through it. And he does this by going out of his way to draw attention to other links in the chain where irregular connections had been no bar to God. According to the law they should have been; for 'no descendant of an irregular union, even down to the tenth generation, shall become a member of the assembly of the Lord'.[106] Yet here, says Matthew, is the pedigree of the Lord's Anointed!

Luke mentions no women in his genealogy, and indeed for Matthew they are strictly redundant, since the line is traced through the male. But Matthew elects, on four apparently random occasions, to specify the women from whom (*ek*) the child was born. The one thing they apparently have in common is the dubiety of their sexual liaisons.[107]

The first is Tamar,[108] the mother of Perez and Zarah, who got them by deceptively contrived incestuous union with her

'his betrothed' as an assimilation to 1.27 (so J. M. Creed, *St Luke*, Macmillan 1930, *ad loc*). Subsequently Joseph and Mary are referred to as the 'parents' or 'father and mother' of Jesus without question or explanation (2.27, 33, 41, 43, 48). The material in the second chapter may well come from a cycle of tradition which knows nothing of the virgin birth, since 2.17–19, 33 and 48–51 show no awareness of the knowledge vouchsafed to Mary in 1.26–38.

[106] Deut. 23.2.

[107] Johnson, op. cit., pp. 152–79, has an extended discussion of the significance of the four women, and he lists the various interpretations given by commentators. The only other possible common factor is that in contemporary rabbinic thinking they may all have been regarded as non-Israelites. But even if this was so, there is no suggestion that Matthew (unlike Luke, who traces Jesus' ancestry behind Abraham to Adam) is using his genealogy as a justification for the church's universal mission. If he had had this in mind, he needed only to have given Ruth her regular biblical and rabbinic title, 'the Moabitess'. Johnson's own explanation, which he offers 'tentatively . . . as one of the possible solutions', seems strangely pointless. He thinks Matthew is reflecting internal *Jewish* polemic of the Sadducees and others who argued for an Aaronic Messiah against the Pharisees' case for a Davidic Messiah, by quoting well-known 'blots' on the Davidic escutcheon. He admits, however, that Rahab, whom Matthew alone tells us was the mother of Boaz, is never connected with the ancestry of David either in Scripture or in the entire rabbinic tradition. In any case, the introduction of the women could scarcely serve any obvious *Christian* purpose unless it were to answer attacks on the irregularity of Jesus' birth.

[108] Matt. 1.3.

father-in-law Judah, in the guise of a temple-prostitute[109] –
a role specifically forbidden to an Israelite.[110]

The second is Rahab,[111] the common harlot, who seems to have
been a surprising feature of Christian apologetic, being mentioned also in Hebrews[112] and James[113] – though nowhere else in
scripture outside the original story of Joshua.[114]

The third is Ruth,[115] the most moral of them all, though as a
Moabitess she was, according to rabbinic tradition, the fruit of
incest between Lot and his daughters, of whom Moab and Ammon
were born.[116] But she obtained entry to the Messianic line,
through marriage to Boaz, only by some fairly shameless sexual
exploitation at the prompting of her mother-in-law;[117] and
Naomi's feat in thus acquiring succession is specifically compared
to that of Tamar, who again is nowhere else recalled in scripture:
'May your house be like the house of Perez, whom Tamar bore
to Judah, through the offspring the Lord will give you by this
girl.'[118]

The fourth woman is Bathsheba,[119] who though legally married
to David by the time Solomon was conceived,[120] is deliberately
referred to by Matthew not by name, like the others, but as 'the
wife of Uriah'. It is hard to see any intention in this other than to
draw attention to her reprobate status and character.[121] She had
already committed adultery with David[122] – and that in a state of

---

[109] Gen. 38.
[110] Deut. 23.17.
[111] Matt. 1.5.
[112] Heb. 11.31.
[113] James 2.25.
[114] Josh. 2–6.
[115] Matt. 1.5.
[116] Cf. Johnson, op. cit., p. 166, who cites the sources.
[117] Ruth 3–4.
[118] Ruth 4.12.
[119] Matt. 1.6.
[120] II Sam. 12.24.
[121] Recognition of this goes back a long way. Cf. Thomas Aquinas, *Summa*
III.31.3 ad 5: 'As Jerome says on Matt. 1.3: "None of the holy women are mentioned in the Saviour's genealogy, but only those whom Scripture censures, so
that he who came for the sake of sinners, being born of sinners, might blot out all
sin." Thus Thamar is mentioned, who is censured for her sin with her father-in-
law; Rahab who was a whore; Ruth who was a foreigner; and Bethsabee, the
wife of Urias, who was an adulteress. The last, however, is not mentioned by
name, but is designated through her husband; both on account of his sin, for he
was cognizant of the adultery and murder; and further in order that, by men-
tioning the husband by name, David's sin might be recalled.' Needless to say,
Aquinas does not go on to draw any implications with regard to the fifth woman
mentioned.
[122] II Sam. 11.4.

ritual impurity for which alone the penalty was for both to be cut off from their people[123] – and was only his wife now by dint of Uriah's murder. Luke[124] in contrast traces the line through another son, Nathan, who was born to David before his entanglement with Bathsheba.[125]

Finally, and fifthly, there is Mary, who is introduced by the same formula as the rest.[126] The implication is not one of moral condemnation. On the contrary, Tamar was commended in Jewish interpretation,[127] the Targums stressing not her immorality but the desire – blessed by God – of this innocent woman for a share in the royal line from which men had unjustly sought to exclude her. And, as we saw, Naomi's stratagem for Ruth is proudly likened to it with the significant words: 'May you do great things in Ephrathah and keep a name alive in Bethlehem.'[128] Mary is similarly blessed by God. Yet there is nothing to suggest that Matthew intends us to see in her the spotless virgin of ecclesiastical tradition, or even Luke's obedient maiden.[129] Clearly he is presenting her child as being 'of the Holy Spirit'[130] and sees 'the whole thing' as fulfilling Isaiah's prophecy of a virgin birth (as in his Greek-speaking church he was able to interpret it).[131] He will not admit for one moment the validity of the Jewish slurs. But his line of apologetic is strikingly different from that which he adopts in regard to the empty tomb. He does not simply deny the irregularity as pure fabrication. Evidently he could not. On the contrary, he implicitly acknowledges it, and

[123] Lev. 20.18.   [124] Luke 3.32.
[125] II Sam. 5.14.
[126] Matt. 1.16. Cf. F. C. Burkitt, *Evangelion da Mepharreshe* II, Cambridge University Press 1904, p.260: 'Throughout the whole genealogy the Evangelist appears to be telling us in an audible aside that the heir had often been born out of the direct line or irregularly. Thamar the daughter-in-law of Judah, Rahab the harlot, Ruth the Moabitess, and the unnamed wife of Uriah, are forced upon our attention, as if to prepare us for still greater irregularity in the last stage'; quoted, Vincent Taylor, *The Historical Evidence for the Virgin Birth*, Oxford University Press 1920, p.90, who adds: 'There can be little doubt but that the writer's purpose is to rebut Jewish slanders already current regarding the birth of Jesus.'
[127] Cf. Renée Bloch, 'Juda engendra Pharès et Zara de Thamar (Matth. 1.3.)', in Joseph Trinquet (ed.), *Mélanges bibliques redigées en l'honneur d' André Robert*, Paris 1958, pp.381-9.   [128] Ruth 4.11.
[129] Luke 1.38.   [130] Matt. 1.18, 20.
[131] Matt. 1.22f.; Isa. 7.14LXX. In Hebrew the word simply means a young woman.

from the evidence of the past sets out to show that it is entirely compatible with it all being of God and with Jesus being the Christ. The climax of his story is the acknowledgment and naming of the child by Joseph, at the direct instruction of God, and it is *this* that makes him, like his father, 'son of David'.[132] Jesus is thus engrafted into the Messianic line, and it is 'exactly by the irregularity' that 'the action of God and his spirit are made manifest'.[133]

Many years ago I wrote an article entitled 'Hosea and the Virgin Birth',[134] to show that the possibility of Jesus' being born of an irregular union was strikingly in line with the pattern of the divine good pleasure in deliberately choosing to raise children of promise, who were to 'be called Sons of the Living God',[135] from Hosea's faithless spouse, 'a woman loved by another man, an adulteress'.[136] For thus the scandal of the divine love is revealed as an affront to all legal righteousness, being vindicated in one who is born, as well as dies,[137] under the curse of the law. It did not occur to me at the time that this was a line of apologetic to be found in the New Testament, not simply of the Christian church (of which it is used independently by two writers),[138] but of Christ himself.

I am not, of course, arguing that this proves anything historically – though it is surely a line that would scarcely have been invented without cause.[139] All I am saying is that it is a possibility

[132] Cf. Matt. 1.20, 'Joseph, son of David'.

[133] Stendahl, op. cit., pp.94–105. I was much indebted in all this to the draft of the article by Leaney, 'Mary and the Virgin Birth', quoted above. Leaney, however, was supposing (I have not seen his final version) that the truth which Matthew is defending against calumny is that Jesus was the son of Joseph and Mary by pre-marital intercourse (position (*b*) above). If so, he surely made his task very much more difficult than it need have been. Pre-marital intercourse between betrothed couples does not appear to have been regarded as scandalous. Indeed, according to the Mishnah (*Kiddushim* 1), it was one of the three recognized ways of effecting a betrothal. Cf. Phipps, op. cit., pp.39f. and the literature there cited.

[134] John A. T. Robinson, 'Hosea and the Virgin Birth', *Theology* LII, October 1948, pp.373–5.

[135] Hos. 1.10.

[136] Hos. 3.1; cf. 1.2f.

[137] Gal. 3.13.

[138] Rom. 9.25f.; I Peter 2.10.

[139] Stauffer, op. cit., p.25, concludes much more definitely: 'To sum up, *Jesus was the son of Mary, not Joseph*. That is the historical fact which is recognized equally by Christians and Jews, friends and foes. This fact is symbolic and am-

that cannot be dismissed on the ground of inappropriateness, let alone impropriety. We shall never know humanly speaking who was Jesus' father. But can we be free to be as indifferent as we are ignorant – on the ground, as Matthew bodly asserts, that his divine significance is entirely unaffected? I suspect that most Christians would have difficulty in saying, Yes.

And can we say the same of Jesus's own sexuality? Again, it appears not, from the furore occasioned by Hugh Montefiore's mere raising of the question whether Jesus might have been homosexual in tendency.[140] He put it forward very tentatively as 'an explanation which we must not ignore' for some of the facts, again suggesting that it may tell us something of God's self-identification with the outsider and the unloved. I shall return to the reaction it occasioned in the next chapter.

Meanwhile the real difficulty for many is to admit that Jesus had *any* sexuality – *and was therefore a normal human being.* If only to show how far we have moved, it is amusing to observe across the interval of a hundred years the horror of the reviewers at Seeley's hint in *Ecce Homo* that Jesus might have had ordinary (though still very Victorian) feelings about sex. The delicate suggestion that, confronted by the woman taken in adultery, he looked on the ground through embarrassment provoked the response from *The Quarterly Review*:

> The coarseness and latitude of the interpretation was never, we believe, exceeded by any comment which was not designed to be profane.[141]

Another anonymous pamphleteer,[142] who complained of the 'indecorous, not to say indecent, mode of writing about our blessed Saviour', was reduced to speechlessness by some apparently innocuous words written in connection with Mary Magdalen:

> It is commonly by love itself that men learn the sacredness

biguous, like all the circumstances of Jesus' history. The Christians saw in it a divine act of creation. The Jews spoke of Mary's adultery.'
[140] Hugh Montefiore, 'Jesus the Revelation of God', in *Christ for Us Today*, pp.108–10.
[141] *The Quarterly Review* CXIX, April 1866, p. 518. The review is unsigned.
[142] *Notes on 'Ecce Homo'*, London 1866.

of love. Yet, though Christ never entered the realm of sexual love, this sacredness seems to have been felt by him far more deeply than by other men.[143]

'Comment,' he adds, 'on this humanitarian idea is superfluous.' Imagine his reaction to the question suggested at a Council of Churches' Conference on Family Life in Canada just a century later in 1966 as 'a good one to ask yourself':

When the woman wiped Jesus's feet with her hair, she performed a highly sexual action. Did Jesus at that moment experience an erection?[144]

Of course there is no answer. The gospels are not there to answer such questions. It *is*, however, a good question to ask *ourselves*, to test our reaction. Maybe Jesus was not in the slightest roused: perhaps, like some men, he attracted women without being attracted by them. Or perhaps he responded in a perfectly natural heterosexual manner. I am simply urging that we can be free to say either. But in practice the answer has been, Neither. The question still remains, of course, whether Jesus may not – like a small minority of human beings – have been without any strong sexual drives. And we must retain this as an open possibility. But that is very different from being required to assume it. In fact the same piety which implicitly presumes it would be most shocked to hear Jesus described as undersexed! But merely to raise the question appears bad taste. To think of Jesus as having had sexual desires of any sort has seemed to offend against his purity – though the novelists have been more realistic.[145] Consequently the church has appeared to present him as sex*less*.[146] And that for most people today is about the most effective way of saying that he was not fully human.

All this is part of the deeply ingrained notion of an impassible

[143] *Ecce Homo*, p. 198.

[144] Quoted by Ernest Harrison, *A Church without God*, McClelland and Stewart, Toronto 1967, p. 61.

[145] E.g. D. H. Lawrence, *The Man Who Died*, Heinemann 1931; N. Kazantzakis, *The Last Temptation*; C. Monterosso, *The Salt of the Earth*, Faber 1967.

[146] Tom Driver, 'Sexuality and Jesus', *Union Seminary Quarterly Review* XX, March 1965, pp. 235–46; Phipps, op. cit., especially chs. 3 and 9.

Christ-figure – one who cannot be acted on, affected or changed. It is reflected, interestingly enough, in the (in many ways) traditionalist Catholic films of the Communist Pasolini. His *Gospel According to St Matthew* was widely acclaimed by Christians, but it showed a Jesus who passed through the midst of men without entering into any real human relations with anyone. And his later *Theorem* presents the same sort of Christ-figure – in the form of a visitor to a family who changed the lives of everyone he touched, but without any suggestion that he was affected by them.

This, above all, is the conception of Jesus' goodness which has undermined the genuineness of his humanity. And it is from there that we must go on to examine what is implied in calling him *the* man, the perfect man. But for many today the first step is to convince themselves that he could be the definition and vindication of a genuine human existence, let alone of a perfect human existence. Our concern in this chapter has not been in any way to diminish, let alone to depreciate – though inevitably, I fear, some will take it so. It has been to allow possibilities, the exclusion of which by piety has made it impossible for men to judge Jesus *extra*ordinary because they cannot even judge him ordinary.

What we have been doing is to explore what for us now is involved in the insistence of the author to the Hebrews, that like 'every high priest' Jesus was a man 'taken from among men'.[147] This cannot merely mean selected from among the men who happened to be alive at that moment, one of whom had been 'planted' there as God's agent. It must include, as the writer says earlier, stemming from the common human stock,[148] sharing the same genetic inheritance, like the children of one family.[149] By comparison with this, *how* he was conceived is (as Schleiermacher recognized) quite secondary, and (as I believe Matthew saw) strictly irrelevant to his divine significance.

This is a point of wider application and importance today. In his recent Eddington Memorial Lecture,[150] John Hick made the point that in our age we must come to terms with the fact that

[147] Heb. 5.1.
[148] Heb. 2.11.
[149] Heb. 2.14.
[150] John Hick, *Biology and the Soul*, Cambridge University Press 1972.

the significance of the individual as a person, what has traditionally been expressed as his 'soul', may have to be compatible with crucial elements of randomness in the genetic process. Similarly, the taking of the Christ from among men could at one level ('according to the flesh') be the outcome of a process of chance and necessity (such as Jacques Monod has described in his book of that title),[151] which embraces hazards far vaster than any that Matthew incorporated – *if* that should turn out to be the manner of the divine operation. Significance, even unique significance, is not *dependent upon* any particular supposition of regularity or irregularity, of mutation or intervention. This raises much bigger questions of how Jesus as a human being can be *both* a genuine product of the process – with all we are now beginning to know that this implies – *and* the clue to its total significance. To these questions we must come back. But if we have laid particular stress on his genetic inheritance as one fairly crucial test of his humanity, it is no more than Matthew did and no more than the science of microbiology is pressing afresh upon our generation. For a Christ who can *only* be an exception to, rather than the supreme exemplification of, what is true of every other human being can scarcely be our man – let alone *the* man.

[151] Jacques Monod, *Chance and Necessity*, Collins 1972.

THREE

THE MAN

In the previous chapter we tried to take seriously the requirement (which no one theoretically would dispute) that if Jesus Christ is to be anything for us at all he must have been genuinely a man, with the peculiarities and limitations of one unique individual. But we noted the reluctance to press this to the limit, and this reluctance is connected with the desire, which we must go on to consider, to see in him more than *a* man – and to admit nothing that might prejudice that 'more'. One of the most powerful reasons against admitting that Jesus was in every sense a man has been that if he were simply an individual human being, his life and death would merely be significant for what he himself was and did. But if he is to be the Christ, he must point beyond himself. He must (as we saw at the beginning) be the clue to the nature of both man and God. He must be a representative figure, standing for all mankind and standing for God. The latter demand we shall be considering later. But first let us look at the former.

What does it mean to say of Jesus Christ that he is 'the proper man', the norm of what a truly human existence should be? This includes what Christians have wanted to say of Jesus in speaking of him as *the* Son of Man, the archetypal man, the last or definitive Adam, the completely integrated self, the one who can truly say 'I am'. And it is not only Christians who have found themselves wanting to make this response. Buber, the Jew, has left his testimony:

> How powerful, even to being overpowering, and how

legitimate, even to being self-evident, is the saying of *I* by Jesus! For it is the *I* of unconditional relation in which the man calls his *Thou* Father in such a way that he himself is simply Son, and nothing else but Son.[1]

But what does it mean to see this ideal of normality and universality in any one individual, and what relation does it bear to the Jesus of history? It has tended to be taken as axiomatic in Christian thinking and devotion that Jesus was complete and perfect in every respect. He must have had everything, he must have been everything – or he could not have been the Christ. And this has been a powerful influence in the separation of him from ordinary humanity. He has been set on a pedestal by himself, an immaculate paragon, of whom it was impossible to think that he should fall short in anything. And as such he quickly becomes unique not because he is normal but because he is abnormal. What we want to say of him as *the* man paradoxically undercuts his humanity. And this is a powerful factor today in making him for many an unreal figure with the static perfection of flawless porcelain, rather than a man of flesh and blood. So pervasive and damaging is this estimate that it is necessary to give some attention to it. For one has merely to breathe the suggestion that Jesus might not have been perfect, to have more bees about one's head than if one raises the question whether he might have been homosexual. Indeed, assertion of the latter is immediately taken to be denial of the former.[2]

But what is meant by saying that Jesus Christ was 'a perfect man' as opposed to 'perfect man', that is to say, 'completely human', which is what the phrase *teleios anthrōpos* always meant in patristic usage[3] – notably in the *teleion en anthrōpotēti* (complete in regard to his humanity) of the Chalcedonian Definition?

---

[1] Martin Buber, *I and Thou*, T. and T. Clark 1937, pp.66f.
[2] Cf. *The Times*, 28 July 1967: ' "There is no evidence whatever to support Canon Montefiore's reported ideas," Dr Ramsey said. "Christians believe that Christ's dealings with both men and women were those of a perfect man." '
[3] Cf. Grillmeier, op. cit., p.137: 'As a christological expression "perfect man" merely affirms the true reality of Christ's Incarnation.' In Hippolytus, *Ref. omn. haer.* 17, one of its first appearances, *anthrōpos teleios* stands parallel to *alēthōs genomenos anthrōpos* (truly become man).

We may ask the question under two heads – though it is ultimately impossible to separate them. What does it mean to say that Jesus *had* everything that a man could have? And, What does it mean to say that he *was* everything that a man could be?

The man who had everything

The former is easier to answer, though even here there has been a strange reluctance to concede that Jesus was not endowed with every perfection: physical, mental and spiritual.

Even at the physical level, whereas Christians have happily absorbed the tradition that Paul was an ugly little man with a snub-nose, who might have been an epileptic, Jesus has been assumed to be the perfect specimen of humanity, as Aquinas put it, 'of becoming and middle stature',[4] with no imbalance of any kind. This, of course, lies behind the immediate reaction that if he had been homosexual he could not have been perfect – though on this model the golden mean between the two poles of heterosexuality and homosexuality in all of us is the man who is bisexual, who indeed in many societies has been regarded as the ideal. But Jesus must have been right-handed or left-handed (unless we are to say he *must* have been ambidextrous!), belonged to one particular blood-group, and had the characteristics of one psychological type rather than another. Perhaps it is the last notion that is the most threatening. I was recently asked to reply to an article which

---

[4] *Summa* 33.2 ad 2: *decentem et mediocrem quantitatem.* This statement occurs in a fascinating reply to the objection that if (as Aquinas is arguing) Christ's body received its soul at the instant of conception, whereas all other men have theirs infused only after an interval, this head-start would mean that he should either have been born sooner or have been a bigger child than others. Aquinas answers that there is a 'certain latitude' in the amount of matter at the moment of 'animation', large men having more. So in order to end up middle-sized, Jesus must have started with less. 'Nevertheless that quantity was not too small . . . since it would have sufficed for the animation of a small man's body.' This is a nice way of saying that Jesus was abnormal – but not too abnormal! In the same argument in *Sentent.* III 3.5.2, he accepts the traditional estimate of the interval before the embryo becomes a distinct body (and can therefore receive a soul) as forty days (according to Aristotle) or forty-six (according to Augustine). Had Jesus been a girl it would have been at least ninety days, and then the 'certain latitude' would indeed have been stretched!

sought to show that Jesus was a manic-depressive.[5] It was far from conclusive, because the evidence is insufficient (if only in its chronological sequence) for any such reconstruction. But even to suggest in a sermon that this was an open question, or that he might, alternatively, have been schizoid in tendency, would be enough to blow the top. Yet, as I said earlier, the film *The Gospel According to St Matthew*, which was welcomed by many churchmen, presents a Jesus who appears to make no real human relationships with anyone. (The question still remains whether it may not in this be faithful to the particular gospel it portrays.)

Quite apart from what this idea that 'Jesus could not have been perfect if . . .' says to those who are constitutionally homosexual, schizoid or snub-nosed, the basic question surely is: Is there anything in the New Testament to suggest that this is the kind of perfection any of his contemporaries thought of seeing in him? One cannot read Mark's gospel, and even more John's, without seeing grounds for the fears of those, including his family, who questioned his mental balance.[6] Indeed he himself insisted on the single-minded obedience that does not require any of these well-rounded perfections. In fact, they may be an actual hindrance. A man may have to enter life without hand or foot or eye,[7] or indeed without testicles at all.[8] The norm for the Bible is that a person should be God's true man, not the complete man of renaissance humanism, the all-rounder of whom it could be said, You name it: he's got it. Indeed Jesus' strength was precisely that he called men to the narrow gate, going unerringly for the one thing necessary, risking being taken for a fanatic. As another writer put it in the same exchange I have referred to on Jesus' sanity:

> Jesus was not an average level-headed man, such as parents of a daughter would welcome as a son-in-law. He was an off-centre, minority type, along with such men as the Hebrew prophets before him or William Blake and Søren Kierkegaard

[5] Raymond Lloyd, 'Cross and Psychosis', *Faith and Freedom* XXIV, Autumn 1970 and Spring 1971, pp.13–29 and 67–87. My reply 'Was Jesus Mad?' followed in XXV, Spring 1972, pp.58–64.

[6] Mark 3.21; John 7.20; 8.48, 52; 10.20.

[7] Mark 9.43–48; Matt. 5.29f.   [8] Matt. 19.12.

in times nearer our own. Such men are 'the salt of the earth', not our staple diet. It would not be good for everyone to aim, in simple general terms, at being 'like Jesus'.[9]

There would be few today who would question that Jesus' knowledge was limited,[10] and indeed at points wrong[11] – though the latter was being disputed by Frank Weston as recently as the First World War ('We cannot for a moment believe that the Incarnate ever spoke a single word, of which in his universal life as Logos he could not say: "That is not exactly and finally true" ')[12] and indeed by Eric Mascall today ('Positive error is altogether excluded from the utterances that Christ makes').[13] But no one is presumably going to follow the flights of the seventeenth-century commentators on Thomas Aquinas[14] who held that Jesus was the 'greatest' as dialectician, philosopher, mathematician, doctor, politician, orator, painter, farmer, sailor, soldier (or anything else you care to mention), nor emulate the Lutheran dogmaticians who ascribed to him every excellency of

[9] Francis Terry, 'Cross and Sanity', *Faith and Freedom* XXV, Autumn 1971, p.11.

[10] Symptomatic of much traditional interpretation has been the way in which Jesus, even as a child, has been seen as 'teaching' the doctors of the law when Luke merely represents him as 'listening to them and putting questions' – however intelligent his questions and answers (Luke 2.46f.). But a tendency to see Jesus as the 'wonder child' set in very early, with the Gnostic infancy narratives, cf. e.g. 'The Childhood Gospel of Thomas', in E. Hennecke (ed.), *New Testament Apocrypha* I, Lutterworth Press 1963, pp. 388–401.

[11] Cf. from a modern Roman Catholic point of view, R. E. Brown, 'How Much Did Jesus Know?', in id., *Jesus, God and Man*, Geoffrey Chapman 1968, pp.39–102, and from a Protestant, C. K. Barrett, *Jesus and the Gospel Tradition*, SPCK 1967, pp. 105–8.

[12] Frank Weston, *The One Christ*, Longmans [2]1914, p.226; cf. id., *The Christ and His Critics*, Mowbrays 1919, chs. 10 and 11. Forbes Robinson was prepared to concede the fallibility (as distinct from the peccability) of Christ in an essay written for the Burney Prize at Cambridge of 1891–2, *The Self-Limitation of the Word of God as Manifested in the Incarnation*, Longmans 1914, pp.100–4. In this he goes further than Gore was ready to go either in his contemporary Bampton Lectures, *The Incarnation of the Son of God*, John Murray 1891, or even at the end of his life in *Belief in Christ*, John Murray 1922; reprinted in *The Reconstruction of Belief*, John Murray 1926, where he still denies to Christ the possibility of any mistake or error – merely the acceptance of current assumptions for the sake of argument with his contemporaries. Forbes Robinson's general position closely foreshadows that of Weston, but he receives no mention in the histories of the doctrine.

[13] E. L. Mascall, *Christ, the Christian and the Church*, Longmans [2]1955, p.60.

[14] The Salmanticenses in their *Cursus Theologicus* XXI.22.2. n.29; quoted by R. E. Brown, op. cit., pp.44f. Aquinas himself is altogether more restrained.

body and soul[15] – perfect health,[16] immortality and supreme
beauty of form – including one German, found by Barth,[17] who
claimed to know that among these perfections belonged the fact
that Jesus never laughed. In fact, as Barth rightly insists, humanly
speaking Jesus is not to be regarded as 'a great man'.[18] It would be
more true to say of him that he had nothing than that he had
everything,[19] and so far from putting men in mind of a Greek
god, it was rather of one of whom it was written, 'He had no
beauty, no majesty to draw our eyes, no grace to make us delight
in him'.[20] Indeed, this *was* the image of the Christ during the
period of the persecutions: a Jesus 'without honour and without
form',[21] 'wretched, dishonoured, unsightly'.[22]

It was only later that everything was loaded on to him. All
such excess of piety rests on a false understanding of the relation of
the universal to the particular – that *the* man must have everything
that anyone else has, rather as the master key fits all the locks
opened by each of the separate keys. But universality is not denied
by particularity. The individual may be the antithesis of the
general, but it is not of the universal.[23] Rather than argue this in
the abstract, however, let me make the point by an illustration.
Henry Scott Holland wrote in his memoirs of the face of Edward
King, Bishop of Lincoln:

> It seemed to say 'This is what a face is meant to be. This is the
> face that a man would have, if he were, really, himself. This is

---

[15] Luther himself was again much more restrained, stressing the lowliness and
weakness of Christ, though 'he expresses in passing his opinion that Christ was
also physically well built and finely proportioned (WA 40/II 484.25)' (Siggins,
op. cit., p.35).

[16] From an earlier period Athanasius (*De Incarn.* 21 and 22) held, typically, that
Christ's body could not have fallen sick or lost its strength: the weakness of death
came only at the hands of others.

[17] Hollaz: Barth, CD I 2, p.153.   [18] CD IV 2, pp. 167f.

[19] Matt. 8.20; Luke 2.7.   [20] Isa. 53.2.   [21] Justin, *Dial.* 14.8; 88.8.

[22] *Orac. Sib.* 8.256f. On the 'unsightly and hateful Christ' cf. Grillmeier, *Der
Logos am Kreuz*, Munich 1956, pp.42–7 (contrasted with the 'fair' Christ, pp.47–9),
and the references there cited from Justin, Clement, Irenaeus, Tertullian, Hippolytus, the Sibylline Oracles and the Acts of Thomas.

[23] Indeed it has been said that 'Christianity became Catholic by successfully
resolving the apparent contradiction between universality and identity' (J.
Pelikan, *The Finality of Jesus Christ in an Age of Universal History*, Lutterworth
Press 1965, p. 5).

the face that love would normally wear.' We felt as if we had been waiting for such a face to come and meet us – a face that would simply reveal how deep is the goodness of which humanity is capable. Oh! if all men could be just like that! So typical was its naturalness. Yet, of course, this did not diminish its intense individuality. It was only that this most vital individuality was so whole and sound and normal and true, that it seemed to be the perfect expression of what a man might be.[24]

To be a 'universal man' is not to have every human quality, but to be the sort of person of whom we recognize *in* the individual that which transcends the individual. We see in him what *each* of us could be – in his own unique way.[25] What attracts and judges us is not the man who has everything – that merely oppresses us – but the man in whom we can glimpse a vision of the essential. That man we feel has got there, and we say, with Hamlet: 'He was a man.'[26] This is compatible with his being quite limited, yet having done his own thing with total authenticity. It is also compatible with our being able in varying degree to see the same thing in other people and to see different things in other people which speak to us of the same thing.

In an evolutionary world, the idea of one man from the past who has already had everything a man could have seems to place a false ceiling on the human potential. It presents a static ideal on which no advance is possible. Indeed, the claim that Jesus was 'perfect' needs so much explanation and qualification that perhaps it would better be dropped. We can imagine him asking, '*Why* do you call me perfect?' as he asked, 'Why do you call me good?'[27]

---

[24] Henry Scott Holland, *A Bundle of Memories*, Wells Gardner 1915, pp.48f. For an assessment of Scott Holland's own contribution to Christology, cf. the tribute by D. M. MacKinnon, 'Scott Holland and Contemporary Needs', *Borderlands of Theology and Other Essays*, Lutterworth Press 1968, pp. 105–20.

[25] Cf. H. P. van Dusen, *Dag Hammarskjøld: A Biographical Interpretation of 'Markings'*, Faber 1967, p.91: 'Dag Hammarskjøld, in his inner as in his public life, was not a "sport", an eccentric. On the contrary he was a man as all of us, in the lesser measures of our slighter gifts and fumbling responses, should aim to be'; and Aubrey Hodes, *Martin Buber: An Intimate Portrait*, Viking Press, New York 1971, pp.67f., who quotes Heinz-Joachim Heydorn's remark, 'Buber has accomplished what one can only say of a very few: he has reached the limits of his own being . . . and through this has made the universal transparent.'

[26] *Hamlet* I.i.187.   [27] Mark 10.18.

What is the psychological need that *requires* this idealization? It is easy to sense the splutter and misunderstanding that would greet this suggestion in many circles. But we should also sense the relief and release. I remember a woman once saying in a group, 'I've been "had" by this "perfection" thing.' There has been a problem of 'over-belief', of *having* to ascribe everything to Jesus for fear of under-belief.

Another who reacted sharply against this 'perfection thing' was William Blake. He indeed actually *wanted* a snub-nosed Christ, like himself:

> Thine has a great hook nose like thine,
> Mine has a snub nose like to mine.[28]

But he went much further in protest against what it seemed to him Christians had made of Christ:

> Was Jesus Gentle, or did he
> Give any Marks of Gentility? (b, 1f.)
>
> Was Jesus Humble? or did he
> Give any Proofs of Humility? (c and d, 1f.)
>
> Was Jesus Chaste, or did he
> Give any Lessons of Chastity? (e, 1f.)
>
> Was Jesus Born of a Virgin Pure
> With narrow Soul & looks demure?
> If he intended to take on Sin
> The Mother should an Harlot been,
> Just such a one as Magdalen
> With seven devils in her Pen (i, 1–6);

and he sees Jesus as conquering evil not by never falling but by living 'above Controll' (i, 44).

---

[28] William Blake, *The Everlasting Gospel* a,3f. Cf. the prose jotting, 'I always thought that Jesus Christ was a Snubby or I should not have worshipped him, if I had thought he had been one of those long spindle nosed rascals!', quoted by J. G. Davies, *The Theology of William Blake*, Oxford University Press 1948, p. 110.

Blake indeed felt that his Christ and the church's were anti-thetical:

The Vision of Christ that thou dost see
Is my Vision's Greatest Enemy (a, 1f.).

Nevertheless, he still wished passionately to focus his desires and longings for humanity in Jesus, in whom he recognized:

The Naked Human form divine (e, 66),

and saw contained:

As One Man all the Universal Family, and that One Man
We call Jesus the Christ.[29]

For, despite every contradictory vision, this Man retained for him, as for others, the lure of a perennial catholicity.

To call Jesus the Christ is to acknowledge that somehow he has that which has made men say, in their thousand different ways, 'This is *it*'. *What* we see in him, how *we* designate the truly human, depends on what speaks to us, on what for us says 'This is the man'. And that will differ to some extent with every generation and every individual. This is the point of Carlo Monterosso's striking novel *The Salt of the Earth*, which consists of four quite different portraits (all of them far from 'perfect') of Jesus as seen by four of his followers.[30] We respond because we recognize

[29] Blake, *Jerusalem* 38.19f.
[30] There is an interesting ancient parallel in the apocryphal *Acts of John* 88–93, where at the call of the sons of Zebedee the following conversation occurs: James: 'What would this child have that is upon the sea-shore and called us?' John replies: 'What child?' And James says again: 'That which beckoneth to us.' John answers: 'Because of our long watch we have kept at sea, thou seest not aright, my brother James; but seest thou not the man that standeth there, comely and fair and of a cheerful countenance?' But James is unable to see him. Hardly have they reached land when another figure appears to them. John sees a bald-headed man with a thick, flowing beard, but James a 'youth whose beard was newly come'. The beloved disciple moreover now sees 'a small man and un-comely, and then again as one reaching unto heaven'. When he touches Jesus his body is sometimes immaterial and unreal, then again, 'smooth and tender, and sometimes hard like unto stones'. Finally, the form of Jesus is quite unearthly, hovering free over the earth: 'And oftentimes when I walked with him, I desired to see the print of his foot, whether it appeared on the earth (for I saw him as it were lifting himself up from the earth). And I never saw it' (quoted by Grillmeier, *Christ in Christian Tradition*, p. 83).
The presupposition here is that Christ actually changes his bodily shape in docetic fashion. But through the recognized mythology of metamorphosis the

in him 'our' thing. Yet if, to use John A. Phillips' words I quoted in the first chapter, 'faith and discipleship do not and cannot require one to become less than a man of one's own time', we must equally insist on the second half of his sentence: 'neither do they necessitate removing Jesus from his own time and place in history'.[31] If we are not just to modernize Jesus, to see in him what we want to see (as the Gnostics did), we must be prepared to put our recognition to the test of history (as they were not).

To give a current example, we may respond because we see in Jesus the truly 'free' man, and Paul van Buren, following Barth, has given a convincing sketch of Jesus in this role.[32] Yet the word 'free' is never used of Jesus in the gospels.[33] Nevertheless, the test is whether Jesus was the sort of person, both in terms of what he was free from and even more of whom he was free for, who constrains *us* to that recognition. I believe he was, and that this designation is valid and indeed vital. Yet the historical problem cannot be burked. The credibility gap cannot be too great. For, as van Buren says:

> If historians could establish . . . that Jesus had made an agree-ment with the authorities to spend his remaining days in the wilderness in silence and let some other person be crucified in his place, thereby revealing that he was as insecure and self-interested as his enemies, Christian faith as the New Testament presents it would cease to be tenable.[34]

To this test I shall be returning.

The man who was everything

But now we must turn to the more difficult question of the two

Gnostics were seeking to express the psychological fact that different people 'see' such different things in the Christ figure. Such apocrypha performed in the ancient world the function of historical novels.

[31] Phillips, op. cit. (see p. 18, n.55), p. 292.

[32] Van Buren, *The Secular Meaning of the Gospel*, pp.121–4; Barth, CD IV 2, p.161; cf. F. G. Downing, *A Man for Us and a God for Us*, Epworth Press 1968, especially ch.3; Ernst Käsemann, *Jesus Means Freedom*, SCM Press 1969.

[33] The nearest is John 8.36: 'If then the Son sets you free, you will indeed be free.'

[34] Van Buren, op. cit., p.126.

from which we began. Did Jesus have to *be* (as well as to *have*) all that a man could be? What do we mean by saying that he was morally perfect, and how do we know?

There is no doubt that Jesus was remembered by his followers as a supremely *good* man. 'He went about doing good'[35] was how the early Christian preaching summarized his ministry. And not only his followers appear to have formed this impression. The recently published testimony of the Jewish historian Josephus, as found in the tenth-century Arabic chronicle of Agapius, which has been convincingly argued[36] to be more original than the (doctored and long-suspect) Greek text, begins:

> At that time there was a wise man who was called Jesus. And his way of life was good, and he was known to be virtuous.[37]

In the pages of the gospels themselves there meets us a man of radical integrity, obedience, courage, freedom, and sheer victory – undeflected and undefeated by whatever men might do to him. This does not mean, of course, that we should accept the portrait as unvarnished history. But even in this there is nothing to suggest the *kind* of goodness that Christian doctrine and still more Christian piety have so often demanded that he should have had – what I called earlier the static perfection of flawless porcelain. The ideal of perfection which has been applied both to Mary and to Jesus – that of immaculateness, of being untouched and un-spotted by sin – corresponds to the late Jewish ritual conception of the holy as the opposite of the common and unclean. But there is every reason to suppose that any goodness Jesus had was won – and hard-won – out of the struggle with evil within him and around. It is noteworthy that the Epistle to the Hebrews, which is the only New Testament document to refer to Jesus' perfection, always uses of him the verb 'perfected',[38] never the adjective

[35] Acts 10.38.

[36] Shlomo Pines, *An Arabic Version of the Testimonium Flavium and its Impli-cations*, Jerusalem 1971.

[37] The Greek text, *Antt.* 18.63f., runs: 'About this time there lived Jesus, a wise man, if indeed one ought to call him a man.' There are similar differences in a Christianizing direction throughout.

[38] Heb. 2.10; 5.9; 7.28.

"perfected" not "perfect"

'perfect'. (The sole occurrence of the phrase 'the perfect man'[39] is not a description of Jesus but of humanity fulfilled in Christ.) And it insists that he 'learned obedience in the school of suffering'[40] – through the things, that is, that touched him, affected him, changed him. The writer has his doctrinal motives for stressing this. But it is hardly a picture that the early Christians would have invented: they would be more likely to have created a picture of effortless superiority to all human weakness, such as we find later. I am persuaded, in fact, that in its material on Jesus' temptations, and particularly in its echo of Gethsemane,[41] the Epistle to the Hebrews reflects knowledge of good oral tradition, with affinities to, but no literary dependence on, Luke and John.[42] Indeed, I personally believe with Montefiore[43] that it is likely to be earlier than any of the gospels – certainly before AD 70.[44] In any case, its value lies in giving us the most forceful evidence that Jesus was remembered as a man of like passions with ourselves who had to win through in the same way as everyone else.[45]

[39] Eph. 4.13.

[40] Heb. 5.8. The same applies to the only use of the word 'perfected' in the gospels, though there it has a wider sense: 'Today and tomorrow I shall be casting out devils and working cures; on the third day I reach my goal (*teleioumai*) . . ., because it is unthinkable for a prophet to meet his death anywhere but in Jerusalem' (Luke 13.32f.).

[41] Heb. 5.7.

[42] Luke 22.44; John 12.27. Cf. the long and careful discussion in C. Spicq, *L'Épitre aux Hébreux* I, Paris 1952, pp.99–104.

[43] H. Montefiore, *The Epistle to the Hebrews*, A. and C. Black 1964, p.28. He actually places it before I Corinthians in AD 52–54.

[44] Omission of any reference to the destruction of the temple and the end of its sacrificial system, which would have clinched the writer's entire argument, is, I believe, otherwise inexplicable. He always speaks of the system in the present tense: if it all lay in ruins he could hardly have failed to point the moral.

[45] It is also possible that Heb. 2.6–9 may contain the sole echo in the epistles of the memory of Jesus as 'the Son of Man', and that as a title of humiliation leading to glory, as in Dan. 7.13–22 (cf. Mark 8.31; 14.62; Matt. 8.20 = Luke 9.58; etc). The writer cites Ps. 8.4–6 ('What is man, that thou rememberest him, or the son of man that thou hast regard to him?') of man in general, but then immediately applies the verses to Jesus, in whom alone they are as yet completely fulfilled: 'In Jesus, however, we do see one who was made little lower than the angels, crowned with glory and honour because he suffered death, so that . . . he should stand for us all.' Montefiore comments, op. cit., p.57: 'Our author probably knew of Jesus' self-designation as the Son of Man, and this may have influenced his choice of this *testimonium*.' If so, this is significant evidence, since 'the Son of Man' evidently played no part in the later theology of the church. It may be a further indication that in the Epistle to the Hebrews we stand near to a source for the

This is something so elemental and to us so obvious that it is astonishing how reluctant Christian theologians have been to admit it, let alone to emphasize it. As we saw earlier,[46] one can go through the whole of Alexandrian and mediaeval theology without finding it referred to as more than a condescension to human weakness or a concession to appearances. One of the notable contributions of Luther to Christology is that against the stream of his inheritance he should have recognized not simply that Christ *was* a person, who became man, but that he had to *become a person* through the normal processes of maturation and moral growth.[47] But the recognition made little impact on subsequent thinking.

It is quite astonishing, for instance, that a man like Schleiermacher, who believed so much in starting from experience and who even has a special 'postscript' on the scriptural witness at this point,[48] could read the New Testament evidence as presenting a Christ wholly free from any inner conflict, effort or doubt.[49] As he sees it, temptation for Jesus must not be taken to mean 'that there was even an infinitely small element of struggle involved'.[50] Pleasure and pain were mere symptoms 'without any determinative or co-determinative power',[51] and 'death can have been no

---

memory of the historical Jesus – though obviously the writer was himself dependent on the tradition of others.

[46] See pp.39f. above.

[47] Cf. the sympathetic account of this in J. A. Dorner, op. cit. II, T. and T. Clark 1862, pp.89–100.

[48] Schleiermacher, *The Christian Faith*, pp.421–4. He omits altogether the passages from Hebrews cited above and his sole reference to Gethsemane (Matt. 26.36) is to note it as a passage in which 'a high degree of grief is ascribed to Christ'. There is no mention of the clear conflict of wills (Mark 14.36 par.) and he passes over entirely the more 'agonizing' Lukan version. However, the prize for the exegesis of this incident must surely still go to Hilary who, when faced with the 'sweat like clots of blood' in Luke 22.44, says that this is no sign of infirmity, because it is contrary to nature to sweat blood: the phenomenon must therefore be regarded as a display of power (*De Trin.* 10.24)! Contrast the great Antiochene exegete, Theodore of Mopsuestia: 'Suppose as you would have it, that the Deity took the role of the *nous* (or soul) in him who was assumed. How was he affected with fear in his suffering? Why, in the face of immediate need, did he stand in want of vehement prayers—prayers which, as the blessed Paul [*sc.* the author to the Hebrews] says, he brought before God with a loud and clamorous voice and with many tears? How was he seized of such immense fear that he gave forth fountains of sweat by reason of his great terror?' (*Hom. Cat.* 5.10).

[49] Schleiermacher, op. cit., p.382.

[50] Ibid., p.414.   [51] Ibid., p.415.

evil' for him.[52] His development was an unbroken transition from 'the condition of purest innocence to one of purely spiritual fullness of power, which is far removed from anything we call virtue' (i.e., the goodness won of moral victory).[53]

Even Seeley, for all his humanitarian interest in *Ecce Homo*, sees the gospels as presenting a portrait of one in whose 'mode of thinking, speaking or action' 'no important change took place'.[54] Such a judgment reflects, of course, the fact that the gospels are precisely not 'biographies' (as he always calls them): they are not concerned to trace or record Jesus' human development. But we should be careful to draw the correct inference from this. There is a tendency in some New Testament circles to conclude that merely to approach the evidence with this interest is to ask the 'wrong question'. But there is no reason for *us* not to ask it. Indeed, not to do so is tacitly to leave the impression that because the gospels are not interested in Jesus' development, there was none – just as simply to accept their silence about his sexuality is to leave the impression that he was sexless. And both the static and the sexless Jesus are powerful versions today of the cardboard Christ.

We can and must ask the question, and indeed assume that if he was fully human Jesus did *not* suffer from arrested development, but that the growth, mental as well as physical, recorded of his boyhood[55] (which Barth delights to observe is described by a Greek word [*prokoptein*] meaning 'to extend by blows, as a smith stretches metal by hammers'),[56] continued throughout his life. Indeed, the very fact that the evangelists have no theological interest in this gives us the more reason for trusting what signs of change and development we may be able to detect. For they cannot be put down to doctrinal motivation.

Any reconstruction of Jesus' inner history is notoriously full of pitfalls; but I believe that the gospel tradition bears out of him, like everyone else, the truth of Newman's dictum that 'here below to live is to change, and to be perfect is to have changed often'.[57] It

---

[52] Ibid., p.416.   [53] Ibid., p.383.   [54] Seeley, op. cit., p.14.
[55] Luke 2.40, 52.   [56] Barth, CD I 2, p.158.
[57] J. H. Newman, *Essay on Development*, Longmans 1878, p.40. Newman himself never, of course, applied this to Christology, on which indeed he tended in the very opposite direction. Nicholas Lash has kindly supplied me with the

would be far too great a diversion to argue the case in detail, but, simply in order to destroy the image of a cardboard figure which is itself so destructive, it can, I believe, be shown that there were at least three different understandings by Jesus of his mission at different stages of his career.

The first, if we accept, as I think we now should, the substantial historicity of an early Judaean period attested by the Fourth Gospel,[58] belonged to the stage when Jesus worked in close accord with John the Baptist, basically accepting the role of the 'mighty one' John marked out for him. This role was essentially that of the Elijah figure described in Malachi 3 and 4. I believe the Fourth Gospel is right in seeing the cleansing of the temple as Jesus' first symbolic piece of 'direct action' in this capacity, following closely the programme of the messenger who was to 'come suddenly to the temple', to 'purify the sons of Levi till they present right offerings to the Lord' and cease to 'rob God'.[59] According to the Synoptists, when challenged by the Jews for the authority for this action,[60] Jesus replied by referring them to the authority of John.[61] In the position which the incident occupies in the first three gospels,[62] late in the ministry and long after the Baptist has disappeared from the scene, this reads like a clever riposte to a trick question. But if it happened at the stage at which the Fourth Evangelist places it, it is entirely apposite. For the sanction behind it *was* the sanction behind the Baptist's mission: Jesus was acting out the role John had designated for him.

It was this role of which the Baptist was subsequently to ask from prison whether Jesus could really be the fulfilment: 'Are you the coming one (of whom I spoke)?'[63] For it did not appear to be working out like that. And indeed it was not. Whereas the mighty one of John's prediction would 'gather the wheat into his granary but . . . burn the chaff on a fire that can never go out',[64] Jesus is

---

following references to his writings: *Parochial and Plain Sermons*, Longmans 1868, III, p.129; *Essays Critical and Historical*, Longmans 1872, I, pp.74, 87; *Select Treatises of St Athanasius*, Longmans 1881, II, pp.94, 146, 161–72, 293–303; *Letters and Diaries*, ed. S. Dessain, Nelson 1961–, XI, p.135; XIII, p. 3; XV, pp.56–8.
[58] Cf. my *Twelve New Testament Studies*, especially chs. 1, 2, 4 and 7.
[59] Mal. 3.1–10. [60] Mark 11.27f. par. [61] Mark 11. 29–33 par.
[62] Mark 11.15–19 par. [63] Matt. 11.2f. = Luke 7.18–20.
[64] Matt. 3.12 = Luke 3.17.

proclaiming, 'I did not come to invite virtuous people, but sinners.'[65] After John's arrest there appears to have been a reassessment and change of direction – reflected perhaps in the symbolic story of the desert temptations. Jesus comes into Galilee in a different role, that of liberator, healer and saviour, which received its classic expression rather in Isaiah 61[66] and 35.[67] And it is the latter passage that he gives to John as the sanction for his actions, urging him and others not to be offended.[68] Despite the disciples who expect him still to endorse the Elijah role in the destruction of the Samaritan villages,[69] it is this that gives rationale to the Galilean period.

But again it changes, and I believe those are right who detect in the feeding of the five thousand the second climacteric.[70] The observation of the Fourth Gospel that the desert crowd wanted to make him king[71] explains the extraordinary end to the story in Mark,[72] where Jesus 'compels' the disciples to get in the boat and then handles himself the business of dispersing the crowd. Evidently he could not trust them. For the role of liberator and saviour was running dangerously into that of political Messiah. So it, too, had to be rethought in seclusion[73] and the disciples' loyalty tested again.[74] Peter's response (learnt of the Galilean ministry) 'You are the Christ', far from being ecstatically re-

[65] Mark 2.17.

[66] Quoted in the programmatic sermon at Nazareth (Luke 4.16–21). This is doubtless the evangelist's composition, but summarizes accurately enough the thrust of the Galilean ministry as represented in Mark and Q.

[67] Matt. 11.5 = Luke 7.22.

[68] Matt. 11.6 = Luke 7.23.

[69] Luke 9.54 (cf. the scribal gloss 'as Elijah did'). It is possible that Luke, whose chronology allows for only one journey through Samaria and who was thus compelled to include this incident here, may have misplaced what originally belonged to an earlier journey (e.g. that recorded in John 4.4) when Jesus was beginning to dissociate himself from the role of Elijah, which still stuck to him later (Mark 6.15; 8.28). Cf. on all this my article, 'Elijah, John and Jesus', *Twelve New Testament Studies*, pp.28–52.

[70] Most recently Dodd, *The Founder of Christianity*, pp.131–9. Cf. T. W. Manson, *The Servant Messiah*, Cambridge University Press 1953, pp.69–71; H. Montefiore, 'Revolt in the Desert?', *New Testament Studies* VIII, 1962, pp.135–41; C. W. F. Smith, *The Paradox of Jesus in the Gospels*, Westminster Press, Philadelphia 1969, ch. 5.

[71] John 6.15; cf. the identification in Luke 23.2, 'Christ, a king'.

[72] Mark 6.45.   [73] John 6.15.

[74] Mark 8.27–38 par.; John 6.66–71.

ceived,[75] has immediately to be corrected by new teaching about
the Son of Man who must suffer and die.[76] 3)

The sanction for this third role, of the Servant-Son of Man, the
representative of his people who would bring redemption and
come to vindication only through humiliation and defeat, was to
be found in Daniel 7 and Isaiah 40–53 (whether or not Jesus himself drew out the scriptural links).[77] Small wonder it set up such
resistance when it was first broached, and right to the end it was
met with incredulity and misunderstanding.[78] The final treachery
of Judas and the subsequent disillusionment of the crowds[79] may
well reflect the disappointment that Jesus had once more betrayed
a more 'positive' programme.

If there is anything at all in this schematic reconstruction, it
shows Jesus being changed by events, learning his obedience in
the school of reappraisal and suffering. This takes no account of
suggestions such as that of Schweitzer, relying heavily on one

[75] As I noted earlier, the word *epitimaō*, 'rebuke', occurs three times in Mark
8.29–33, and Peter is roundly called 'Satan'. The acclaim in Matt. 16.16–19 is
widely agreed to have been inserted here from a different context and focusses in
the recognition of the 'Son-Father' relationship (as in Matt. 11.25–27), which is
very different. Cf. O. Cullmann, *Peter: Disciple, Apostle, Martyr*, SCM Press 1953,
pp.170–84; id., *The Christology of the New Testament*, SCM Press ²1963, pp. 280f.

[76] Mark 8.31 par. There is the same transition from Messiah language on
others' lips to Son of Man language on Jesus' own in Mark 14.61f. par.

[77] I believe he did in the case of the Son of Man at the trial saying (Mark 14.62),
where the Danielic sense of an earthly human figure, representing the saints of the
Most High and coming to God in vindication and power by a great reversal of
human judgment, fits the context like a glove. This was not how the church
subsequently used the testimonium of Dan. 7.13 (cf. Mark 13.26 par; and my
Jesus and His Coming, SCM Press 1957, pp.43–52). In the case of the Servant
concept, I suspect the truth will be found to lie somewhere between the position
of T. W. Manson, *The Servant Messiah*; O. Cullmann, *The Christology of the New
Testament*, pp.51–82; and Joachim Jeremias, *The Servant of God*, SCM Press 1957,
who tend to see it everywhere, and that of Morna Hooker, *Jesus and the Servant*,
SPCK 1959; and C. K. Barrett, 'The Background of Mark 10.45' in A. J. B. Higgins
(ed.), *New Testament Essays: Studies in Memory of Thomas Walter Manson*, Manchester University Press 1959, pp.1–18; id., *Jesus and the Gospel Tradition*, pp.39–41,
who tend to see it nowhere. *If* Mark 10.45 and 14.24 go back to Jesus, it is difficult
not to hear *some* echo of Isa. 52–53. Cf. James L. Price, 'The Servant Motif in the
Synoptic Gospels', *Interpretation* XII, January 1958, pp. 28–39.

[78] E.g. Mark 10.32–45; Luke 22.24–27; John 13.1–38; Acts 1.6.

[79] These proclaim him as Davidic Messiah *despite* Jesus' acted parable of the
donkey (Mark 11.1–10 par.). The affirmation as 'King of Israel' is in John's
account *followed* by the words 'but Jesus found a donkey and mounted it' (John
12.13–15), as though to say, 'King, yes (cf. Zech. 9.9), but not in that sense' (cf.
John 18.33–37).

unsupported text of Matthew,[80] that Jesus was forced by the non-arrival of the kingdom to a radical change of tack, or that he died a broken, disillusioned man. I personally find such an interpretation unpersuasive.[81] But that he was, like anyone else who has tried to change the world, himself changed by it, seems indisputable.

A vignette of this is preserved in the Markan tradition from just such a moment when the need for rethinking had led him to withdraw and 'he would have liked to remain unrecognized'.[82] Pestered by a Syro-phoenician woman, he is forced to an action which at the beginning he had apparently no intention of performing.[83] His refusal is often interpreted by preachers[84] (and perhaps by Matthew)[85] simply as a test of the woman's faith, as if he knew all along what he would do. But this is not how we

---

[80] Matt. 10.23: 'I tell you this: before you have gone through all the towns of Israel the Son of Man will have come.' Whatever the original meaning of this difficult saying (and I have ventured a very tentative opinion in my *Jesus and His Coming*, pp.91f.), Schweitzer's interpretation (op. cit., pp. 357–63) depends on Matthew's attachment of it to a portion of the Markan apocalypse which he has transferred to the mission of the Twelve – 'an entirely arbitrary combination of the sources' (N. A. Dahl, *Kerygma and History*, Abingdon Press, Nashville 1962, p.157).

[81] Raymond Lloyd in his article quoted above, 'Cross and Psychosis', argues that Jesus suffered a 'total breakdown and complete loss of mood control' from which he never recovered. The only text on which this can be based is the cry of dereliction from the cross, 'My God, my God, why hast thou forsaken me?' (Mark 15.34). Clearly this could not have been invented, but equally clearly Mark does not read things this way (cf. 15.35–39), still less Luke, who makes Jesus' last words read, 'Father, into thy hands I commend my spirit' (Luke 23.46). The memory of Jesus preserved in the Epistle to the Hebrews is that he *was* 'perfected' – in other words, that the effect of his sufferings was that he achieved the very integration which Lloyd says was denied and cut short by the cross. It is easy to dismiss this by saying that of course the early church *had* to assert this. But I question whether it would gratuitously have invented a Christ who had to be *made* perfect. Moreover, it left in the record things which it should have erased if it was really trying to cover up the record of a broken man. Indeed, it is precisely these things which supply the evidence on which it is possible (though I think neither necessary nor probable) to build such a construction as Lloyd does. See more fully my reply, cited above, 'Was Jesus Mad?'

[82] Mark 7.24.

[83] Mark 7.25–30.

[84] Cf. Roy A. Harrisville, 'The Woman of Canaan: A Chapter in the History of Exegesis', *Interpretation* XX, July 1966, pp.274–87, who comments: 'The history of nineteenth- and twentieth-century theology could well be written by the light of our text' (p.286).

[85] Matt. 15.28.

should read the story of any other man. Jesus evidently starts with all the inbuilt racial prejudices of the Jew, describing the Gentiles as dogs.[86] Indeed, he could not have been what it meant to be a Jew of the first century without a whole complex of national memories, repressions and alienations. He reacts instinctively, as I believe he does in the similar story in the Fourth Gospel,[87] where the court official (*basilikos*) who seeks help for his sick boy is dismissed with the categorizing plural, 'Oh, you people, all you want to see is signs and wonders' – for the man was a representative of Herod's house, the half-breed quisling king.[88] But in each case the greatness and goodness of Jesus lay not in his being exempt from these distorting limitations but in his power, shown also in his attitude to the Samaritans,[89] to break through and come out the other side of them. As a result of such experiences he emerged a different and a bigger man.

There is every reason from the gospel evidence, as well as from the Epistle to the Hebrews, to suppose that Jesus was fully a man like ourselves, sharing the same unconscious drives and libido,[90] with a temper and an intolerance, an anxiety and a fear of death, as strong as anyone else's.[91] Like any other human being, he had a dark side as well as a light, what Jung calls 'the shadow' – the

[86] Cf. Matt. 7.6; Phil. 3.2; Rev. 22.15. But the diminutive *kunaria* may be intended as playful. This is listed, somewhat improbably, among 'Thirty humorous passages in the Synoptic Gospels' by Elton Trueblood, *The Humor of Christ*, Harper, New York 1964.

[87] John 4.46–54.

[88] He is precisely the sort of person represented in Luke 8.3 by 'Chuza, a steward of Herod's', whose wife Joanna is (surprisingly) among those who provide for the disciples out of their own resources. Perhaps the explanation is after all to be found in John 4.53, where we are told that the official and 'all his household' became believers.

[89] Matt. 10.5; Luke 9.52–55; 10.33; 17.11–19; John 4.4–42. In John 8.48 he is even called in abuse a 'Samaritan' – the equivalent perhaps today of a 'nigger-lover'.

[90] See the discussion of this in W. R. Matthews, *The Problem of Christ in the Twentieth Century*, Oxford University Press 1950, pp.46f. Cf. the comment of Grillmeier, op. cit., p.315: 'Jerome dares to speak of *passiones* and *libidines corporis* in Christ, and in this he is very modern.' The furthest most of the Fathers would go was to admit *propatheia* – the condition that occurs before the onset of real passion, by which time the soul loses its state of equilibrium.

[91] Mark 14.33–36 par.; John 12.27; Heb. 5.7, where *apo tēs eulabeiās* should almost certainly be taken to mean 'out of his anxious fear' and not 'because of his piety'.

symbol of all those instinctive, 'unclubbable' aspects of the personality, dangerous in expression and resistant to conscious moral control, which are repressed and projected on to others. As Nels Ferré puts it:

> When Jesus looked around with anger,[92] such anger may not merely have been righteous concern, which seldom in its purity expresses itself in anger, but may also have been the result of mixed motives. He was grieved at the hardness of their heart; but all the same his own breaking of the Sabbath in the interest of healing very likely did not come about without some inner strife, part of which probably went below conscious conflict.[93]

Francis Terry makes a similar point about Jesus' class-conditioning:

> Jesus was an outspoken anti-establishment man on the side of the 'have-nots' against the 'haves', and, when talking of the Scribes and Pharisees, may well be called 'Voltairean'. Common experience shows that such attitudes usually include a certain pleasure in scoring points off self-satisfied and successful people, and that this has its roots in the resentments felt by the unrecognized and underprivileged. Do we not recognize something of this sort in Jesus – especially, perhaps, in the contrast between some of his remarks about the Pharisees and some of his exhortations not to judge people? But to say this is no more than to admit that Jesus was involved in the common texture of human relationships.[94]

These remain no more than open questions. But Jung[95] is surely justified in accusing Christians of having split the Christ-image by understanding perfection, *teleiōsis*, to mean the absence of evil, rather than wholeness, completion, or what he calls

---

[92] *Met'orgēs* (Mark 3.5); cf. *orgistheis* (Mark 1.41; to be preferred here, with the NEB, as clearly the harder reading), and *embrimēsamenos* (Mark 1.43; John 11.33, 38), a vivid word which originally seems to mean 'snorting'.
[93] Ferré, *Christ and the Christian*, p.89.
[94] Terry, 'Cross and Sanity', p.12.
[95] Jung, *Aion*, pp.41f.

'individuation' (or undividedness). In Christian tradition, he says, the Christ-image has been weakened in psychological power as an archetype of the self because the shadow, the dark double (which is not in itself evil), is split off into an irreconcilable counterpart, the anti-Christ. The Christ becomes identified simply with one half of the personality. Instead of overcoming the separation by taking the unacceptable into himself and transcending it, he is viewed, in the vivid terminology of the Gnostics (whom Jung rightly saw as the psychologists of the ancient world), as 'casting off the shadow' with which he was born.[96] But the effect of this is to make him unreal as a man. For docetism is always the other side of the penny of Gnosticism.[97] If Jesus was genuinely a man, he was 'made perfect' (which does not mean that he was morally improved, but that he achieved integration) in the only way men can grow, by acceptance and incorporation of the whole of his self, rather than by rejection and repression of a part.[98]

The psychologist L. W. Grensted, in the appendix on 'The Sinlessness of Jesus' to his book *The Person of Christ*, noted, for what it is worth, how in Jesus' life-struggle the unacceptable is presented in the gospels as progressively internalized and absorbed. In the wilderness temptation it is objectivized and projected as the Devil. At the Transfiguration the cross is represented 'not by Satan, but by the friendly figures of Moses and Elijah'. In Gethsemane there is 'no longer . . . a casting out of these elements in humanity which are the source of the conflict', but in a final shuddering struggle, which Mark introduces with the words 'he began to be panic-stricken and distraught', the embracing of them as the will of the Father.[99] This progression may be purely fortuitous. But clearly the evangelists had no conscious awareness of it, and it is difficult, therefore, to put it down simply to doctrinal motives.

[96] Cf. the references, Jung, op. cit., p.41.
[97] Cf. p.75f. above.
[98] Cf. H. A. Williams, 'Theology and Self-awareness' and Rosemary Haughton, *On Trying to be Human*, Geoffrey Chapman 1966, ch. VII, who writes: 'If the devil in man is really part of human nature he can only be rejected at the cost of repudiating the possibility of being fully human' (p.162).
[99] L. W. Grensted, *The Person of Christ*, Nisbet 1933, pp.279f.

Perhaps it is in this sense that we can use the traditional language that Jesus 'became man' – not by becoming a man from being something else (no one can do that), but by *becoming* fully and completely human. As the author to the Hebrews says again, 'He had to be made like his brethren in every respect, so that he might *become* a merciful and faithful high priest'.[100] Indeed this process is particularly necessary for anyone who is to be able to save or to salve others. For only a person who has not cut off part of himself can be free to relate to men as Jesus did. To accept the unacceptable in others depends upon not finding it a threat to oneself. What seems to have impressed his contemporaries was precisely his self-possession, his poise, his authority, his 'peace'[101] – what he made *out* of the inner tensions and the outward conflicts that marked and scarred his entire public life.

The sinless Christ

According to every recognized standard of his day Jesus was a 'sinner', a law-breaker, an outcast, accursed of God. Yet it was of this man that Christians were saying within a generation (and it comes astonishingly early and apparently independently in several writers) that he was 'innocent of sin',[102] that he committed no sin',[103] that he was 'without sin'[104] or 'blemish'.[105] And this judgment was never seriously questioned till a hundred years ago. Grensted begins his appendix just referred to with the words:

> That our Lord was sinless has been continuously and from the beginning the faith of the whole Christian church. It would be hard to find any dogmatic statement which more completely fulfils the Vincentian Canon ['What has been believed everywhere, always and by everyone']. Only a very few writers who would call themselves Christians at all have ventured to

[100] Heb. 2.17 RSV. This writer constantly stresses that Jesus has to become what he is: 1.4; 5.5,9; 6.20; 7.26.
[101] Cf. supremely the reflection of this in the last discourses of John 14.27–31; 16.31–33.
[102] II Cor. 5.21.   [103] I Peter 2.22.
[104] Heb. 4.15.   [105] Heb. 9.14; I Peter 1.19.

take up the challenge: 'Which of you convicteth me of sin?'[106]

Yet James Stalker, writing the article on 'Sinlessness' in Hastings' *Dictionary of Christ and the Gospels*,[107] already saw clouds upon the horizon:

It is quite within the bounds of possibility, or even probability, that this belief may have to be earnestly contended for in the not distant future.

What are we to make of it today?

First of all, we should recognize that it is in the first instance a theological rather than a historical judgment. It is not simply an extrapolation from the historical evidence.[108] From the latter it is impossible, even for those who know a man best, to prove a universal negative, that in his most private moments or the secret recesses of his heart he never sinned – or even a universal positive, that he was always perfect, always loving. And the contexts in which the New Testament speaks of Jesus as being without sin make the theological interest plain. For in order to 'do away with sins' he had, according to the sacrificial theory of the day, himself to be spotless, whether as priest[109] or as victim.[110]

Knox sums up what he diagnoses as 'the poignant dilemma' of the early Christians about the humanity and the sinlessness of Jesus in these words:

How could Christ have saved us if he were not a human being like ourselves? How could a human being like ourselves have saved us?[111]

[106] Grensted, op. cit., p.271.
[107] James Hastings, *Dictionary of Christ and the Gospels*, T. and T. Clark 1908.
[108] Cf., for a profound treatment of the sinlessness and perfection of Christ in relation to history, R. Niebuhr, *The Nature and Destiny of Man* II, ch. 3.
[109] Heb. 4.15; 7.26–28.
[110] II Cor. 5.21 (cf. NEB margin); Heb. 9.15; I Peter 1.19; 2.22–24; I John 1.7–2.2; 3.3–5.
[111] Knox, *The Humanity and Divinity of Christ*, p.52. See the whole argument of pp.39–52. He presents the ultimate choice for Christology thus: 'One may believe that Jesus was *not* an actual normal man, a man like us, and that he could be the Saviour only *because* he was not; or one may believe that he *was* an actual normal man – and moreover the particular man he was – and that he could become the Saviour only because he *was*' (p.88).

We must leave till the next chapter the pressures on the humanity of Jesus arising from the judgment that he was more than 'a human being'. For now let us concentrate on those arising from the need that he be not too much 'like ourselves'.

As we have seen, both Paul and the author to the Hebrews insist as strongly as they can that the humanity of Christ must be complete if he was to do anything for our condition from the inside, and the latter makes the additional point that he had to be perfected and not merely perfect. But each draws back at the point of total identification. They can think of him as sharing our weakness, but not our sinfulness. But this presents them with an acute dilemma. Paul goes so far as to say, 'For our sake God made him one with the sinfulness of men'.[112] Yet he describes this by saying that God sent his Son *in a form like* that of our own sinful nature'.[113] The last thing he intends by this is a docetic denial that Christ was really one of us. Yet what Knox calls the 'pressure towards modification' is evidently at work. Equally, the author to the Hebrews is also treading very delicately. Whereas in every other respect his argument requires that Jesus in order to be *our* high priest must totally share our condition, he does not draw out the logic of his observation that 'every high priest . . . is able to bear patiently with the ignorant and erring, since he too is beset by weakness; and *because of this* he is bound to make sin-offerings for himself no less than for the people'.[114] Indeed, at this one point he actually makes a virtue of Jesus's *unlikeness* to us: 'Such a high priest does indeed fit our condition – devout, guileless, undefiled, separated from sinners.'[115] He uses the same word (*eprepen*) with which he had previously argued on the other side, that 'it was clearly fitting that God . . . should, in bringing many sons to glory, make the leader who delivers them perfect through sufferings. For a consecrating priest and those whom he consecrates are all of one stock'.[116]

The same dilemma comes out when he wishes to insist on the reality of Christ's temptations: 'For ours is not a high priest unable to sympathize with our weakness, but one who, because of

---

[112] II Cor. 5.21. [113] Rom. 8.3. [114] Heb. 5.1–4.
[115] Heb. 7.26. [116] Heb. 2.10f.

his likeness to us, has been tested every way, only without sin.'[117] Knox's comment on this passage is, I think, judicious:

meaning of "tempted"

> He means, of course, that Jesus, when he was tempted, did not *consent* to sin, did not succumb to its enticements. But, we may ask . . . Am I really tempted if I do not, however briefly or tentatively or slightly, consent? Have I been really tempted if I have rejected only that which entirely repels me or that from which I stand entirely aloof? Can we, then, think of Jesus as tempted – and moreover tempted in all respects as we are – and yet as not knowing from within the existential meaning of human sinfulness? I am not saying that we cannot; I am saying that there is no obvious way in which we can.[118]

Really to feel the pull of evil, one must see it as more attractive than the good. And it is surely a mere quibble to say of Jesus with P. T. Forsyth, 'The only temptation with real power for him was a temptation to good – to inferior forms of good'.[119] Why should the inferior appear superior? It can do so only if it is already being regarded from some viewpoint other than God's.

The line between temptation and sin is, as Knox sees, a very fine one. From the other side Moule has written with equal sensitiveness:

> In a desperately long battle, a soldier may yearn with every muscle in his weary body to gain the relief of desertion; but it is possible for him, at the same time, never to deviate a hair's breadth from the steady 'set' of the current of his loyalty to his country or his cause. Physically – even mentally – he may consent to the relief he longs for, but the 'set' of his will remains constant in its direction. In another context, and by way of another example, one might say that this 'set' of the will will negate what might otherwise have been 'looking lustfully' on a woman (Matt. 5.28).[120]

---

[117] Heb. 4.15.

[118] Knox, op. cit., p.47.

[119] P. T. Forsyth, *The Person and Place of Jesus Christ*, Independent Press 1909, p. 303.

[120] C. F. D. Moule, 'The Manhood of Jesus in the New Testament', in Sykes and Clayton (eds.), *Christ, Faith and History*, p.106.

Temptation does not of itself involve disobedience, but it must, I think, involve what Tillich calls 'estrangement'. He asks:

> Under what conditions is a temptation serious? Is not one of the conditions an actual desire toward that which has the power to tempt? But if there is such a desire, is there not estrangement prior to a decision to succumb or not to succumb to the temptation?[121]

Yet still, he maintains, there is a real distinction between 'desire' and 'concupiscence'.

The problem is the more acute if we widen sin, as Paul always does, to include not merely conscious transgression but the whole objective state of having-gone-wrongness – the very state with which Christ was identified, or he could have achieved nothing. In this situation, as we know, we find ourselves caught up in a sinful society which limits and distorts our outlook before we start and which presents us in almost every decision with a choice of evils.

Martin Kähler saw the problem acutely:

> How could he have been sinless in the midst of a world, a family and a people so full of offence? How could the boy Jesus develop in a pure and positive way when in his years of infancy, filial dependence, and immaturity he was surrounded by bad influences, and when his whole education, however well meant, must have been on the whole distorted?

But it drives him to the opposite conclusion:

> It is conceivable only because this infant entered upon his earthly existence with a prior endowment quite different from our own, because in all the forms and stages of his inner life an absolutely independent will was expressing itself.

Jesus thus becomes wholly other from us:

> The distinction between Jesus Christ and ourselves is not one of degree but of kind. . . . The inner development of a sinless

---

[121] Paul Tillich, *Systematic Theology* II, p.147.

person is as inconceivable to us as life on the Sandwich Islands is to a Laplander.[122]

Yet if Jesus was not subject to the common human conditioning, if he did not feel from within the loves and hates and social estrangements of his own nation, then he was not really a Jew of his time; and certainly, if he was not constantly confronted with a choice of evils, his choices are irrelevant to ours. Sebastian Moore puts it with characteristic directness:

> If the life of Jesus does not, for me, put up any questions of the sort that the life of Napoleon, of J. F. Kennedy, of Gautama Buddha, of Hughie Long put up, then I am a docetist. My Christ has not a real humanity. He is a theological construct. He never existed. If you have never seen Jesus, in your mind's eye, as faced with inescapable political social and personal-integrity options, then you are a docetist. Your Christ never existed. He is a puppet in a theologian's puppet show.[123]

Jesus' goodness is relevant to us if *in this situation* in which we live his obedience was such that he chose God's will even though, as in Gethsemane, it was clearly *not* what he wanted – and the evangelists use the strongest expressions for the *'nevertheless* not my will but thine'.[124] 'In his flesh, too,' says Bonhoeffer, 'was the law that is contrary to God's will.'[125] Jesus' obedience was

---

[122] Martin Kähler, op. cit., pp.53f. In all this Kähler is merely re-expressing the views of Schleiermacher. But Schleiermacher's great antagonist Barth could also write of Jesus: 'He was an absolutely alien and exciting *novum*' (CD IV 2, p.167).
[123] Sebastian Moore, 'The Search for the Beginning', in Sykes and Clayton (eds.), op. cit., p.84 [the US politician was in fact 'Huey' Long].
[124] Mark 14.36, *all' ou*; Matt. 26.39, *plēn ouch*; Luke 22.42, *plēn mē*. Dodd has pointed out how fundamental to the whole New Testament picture is this *contrast* (overcome by obedience) between Jesus' will and that of God. With Luke 22.42 ('Yet not my will but thine be done') he compares: John 5.30 ('My aim is not my own will, but the will of him who sent me') and 6.38 ('I have come down from heaven, not to do my own will, but the will of him who sent me'); Heb. 10.7,9 ('I have come, O God, to do thy will'); and Rom. 15.3 ('For Christ too did not please himself'). He comments: 'Where a trait is so deeply, so widely and so variously imprinted upon the New Testament writings, we have strong ground for believing it to be in the full sense historical' (*Historical Tradition in the Fourth Gospel*, p. 364).
[125] Bonhoeffer, *Christology*, p.112. He continues even more strongly: 'He was not the perfectly good man. He was continually engaged in struggle. He did things which outwardly sometimes looked like sin. He was angry, he was harsh

certainly not automatic or necessary. He was fallible – yet when the crunch came, he did not fail.

If, in terms of the later distinction, we are to say of him that he *could* not have sinned (*non posse peccare*), in the sense that we say of someone we know that it was impossible for him to have committed a murder, it must be because, not in spite, of the fact that he could *not* have sinned (*posse non peccare*). He must have had the freedom to sin or not to sin – or it would not have been *our* freedom that he shared. In other words, we can say, if we wish, that it was *morally* impossible for him to sin – or, as Forsyth put it, 'He could be tempted because he loved: he could not sin, because he loved so deeply'.[126] What we cannot say is that it was *metaphysically* impossible for him to sin – or, as Forsyth also put it: 'Because Christ was true man he could be truly tempted: because he was true God he could not truly sin.'[127] There is a decisive difference between these two, which is constantly blurred – even by so great a theologian as Barth when he insists (rightly) that the real freedom is *not* to sin.[128] Yet what Augustine called the greater freedom not to sin *presupposes* rather than *precludes* the lesser freedom to sin.

But to say, as I believe we must, that Jesus could have sinned like any other human being does not mean reducing his freedom to indeterminacy, as if it were merely a matter of contingency

to his mother, he evaded his enemies, he broke the law of his people, he stirred up revolt against the rulers and the religious men of his country. He entered man's sinful existence past recognition.' If we ask how Bonhoeffer reconciles this with Jesus' sinlessness, he resorts to Luther's paradox of the sinless man who was also *peccator pessimus* in a way which frankly borders on the nonsensical and docetic, ending up in the position that 'even the sinlessness of Jesus is incognito' (p.113): his deeds were not sinless, but *he* was! For a critique of these lectures, cf. J. Pelikan, 'An Early Answer to the Question Concerning Jesus: Bonhoeffer's *Christologie* of 1933', in Martin E. Marty (ed.), *The Place of Bonhoeffer*, SCM Press 1963, pp.143–66; J. A. Phillips, *The Form of Christ in the World. A Study of Bonhoeffer's Christology*, Collins 1967, ch. 6; A. Dumas, *Dietrich Bonhoeffer: Theologian of Reality*, SCM Press 1971, ch.8. But none of them takes up this point.

[126] P. T. Forsyth, op. cit., p. 303.

[127] Ibid., p. 302. Cf. Barth, CD IV 2, p. 93: 'Because and as He was man only as the Son of God, it [sin] was excluded from the choice of His acts. In virtue of this origin of His being, He was unable to choose it. Therefore He did not choose it.' The situation is hardly improved by saying with Forsyth (op. cit., p.301) that he was unaware of the fact that he could not sin – he thought he could; and so his temptations were real!   [128] Barth, CD IV 2, p.93.

which way he acted. In clarification let me cite two writers, one ancient and one modern, who make this point while at the same time insisting that his sinlessness was the outcome of a genuinely *human* freedom.

The first is Theodore of Mopsuestia, who died in 428, and who wrote of Jesus:

> He had an inclination, which was not by chance, towards the good because of his union with God the Word. He was also accounted worthy of this [union] by the foreknowledge of God the Word, who united himself with him from above. Thus, because of all this, he kept straightway with discretion a great hatred of evil, and with boundless love he fixed himself upon good. And receiving a power in accord with the fitting purpose [of the divine economy] and receiving the co-operating energy [*synergeian*] of God the Word, he kept steadfast for the rest [of his ministry] from changing for the worse. On the one hand, this was a purpose he held himself; and, on the other hand, it was something he kept faithfully according to the purpose and by the co-operating energy of God.[129]

Theodore makes it absolutely plain that it was not *because* Jesus was a good man that God united himself to him;[130] yet his union with God from the beginning did not override the human freedom but sustained it.

In the same way, in our day, Tillich writes of Jesus that 'his freedom was embedded in his destiny'. Yet he insists that this destiny denied neither his liberty nor his common humanity:

> The decisions of Jesus in which he resisted real temptation, like every human decision, stand under the directing creativity of God (providence). And God's directing creativity in the case of man works through his freedom. Man's destiny is determined *by* the divine creativity, but *through* man's self-determination, that is, through his finite freedom. In this

[129] J. P. Migne, *Patrologia Graeca* (= PG), Paris 1857–66, vol. 66, 977; in English, R. A. Greer, *Theodore of Mopsuestia: Exegete and Theologian*, Faith Press 1961, pp.51f.
[130] Cf. R. V. Sellers, *The Council of Chalcedon*, SPCK 1953, p. 171.

respect the 'history of salvation' and the 'history of the Saviour' are ultimately determined in the same way as is history generally and as is the history of every individual man.[131]

But the question still remains, Was Jesus that perfect? Can we say, with Schleiermacher, that, 'for every moment of Christ's life without exception' there was not even 'an infinitely small amount of the reality of sin, in the form of tendency'?[132] To this the only honest answer is: We do not know. We simply have not the evidence to say even that he was always obedient, always loving. All we can say is that these were the marks for which he was remembered – by his followers. *Of course* we must expect them to have remembered, and to have improved upon, an idealized portrait. Of course, too, we must expect doctrinal interests – that he was divine saviour and not merely a man heard for his godly fear – to have influenced the picture. Of *nothing* can we be *sure* that it is not the product of the church. But having said this – and said it as strongly as we wish – there are still other factors to be taken into account.

There is first of all the fact, which impresses itself upon me the more I study the gospels, that the early Christians seem to have retained a remarkable reverence for the remembered figure of Jesus. They did not simply put into his mouth, as they might well have done, all that *they* said about him. In fact they show a considerable reluctance to make him claim of himself what they claimed of him – that he was 'Lord' and 'Christ' and 'Son of God'. And, conversely, they constantly (including the Fourth Evangelist) put upon his own lips – and upon no one else's – the mysterious and ambiguous title 'Son of Man', which from the evidence of the Acts and Epistles played little or no part in the church's own preaching. Moreover, in the earliest tradition little attempt is

[131] Paul Tillich, *Systematic Theology* II, pp.149f. Since 'destiny' has in English the overtones of 'fate', and therefore the opposite of freedom, the following from F. Gogarten, *Christ the Crisis*, SCM Press 1970, pp.186f., may help to interpret Tillich's meaning: 'The German word for "destiny" derives from a root which originally means "to set to work". . . . Destiny is the way in which God "sets to work" man's life by giving him the world as his own, so that he may be responsible for it, independent of it, and therefore able to give himself in freedom to be God's own.'

[132] Schleiermacher, op. cit., pp.414f.

made to gloss over aspects of his words or person that could be misunderstood. Mark even makes Jesus say explicitly: 'Why do you call me good? No one is good except God alone',[133] which Matthew expectedly modifies to: 'Good?...Why do you ask me about that?'[134] I say 'expectedly', because this is what we should expect throughout. The surprise is that we do not get it.

In the light of this I think we should give extra weight to two further phenomena in the gospel record.

The first is that the gospels ascribe to Jesus no trace of the consciousness of sin or guilt. It is so universal a mark of saintliness, from Paul onwards, that the saint sees himself as 'the chief of sinners',[135] that the omission cannot but strike us. The obvious answer, of course, is that it has been written out of the record by the church. But the remarkable thing is that its absence is not emphasized[136] or defended[137] – but simply passed over in silence. It is an astonishing omission.

But the second phenomenon, I think, says even more. In regard to Jesus' attitude to the law (especially the ritual laws and the sabbath), the gospel writers are clearly aware of the need to vindicate him against Jewish attacks. But in regard to his personal morals they evince no such pressure – despite the fact that here, too, he clearly incurred the charge of being a 'sinner'. And this is the more remarkable considering the freedom with which they represent him as living and the company they represent him as keeping. They report Jesus as referring (evidently with some wry amusement) to his reputation as a glutton and a drinker,[138] but never think it necessary to refute it. Yet it would not have taken much to twist the Zacchaeus episode [139]into living it up with the exploiting classes instead of identifying with the dispossessed. Nor

[133] Mark 10.18.
[134] Matt. 19.17.
[135] I Tim. 1.15; cf. from his undoubted writings: I Cor. 4.4; Phil. 3.12.
[136] In John 8.46 the question 'Which of you can convict me of sin?' should be translated in the context, with the NEB, 'Which of you can prove me in the wrong?'
[137] In Matt. 3.13–15 the objection answered appears to be not, Why did Jesus accept a baptism of repentance?, but, Why did Jesus (the greater) accept baptism by John (the lesser)?
[138] Matt. 11.16–19 = Luke 7.31–35.
[139] Luke 19.1–10.

would most ministers today be able to survive three circum-
stantial (and, I believe, independent) reports[140] that he had had his
feet (or head) kissed, scented and wiped with the hair of a woman,
whether or not of doubtful repute. The lack of defensiveness with
which such compromising stories are told says a great deal.[141]
Yet no sweeping historical claims are made for his perfection: he
is actually made to disclaim it.

Positive sinlessness is attributed to Jesus, for theological reasons,
within the lifetime of many who could have contradicted the
Christian claim if the credibility gap had been too great. There
are limits, first, to what you can persuade yourself to, then to what
you can get away with, and still more to what you can assert
without even having to defend. If the moral gulf had been that
great, the Christian preaching – of a sinless saviour – would
simply not have been able to survive, given the opposition which
we know it had to counter in every other respect. The astonishing
claim of the church is therefore considerable testimony to the
character of Jesus, whose goodness, as we have seen, even Josephus
apparently conceded. Perhaps Brunner's conclusion is a fair one:

> Even if ultimately the verdict 'without sin' goes further than
> anything that can be grasped empirically, and thus carries us
> into the sphere of faith, yet we know of no situation which
> could shake the truth of these words: 'yet without sin'.[142]

Nevertheless, when everything has been said, 'the perfect man'
is a judgment of faith, not history. *Why* does it need to be made?
The answer to this question is bound up with the other side of
what Christians have wanted to affirm about Jesus, namely, that
he shows us not only man but God. And it is to this side that we
must now turn.

---

[140] Mark 14.3–9 (= Matt. 26.6–13); Luke 7. 36–50; John 12.1–8.

[141] Cf. the story of the woman taken in adultery (John 8.2–11) which, though
it is certainly no part of the Johannine text, is hardly likely to have been invented.
Indeed, it is now a floating piece of tradition precisely because it was *both* embarrassing *and* 'too like Jesus' to have been forgotten or suppressed.

[142] Emil Brunner, *The Christian Doctrine of Creation and Redemption*, Lutterworth Press 1952, p. 324.

FOUR

MAN OF GOD

From man to God

In the last two chapters we have spoken of Jesus as *a* man and as *the* man. And we have had to speak of him thus at a length and with an emphasis that may well strike the uninitiated as excessive. 'Methinks he doth protest too much.' Why should it be so necessary to stress the genuine humanity of this man? Is not the very going on about it suspicious? No one would think to spend so much time insisting on the humanness of Socrates.

The reason is that both the statements that Jesus was *a* man like everyone else and that he was in some sense *the* man (in that he gave us a vision of what humanity might be) have been rendered problematic by the claim that he was more than this – that he speaks to us not only of man but of God. For how could he be genuinely a man if all the time 'underneath', as it were, he was really God? And how could he not have had everything and been everything, without limitation, imperfection or possibility of failure, if he was also divine? It is the pressure to say these things that has complicated the other statements.

Now the pressure to say 'divine' things about Jesus *in some form* is inseparable from saying that he is 'the Christ'. For the mystery of the Christ, as we said at the beginning, is at one and the same time the clue to the meaning of human history *and* to the meaning of God at work in it. In the case of Socrates the pressure does not arise, for *that* claim is not being made of him. But to say of someone that he is the Christ is by definition to say that he is veridical

of God as well as of man: he speaks true of both. In the words of
the patristic formula (however we may interpret it), he is *vere
deus et vere homo*, 'truly God and truly man': he represents to us
the reality of what God is, as well as representing to us the reality
of what man is.

The question that has dogged Christian theology is how this
double reality can be so stated that one aspect of it does not prevail
only at the expense of the other. We have been insisting so far
that nothing must be allowed to encroach upon the integrity of
the humanity. And when now we come to ask how Jesus can be
veridical of God, it is appropriate that we continue from this same
end. In other words, how can he be, not only the man, but the
man of God, without ceasing to be a man in the fullest possible
sense? Only after pressing this to the limit (and it *cannot* be pressed
too far; for, as Luther said, 'The deeper we can bring Christ into
the flesh – but we are never able to do so enough – the better'),[1]
may we go on to ask equally insistently how God can truly be
represented, in all his fullness and initiative, in Christ. And this
approach 'from below' is not just the result of a modern humanistic
bias, nor is it only to be justified (as I believe it can be) in terms of
apologetics, as the way in for our empirical age.[2] It is, insists
Brunner, who was certainly no 'liberal', the approach of scripture
itself; and he quotes a well-known passage of Luther in support:

> The scriptures begin very gently, and lead us on to Christ as
> to a man, and then to one who is Lord over all creatures, and
> after that to one who is God. So do I enter delightfully, and
> learn to know God. But the philosophers and doctors have
> insisted on beginning from above, and so they have become
> fools. We must begin from below, and after that come
> upwards.[3]

---

[1] WA 34/I.147.10; cf. 10/II.68.6.
[2] Cf. T. R. Morton, *Jesus: Man for Today*, Abingdon Press, Nashville 1970,
pp.156f.; John A. T. Robinson, *The New Reformation?*, SCM Press 1965, ch. 2.
[3] WA 10/I2.297.5 (ET, H. R. Mackintosh, *The Doctrine of the Person of Jesus
Christ*, T. and T. Clark ²1913, p.232); cf. WA 57. 99.3: 'His humanity is our holy
ladder, by which we ascend to the knowledge of God. . . . Who wishes safely to
ascend to the love and knowledge of God, let him leave human and metaphysical
rules for knowing the deity, and let him first exercise himself in the humanity of

So, Brunner adds, 'If *God* has opened this way to himself for us . . . we have no right to try to reverse the process'.[4]

But, as he recognizes,[5] this has not been the order in which the church has approached the problem. Despite Augustine's recognition of the pastoral order, *'per hominem Christum tendis ad deum Christum'* ('you come to Christ as God through Christ as man'),[6] theologically the Fathers started with God and asked how God could become flesh without ceasing to be God: they did not start with this man and ask how he could speak to us of God without ceasing to be man. This was particularly true of the dominant (not to say domineering) Alexandrian school. But even the Antiochenes did not really begin from the other end. With the Old Testament, they started more from the unity of God than his triunity, and were more sensitive to what was implied in Jesus being historically a man and in the fullest sense a moral agent. But we must be careful not to 'modernize' them because in this respect we find them sympathetic. An example of this danger is to be seen in Raven's judgment of Theodore of Mopsuestia:

He is the outstanding member of a school in which we can recognize a type of theology not far removed in method or result from that to which the scientific movement has constrained us. He at least starts from history not from dogma, sifts the evidence of the New Testament, accepts its obvious emphasis upon the manhood of Christ, and only then asks himself in what sense the Nazarene is God.[7]

Unfortunately this is a more accurate portrait of the painter than his sitter!

It is important to recognize that the starting-point of the classic

Christ. For it is the most impious of all temerities when God himself has humbled himself in order that he might be knowable, that a man should seek to climb up some other way' (quoted William Hamilton, *The New Essence of Christianity*, Darton, Longman and Todd 1966, p.88).
    [4] Emil Brunner, *The Christian Doctrine of Creation and Redemption*, p.322. Cf. Gogarten, op. cit., pp.1–6 and 281–99; W. Pannenberg, op. cit., pp.33–37.
    [5] Brunner, op. cit., pp.341f.
    [6] *Serm.* 261.7.
    [7] C. E. Raven, *Apollinarianism*, Cambridge University Press 1923, pp.298f.

debate on Christology in the fifth century, which fixed its shape
for the next fifteen hundred years, was determined neither by
scripture nor by experience but by the Arian controversy on the
doctrine of the Trinity, which had reached its resolution at
Nicaea.[8] With Christ established there as a distinct person or
hypostasis of the Trinity, fully God in every sense of the word,
this was the datum that could not be questioned – not the fact of
his existence as an individual, historical person. And this starting-
point separates both the ancient schools of thought more effectively from us than anything that set them in opposition to each
other.[9] And since it colours so much of the language and presuppositions we have received, it is important, at the risk of a
historical excursus, however rapid, to note some of its effects, if
only so that we can be freer to decide whether or not we wish to
be bound by them.[10]

Four ancient presuppositions

1. I would first mention one that does not seem to have been
noticed as much as the others, namely, that of the *individuality* of
the second person of the Trinity. The Alexandrians, as opposed to
the Antiochenes, may have had difficulty in conceiving Christ as
a man. This was because they worked with a scheme of thought
that visualized the Word uniting to himself 'flesh' rather than 'a
man'. Indeed Grillmeier makes his case that the real debate was

---

[8] Cf. M. F. Wiles, 'The Doctrine of Christ in the Patristic Age', in: Norman
Pittenger (ed.), *Christ for Us Today*, SCM Press 1968 pp.85–90.

[9] Gogarten points out that this remains a great gulf even between Luther and
ourselves: 'Although the modern age began with him, he was still a medieval
man' (op. cit., p.298). We live this side of the revolution in historical method
which 'once it gains an entry into theology . . . works like a ferment in it, "transforming everything and finally shattering the whole previous pattern of theological method" (Troeltsch)' (p.292). 'The consequence of this is that if we are not
able to think of Jesus in resolutely historical terms, he and everything a Christology
can say of him loses all reality for us' (p.298).

[10] On all this, cf. (among many others that might be mentioned): G. L.
Prestige, *Fathers and Heretics*, SPCK 1940; R. V. Sellers, *Two Ancient Christologies*,
SPCK 1940, and *The Council of Chalcedon*; E. L. Mascall, *Via Media*, Longmans
1956; Norman Pittenger, *The Word Incarnate*, pp.84–96; J. N. D. Kelly, *Early
Christian Doctrines*, A. and C. Black [3]1968; R. A. Norris, *Manhood and Christ*,
Oxford University Press 1963; A. Grillmeier, *Christ in Christian Tradition*:
W. Pannenberg, *Jesus: God and Man*, pp.287–93.

not between two geographical centres (whose boundaries remained fluid until Cyril[11] galvanized both sides) but between the two thought-structures, Word-flesh (*Logos-sarx*) and Word-man (*Logos-anthrōpos*). What neither school questioned was that the Logos himself as a member of the Trinity was *a* being, *a* person, an 'individual substance', to use Boethius' later definition, 'of a rational nature'. To be sure, by this was not meant a personality in the modern sense, a distinct centre of conscious selfhood, but much more a permanent 'mode of being'[12] of the one personal Godhead. However, the fact that the same terms *hypostasis* and *persona* were used subsequently in the Christological debate to indicate the selfhood of one who, as man, *was* a person in the modern sense of the word, was decisive.[13] Boethius' definition could not have served as a definition of *human* personality for a thousand years, and even led C. C. J. Webb as recently as the First World War to call it 'still perhaps, take it all in all, the best that we have',[14] if it had not occurred in a *Christological* context.[15] And in fact the divine personhood of the Logos was thought of in sufficiently individual terms as actually to be able to constitute the individuality of Christ's human personality.

But if you start the Christological sum with one individual substance (divine), it means you cannot introduce another (human) without finding yourself with the impossible exercise on your hands of trying to put two billiard balls on the same spot. Either the divine displaces the human (as in the doctrine of *anhypostasia* to be discussed below) or the human exists, in Cyril's phrase, 'as another individually beside him' (*heteron par' auton*

---

[11] I am fully aware that the references I make to Cyril do not do justice to his greatness or to his wholly laudable passion for the unity of the person of Christ. But I would agree with the characteristic remark of W. Telfer, reviewing Sellers' *The Council of Chalcedon*: 'Dr Sellers says that no theologian arose among the Antiochenes of the same calibre as Cyril. This may be granted, if that calibre is not made the ideal' (*Journal of Theological Studies*, NS V, 1954, p.111).

[12] The term preferred by Barth in his masterly discussion of the doctrine of the Trinity, CD I 1, pp.412–15.

[13] Interestingly, Luther showed himself aware of the difficulty of using the one term 'person' both for a *hypostasis* of the Trinity and for a human individual. Cf. Siggins, op. cit., pp.223–7.

[14] C. C. J. Webb, *God and Personality*, Allen and Unwin 1918, p. 47.

[15] *Contra Eut. et Nest.* 3.

idikōs). This phrase, as Sellers points out,[16] occurs in varying form in no less than five out of the twelve anathemas that Cyril attached to his Third Letter to Nestorius, and represented his great bugbear. Equally, the Antiochenes were particularly sensitive to the charge that they taught 'two sons', and as vigorously denied it. But the problem was largely created by the terms of the debate. If you do not think of the Logos as 'a being' but as something more like 'the self-expressive activity of God',[17] then you can recognize Jesus as 'a man' in the fullest possible sense, who can *also* be his Word to the world. To this we shall be returning on a number of occasions in the following chapters.

2. The second presupposition introduced by the patristic starting-point was the metaphysical bias or weighting in favour of divinity over against humanity. Christ may have had two equal natures (even though in practice one was more equal than the other), but the person who 'had' these natures was firmly on one side of the line. *He* was divine. No classical statement of the person of Christ was more concerned than the *Tome* of Leo to preserve a true balance between the divine and human, insisting that 'in Christ Jesus' there is 'neither humanity without true divinity nor divinity without true humanity'.[18] Yet the balance is not in fact preserved. The divinity always has the edge. This comes out in a passage I quoted before when stressing the *totus in nostris*:

> In the complete and perfect nature, therefore, of very man, very God was born – complete in what belonged to Him, complete in what belonged to us.[19]

Observe that Leo's phrase is not '*totus in deo, totus in nostris*' but '*totus in suis, totus in nostris*'. God is the subject and Christ's 'own', the place where he really 'belongs', lies on the divine side of the line. The real subject of the birth, and indeed of the entire operation, is God. As Cyril put it,

> He took flesh of the holy Virgin and made it His own from

---

[16] Sellers, *The Council of Chalcedon*, pp.7, 152.
[17] Pittenger, *The Word Incarnate*, p.187 and ch. 8 passim.
[18] *Tome* 5; as in all the Chalcedonian documents, I have used the translation in Bindley, *Oecumenical Documents of the Faith*.   [19] *Tome* 3.

the womb, and underwent a birth like ourselves and came forth
Man . . . , but even though He became Man by the assumption
of flesh and blood He still remained God in Nature and in
truth.[20]

And the underlying assumption in all this betrays itself in the
phrase of Leo's: 'The Divinity was hidden by the veil of the
flesh'.[21] Even in the Chalcedonian Definition itself, where the
homoousion tō(i) patri (of one substance with the Father) is exactly
balanced by the *homoousion hēmin* (of one substance with us), the
latter is immediately glossed by the phrase *homoion hēmin* (like us),
the very word which in relation to God had in the Arian controversy been repudiated as the touchstone of heresy. It is difficult to
escape the conclusion that, however much they insisted otherwise,
the Fathers *did* believe that Christ *was* God but was made *like* us
(in everything but sin).

3. This priority of the divine is fully borne out, thirdly, by the
astonishing doctrine of *anhypostasia*, the view, as Donald Baillie
paraphrases it,[22] that 'Christ was not a human person, but a divine
Person who assumed human nature without assuming human
personality'. Traceable as early as Hippolytus[23] and presupposed
by Athanasius,[24] it was brought to formulation by Cyril, endorsed
(at least implicitly) at Chalcedon, and erected into a dogma by the
Second Council of Constantinople in 553. It remained unchallenged
in the Middle Ages[25] and, though subject to criticism by Luther,[26]

[20] *Ep. Nest.* III.   [21] *Tome* 4.
[22] Baillie, *God Was in Christ*, p. 85.   [23] *Contra haer. Noeti* 15.
[24] Cf. Newman, *Select Treatises on St Athanasius* II, p.293, who spells out (and
endorses) the logic of it as follows:
'That personality, which our Lord had had from eternity in the Holy Trinity,
he still had after his incarnation. His human nature subsisted in his divine, not
existing as we exist, but, so to say, grafted on him, or as a garment in which he
was clad. We cannot conceive of an incarnation, except in this way; for, if his
manhood had not been thus after the manner of an attribute, if it had been a
person, an individual, such as one of us, if it had been in existence before he
united it to himself, he would have been simply two beings under one name, or
else, his divinity would have been nothing more than a special grace or presence or
participation of divine glory, such as is the prerogative of saints.'
[25] Cf. Aquinas, *Summa* III.4.2, who even defends the injudicious remark attributed to Pope Innocent III that 'the Person of God has consumed the person of
man'.
[26] Cf. Dorner, op. cit. II, pp.100–4.

it has been strenuously reaffirmed in our time not only by Catholic orthodoxy, Roman[27] and Anglican,[28] but by those twin pillars of neo-Protestantism, Barth[29] and Brunner,[30] who may have disagreed about the virgin birth, and indeed the doctrine of the two natures, but not about this. Yet it appears so strange and so remote both from common sense and from scripture that it requires a considerable effort of the imagination to understand what can even have been meant by it, let alone why it has been so generally regarded as essential.

It has been used to deny both that Jesus was an *individual* man and that he was a man *independently* of God's self-incarnation in him. Barth wishes to discriminate between these two denials.[31] The former, he is convinced, rests on a misunderstanding. Indeed, we have already argued that to assert that Christ was *the* man need not and cannot mean that he was not genuinely *a* man. But it is far from clear that the second denial, of independence, does not involve denial of individuality. Thus the American writer Louis B. Smedes, who seeks to establish the same distinction, still writes:

> If, however, it were to be said that he [Jesus] as *a* man was in any sense existentially independent of the person of the Son, that he had his existence in himself as did Paul and Peter, then it would be necessary to say that he was *not* a man.[32]

[27] E.g. P. Parente, *L'Io di Christo*, Brescia 1951.

[28] E.g. Mascall, *Christ, the Christian and the Church*.

[29] Barth, CD I 2, pp.163–5; IV 2, pp.47–50, 90–91. He is faithfully followed by T. F. Torrance, 'The Place of Christology in Biblical and Dogmatic Theology', in T. H. L. Parker (ed.), *Essays in Christology for Karl Barth*, Lutterworth Press 1956, pp.16f.

[30] He goes so far as to say 'We cannot sufficiently admire the sureness and delicacy of this definition' (*The Mediator*, Lutterworth Press 1934, p.318) — though his own statement of it is exceptionally unclear. Brunner makes a distinction between Jesus' person, which was divine, and his personality, which was human. But he identifies the latter not with his inner self but with the 'mask' of sin: 'Although he assumed human nature with its possibilities of being tempted, even an historical personality after the manner of men, he did not assume human personality in the sense of the ultimate mystery' (op. cit., p.320; cf. p.346). In his later exposition of the subject, while not denying the doctrine (*The Christian Doctrine of Creation and Redemption*, p.346), he makes much less of it and is concerned to repudiate the suggestion that in *The Mediator* he wished to 'deny to Jesus full human personality' (p.360).   [31] Barth, CD I 2, p.164.

[32] Louis B. Smedes, *The Incarnation: Trends in Modern Anglican Thought*, Amsterdam 1953, p.148.

But John McIntyre, who uses the same analogy, concludes, I think correctly, that in this case:

> The particularity and individuality of the man Jesus would be removed. In fact, it would be impossible to differentiate the *man* Jesus from the man Peter or the man John unless, in some way, the human *hypostasis* were retained.[33]

In other words, independence and individuality cannot finally be separated.

Why Barth and others are so concerned to deny Jesus' independent existence as a human being apart from God I shall return to consider later,[34] when examining the very real objections to any form of 'adoptionism'. But I am persuaded that the truth at stake can be preserved without the theory that Jesus had no human personality (or, by the later refinement of *enhypostasia*, that this was somehow included in his divine personhood).[35] This theory was strongly contested by the Antiochenes as destructive of his humanity, and I am sure they were right.[36] Bonhoeffer dubbed it 'the last refuge of docetism'.[37]

[33] John McIntyre, *The Shape of Christology*, SCM Press 1966, p.97.

[34] See pp. 200-2 below.

[35] The argument is that inasmuch as man is made in the image of God, the essence of manhood was already contained within the divinity of the Son, as it were on a reduced scale, so that the second person of the Trinity could also constitute by inclusion the human *hypostasis* or ego of Jesus. This idea, which may be traced back, with its doubtful implications for independent selfhood, to Apollinarius (though Raven, op. cit., pp.185-8, and Prestige, op. cit., pp.222-6, strongly deny that this is what Apollinarius meant), was elaborated by Leontius of Byzantium and John of Damascus and powerfully defended by H. M. Relton in his book *A Study of Christology*, SPCK 1917. Cf. the criticisms of it by McIntyre, op. cit., pp.95-101. But McIntyre's own 'improvement' on it, following Ephraim of Antioch, that while the two natures are not confused or compounded the two hypostases *are*, so that 'the hypostasis of Jesus Christ is a fusion (*synthetos*) of the human and the divine', would seem to make Christ quite literally a hybrid, a God-man. Indeed, I would judge that if 'the two-nature model' is not to be either docetic or disruptive this is its logical terminus.

[36] Cf. the judgment of Telfer: 'Only the "Antiochene" school protested against "anhypostatic manhood", and it was the finally condemned Theodore of Mopsuestia who saw clearly that unless "the man" in Christ was so far individual as to experience the temptation to pride, the soteriological canon remained unsatisfied. Because this was so, Chalcedon failed to prevent a modified Apollinarianism from becoming the orthodoxy of the Middle Ages' (*Journal of Theological Studies*, NS V, 1954, pp.110f.). This is quoted by Pittenger in his critique of the doctrine, op. cit., pp.100-3; cf. Baillie, op. cit., pp.85-93.

[37] Bonhoeffer, *Christology*, p.81.

Indeed, in the classic statements of it there has been remarkably little embarrassment about the fact that Jesus was on this account superhuman.[38] A good instance of this is the Christology of Bishop Frank Weston, who was as insistent as anyone who has started from the 'Alexandrian' end to stress the utter genuineness of the human limitations of the incarnate Word, and whose book *The One Christ* remains, in the judgment of Archbishop Michael Ramsey, 'one of the greatest of all essays on the Incarnation'.[39] No one can accuse him of the crypto-docetism that constantly threatens to seep through the writings of Cyril. And yet he sees no difficulty at all in Christ *not* being, in his inmost substance and selfhood, a man:

> I think the fundamental error of all who seek a human or divine-human subject of manhood lies in the false belief that the ego of manhood must, in some sense, be necessarily a man. The Antiochene teachers could not conceive of anyone who was not a man exercising human functions humanly and completely; and in this failure they had many followers. Now it may be strongly argued that the ego of manhood in Christ may be superhuman. Provided that his personality possesses all the attributes of human personality as its minimum content, and provided that all his characteristic powers that exceed this human measure can, in some way, be limited, restrained and controlled, there is no evident reason why such a superhuman person should not be the ego of manhood in the Incarnate.[40]

In other words, becoming man means living *as* a man, experiencing a human existence: for, as Leonard Hodgson argues, to be the subject of such experiences *is* to be human.[41] But to *be* a man is more than to experience life as a man. The fact that I, a human being, might decide to experience life *as* a dog – and to know

[38] Cf. Brunner, *The Mediator*, p.345: 'The Person of this human personality does not resemble a human being; here the humanity of Christ ceases.'

[39] A. M. Ramsey, *From Gore to Temple*, Longmans 1960, p.38; see also Brenda C. Cross, 'The Christology of Frank Weston: A Reappraisal', *Journal of Theological Studies*, NS XXI, 1970, pp.73–90.

[40] Frank Weston, *The One Christ*, p.106.

[41] Leonard Hodgson, 'The Incarnation', in A. E. J. Rawlinson (ed.), *Essays on the Trinity and the Incarnation*, Longmans 1928, pp.361–402.

nothing, even of my fellow-men, except through the limitations of the canine nervous system – does not make *me* a dog. Indeed nothing can, unless I *am* one and have been one all along. Weston, commenting on William Temple's essay in *Foundations*,[42] remarked with apparently pained surprise: 'Mr Temple seems to think that unless the subject of the manhood be truly and completely human, manhood is not really assumed.'[43] There are others who would make this rather obvious, but apparently erroneous, judgment.[44]

4. The fourth presupposition of patristic Christology, which was reinforced by Nicaea, was the doctrine of the two natures. The effect of the Arian controversy has been to rule out any middle term between divinity and humanity. Christ was unqualifiedly divine. If, therefore, he was to be unqualifiedly human

[42] William Temple, 'The Divinity of Christ', in B. H. Streeter (ed.), *Foundations*, Macmillan 1912, ch.5.

[43] Weston, op. cit., p.101. Actually Temple makes no such specific statement. It is Weston's interpretation of his mind. Mascall's attempt to assimilate Temple's later views to the doctrine of *enhypostasia* (*Via Media*, pp.115–17) really cannot succeed. He may indeed have said that 'the human personality of Jesus is actually the self-expression of the Eternal Son' and as such 'is assumed in the Divine Person of the Creative Word', but the previous sentence is decisive: 'If we imagine the divine Word withdrawn from Jesus of Nazareth, as the Gnostics believed to have occurred before the Passion, I think that there would be left, not nothing at all, but a man' (William Temple, *Christus Veritas*, Macmillan 1924, p.150).

[44] J. F. Bethune-Baker, whose standard work *An Introduction to the Early History of Christian Doctrine*, Methuen 1903, at least shows that he knew what he was talking about, was forthright: 'We must absolutely jettison the traditional doctrine that his personality was not human, but divine' (id 'Jesus as Both Human and Divine', *The Modern Churchman* XI, September 1921, p.288). This lecture is reprinted in his book *The Way of Modernism*, Cambridge University Press 1927, pp.92–112, where it is incorrectly dated as delivered in August 1923.
Since finishing this present book, I have just been able to read Piet Schoonenberg's *The Christ*, Sheed and Ward 1972. This seems to me a real breakthrough in Roman Catholic Christology. It is not every day that a Roman Catholic theologian, even if a Dutchman, decisively rejects (in a book that carries a *nihil obstat*) both the theories of the anhypostatic manhood and of the two natures of Christ. He stands the former on its head, and argues that it is the *Word* that was *anhypostatic* (i.e., not a person) until it took individuality in the man Jesus Christ. He advances the theory of 'the *enhypostasia* of the Word' which 'becomes in him [Jesus] a historical person', citing Hippolytus, *Contra haer. Noeti* 15: 'The Logos by itself and without the flesh was not completely the Son' (though Hippolytus goes on to say that neither was the flesh 'hypostatic' without the Logos). See especially pp.54–66 and 80–91. This is very much in line with my own argument, and I should have liked the opportunity of noting the correspondences at a number of other points. But I suspect he would not be prepared to go quite as far as I do.

as well, it could only be by holding together two distinct and disparate natures. And the more one wanted to insist, like the Antiochenes, on the reality of the humanity, the more intractable the problem became. The Alexandrians, who were working with a basically Platonic view of God, were prepared to see the line between God and man blurred by divinization. The Antiochenes, with a more Jewish and in some cases more Aristotelian cast of mind, saw God so transcendently 'other'[45] that he could not effectively become one with man, though they had to our mind a profounder and more moral understanding of what full personal union would mean – on which indeed they wished to insist as strongly as anyone else.[46]

This doctrine of two separate 'natures', each with its own inalienable properties, was regarded as essential if Jesus was to be *both* Son of God *and* Son of Man. The so-called *communicatio idiomatum*, or intercommunication of the properties, was not between the two natures – so that the human nature became God-like and *vice versa* – but between each nature and the one subject – so that God himself, for instance, could truly be said to suffer and to die (which in his own nature he could not).[47] There was a

[45] It is incredible to us that the Antiochenes actually accused the Alexandrians of compromising and minimizing the impassibility and immutability of God. They greatly feared what could be read into the Word *becoming flesh*.

[46] Dorner, op. cit. II, p.102, commends 'the accurate and acute glance which Luther took at the history of Christology'. 'He saw that . . . Nestorius esteemed the divine nature to be too lofty for union with, and therefore kept it far from, the human; Eutyches, on the other hand, considered the human nature incapable of receiving the divine as its own, excluded it from participation therein, and thus put a slight on it (though pretending to exalt it by means of absorption).' Luther's great contribution, says Dorner, was to insist, on the one hand, on 'the susceptibility of the human nature to the divine, due to the gracious love of God, and on the other, that the divine nature and its substance, owing to the power exercised over it by love, not only presented no hindrance to a union of natures in the Person of Christ, but was able to possess, and to be conscious of, all that is purely human as its own.' In contrast, the Reformed tradition held to the traditional but sterile *finitum non est capax infiniti*. For a balanced assessment of the truth (and excesses) on both sides, cf. pp.220–48.

[47] It also provided scope for endlessly ingenious paradox, as in H. R. Bramley's Christmas hymn (*English Hymnal*, no. 29):

> Oh wonder of wonders, which none can unfold:
> The Ancient of days is an hour or two old;
> The Maker of all things is made of the earth,
> Man is worshipped by Angels, and God comes to birth.

single personal subject who not merely, as we should say, wore different hats but functioned, as it were, on different circuits. Indeed, particularly with regard to knowledge and will, the impression can scarcely be avoided that he operated with two alternating modes of consciousness,[48] one of which could be switched off or suppressed at will. In Irenaeus' vivid phrase, 'When he was being tempted and crucified and dying, the Logos remained quiescent'.[49] Cyril in particular was a master of the double switch: 'To him,' he said, 'will belong both to know and to seem not to know.'[50] Yet he was equally insistent that Christ was not a split personality: 'For the one and only Christ is not twofold (*diplous*).'[51] Though one must distinguish the natures, one must never divide the person. Indeed, it has been said of the Chalcedonian Definition, 'In an almost literal sense, its first and its last words about Jesus Christ are that he is one.'[52] Nothing in him was done by the man apart from the deity or by the deity apart from the man. One nature, as we should say, 'came through' the other. As Athanasius put it rather nicely,

> He spat in human fashion, yet his spittle was charged with deity, for therewith he caused the eyes of the man born blind to recover their sight.[53]

Yet this quickly runs out into the docetic absurdities of:

> He sleeps in the manger; he reigns on the throne . . .
> A Babe on the breast of a Maiden he lies,
> Yet sits with the Father on high in the skies.

[48] The unfortunate word '*invicem*' in Leo, *Tome* 4, which could mean 'by turns' is, however, clearly not intended to have that meaning but rather, as the Greek version shows, 'by mutual interrelation' (cf. Sellers, *The Council of Chalcedon*, p. 237; Mascall, *Via Media*, p.94). Yet Chrysostom, the preacher, is not so guarded, saying in the name of Christ: 'As God, I curbed nature, supporting a fast for forty days, but afterwards, as man, I was hungry and tired; as God, I calmed the raging sea, as man, I was tempted by the devil; as God, I expelled devils, as man, I am about to suffer for men' (*In quatrid. Lazarum* 1).

[49] *Adv. haer.* III.19.3.

[50] *Apol. contra Theodoret.* anath. 4.

[51] Nevertheless, Tertullian had gone as far as saying, 'We see a twofold condition (*duplicem statum*) which is not unfounded but conjoined in one person, God and man, Jesus' (*Adv. Prax.* 27).

[52] McIntyre, op. cit., p.93.

[53] *Ep.ad Serap.* 4.14. The whole passage is cited in an appended note by Prestige, op. cit., pp.369f.

Nevertheless, two natures were essential; for if he had had only one, there would have been some things he could not have said and done which it is recorded that he did say and do. This is brought out forcibly in a well-known passage in the *Tome* of Leo:

> To feel hunger, thirst, and weariness, and to sleep, is evidently human; but to satisfy thousands of men with five loaves, and to bestow living water on the Samaritan woman, the drinking of which would cause her who drank it to thirst no more; to walk on the surface of the sea with feet which did not sink, and to allay the 'rising billows' by rebuking the tempest, is without doubt Divine. As then, to omit many other examples, it does not belong to the same nature to weep in an emotion of pity for a dead friend, and to raise that same friend from the dead with a word of power, . . . so it does not belong to the same nature to say, 'I and the Father are one,' and 'The Father is greater than I.'[54]

Leo's immediate intention was to allow for the reality of the *human* nature, which the monophysite Eutyches had denied – and indeed it was primarily to safeguard this that the doctrine of the *two* natures was insisted upon. But this *we* do not think to question. Obviously Christ was a man. Our questions relate to the functions for which it is alleged that he required a second, divine nature. In so far as they represent things that Jesus may actually have done or said (as opposed to theological comment by the evangelists), they are evidence for us, as for the New Testament, not of his own independent divinity (to which his deeds and words are never taken to argue, even in the Fourth Gospel), but of what is possible *with God* to *any* man wholly open to the divine power.[55] The response to the healing of the paralytic is typical: 'The people . . . praised God for granting such authority to men.'[56] The furthest that even Matthew, with his heightening of the supernatural, makes Jesus go is to say in Gethsemane, 'Do you

[54] *Tome* 4. It is noticeable that Leo avoids all mention of Christ's knowledge, which forced Cyril into such double talk. Cf. Bruce, *The Humiliation of Christ*, pp.64f., who also notes that Leo says nothing on the personal or impersonal character of Christ's manhood.
[55] Mark 9.22f.; 11.23 par.; Luke 17.6; Matt. 17.20.   [56] Matt. 9.7f.

suppose that I cannot appeal to my Father, *who* would at once send to my aid more than twelve legions of angels?'[57] There is no suggestion that Jesus himself could lay them on *because he was God.* Nor, equally, is there any suggestion, such as comes in later, that he was able to do these things because he was in himself an exceptional 'divine man' (*theios anēr*) in the Hellenistic tradition.[58] As McIntyre sums up the picture of the gospels:

> Even in the great prayer of John 17, when Jesus makes unmistakably plain his awareness of his oneness with the father, there is not the slightest hint that one part of his person is speaking, or that what he is saying might not be entirely true of his whole person. When he faces the final agonies on Calvary, no excuse is offered for his weakness, for example, that it is in his human nature that he is brought low, while his divine nature still reigns in heaven. It was left to later apologetic to invent subtleties, one might even say deceptions, of this sort.[59]

If we wish, as assuredly the New Testament does, to go on to say that Jesus' words and works are not simply those of any man faithful and open to God but the self-expression of God acting in him and through him, this is still not because there were some things he could not say or do as a man, and which therefore required of him a second nature, but because what he said and did must also be seen as 'bespeaking' God as well as man.

In other words, the formula we presuppose is not of one superhuman person with two natures, divine and human, but of one human person of whom we must use two languages, manlanguage and God-language. Jesus is wholly and completely a man, but a man who 'speaks true' not simply of humanity but of God. He is not a man plus, a man fitted, as it were, with a second engine – which would mean that he was *not* a man in any genuine sense. He is a man who in all that he says and does as man is the

---

[57] Matt. 26.53.
[58] For a thorough survey of this concept, of which much use has been made of late in New Testament Christology, cf. Paul J. Achtemeier, 'Gospel Miracle Tradition and the Divine Man', *Interpretation* XXVI, April 1972, pp.174-97.
[59] McIntyre, op. cit., p.84.

personal representative of God: he stands in God's place, he *is* God to us and for us.

Two languages

To the implications of that last statement we must come back later. Now I want to go on to explore the transition I have spoken of from two natures to two languages. This transition is not in fact great if we accept the judgment of what seems to me a discerning essay by R. A. Norris on the real aim of the Chalcedonian Definition. 'The *Definition*,' he says, 'is not talking about Jesus; it is talking about Christian language about Jesus.'[60] In other words, it is not conducting a philosophical analysis into Christ's composition in terms of substance and natures. It is asserting that of this one subject different things can and must be predicated.

> The *Definition* asserts that in the particular case of Christ these two kinds of language [language about God and 'empirical' language] are both to be used to give an account of the same *explicandum*, yet that they are logically different and in some way mutually supplementary. Hence the question arises whether – and how – it can make sense to offer two different *kinds* of explanation for the very same event. This is the form which the problem of Christ's 'natures' takes for modern theology.[61]

But he also makes the important point that, by taking the subject (*hypostasis*) of both the natures (or languages) to be God the Word,

> the Christology of Cyril and the *Definition*, considered from a modern point of view, falsifies the character of the Christological enterprise by in effect distinguishing between the logical subject in statements about Christ and the historical *explicandum* in which the Christological problem has its roots.[62]

[60] R. A. Norris, 'Toward a Contemporary Interpretation of the Chalcedonian Definition', in R. A. Norris (ed.), *Lux in Lumine: Essays to Honor W. Norman Pittenger*, Seabury Press, New York 1966, p.78.
[61] Norris, op. cit., p.79.
[62] Ibid.

Like the gospels, we start from the historical individual Jesus of Nazareth and ask how different statements, human and divine, can be made about *him*.

To the Fathers it seemed self-evident that if Jesus was to be all that was asserted of him as the Christ, he must be the conjunction of two worlds – he had to be a God-man, a single person who *was* both. And the word 'was' must mean the same in each case, if he was to be 'truly' God and man. He must *be* in the fullest metaphysical sense 'God' – 'in person'. And he must equally *have* the full 'nature' of man as well as of God. The fact that these natures had incompatible properties may have necessitated some gracious accommodation, but none of the Fathers would have doubted, for instance, that Jesus *could* have come down from the cross. It was simply that for our salvation he chose not to: he elected to leave that nature in abeyance. As Cyril put it, 'He economically allowed the measures of humanity to have power over himself'.[63] Even so recent and so humanistic a writer as Seeley could speak in his *Ecce Homo* of 'Christ's abstinence from the use of his supernatural power as a device by which he avoided certain inconveniences which would have arisen from the free use of it'.[64]

There can scarcely be anyone today who would not feel uncomfortable with that statement, and it indicates how great a change has come over us in a mere hundred years. For this whole way of thinking strikes us as irredeemably docetic. It has the effect of making Jesus a sort of centaur or bat-man,[65] a hybrid conjunction of two strange species, and we start asking questions such as we ask of the incarnations of the Greek gods, 'Did they have ichor in their veins or blood?'

What is it that has caused this change, and why do statements about the Incarnation in these terms strike us as distorting, whereas they did not do so for our ancestors? The answer is to be sought in the changes which we noted in the first chapter, and

[63] *Quod unus sit Christus* 8.1.319.
[64] Seeley, op. cit., p.40.
[65] I would therefore agree with Barth (CD IV 2, p.115) against Kierkegaard, Berdyaev, Brunner, Tillich and the early Bonhoeffer, that the expression 'God-man' must be avoided, as impossible to safeguard against misrepresentation. Pittenger's 'God-in-Man' (op. cit., p.221) is much nearer to scripture.

particularly in this connection with regard to mythology and metaphysics. For we find it impossible to take the language of mythology or metaphysics, as they did, to describe a second order of being or events, just as real and indeed ultimately more real, above or behind phenomena of this world. And it is these two orders of being that in the theory of the two natures are envisaged as conjoined in Jesus. The reason why this now strikes us as having a docetic effect is that it is a way of thinking we have given up everywhere else. It seems to isolate the Incarnation as a bolt from the blue, a dip of the divine into the human on the arc of a parabola receding as unrepeatably as it came. But originally no such isolating effect was intended or felt. The Incarnation was part of a continuous cosmic drama in which the two worlds, of the natural and the supernatural, constantly interpenetrated. The trouble is that we of the twentieth century, unlike those of earlier centuries, do not naturally see the cosmic process in these dualistic, or two-natured, terms. Hence the Incarnation so presented strikes us as an anomalous exception, not, to adapt Whitehead's phrase,[66] the 'chief exemplification' it appeared to our forefathers.[67]

If, then, we are to make any sense or use of the traditional categories in which Christian theology has spoken of the Incarnation, it is essential that we extend to it the revaluation of them to which we have now become accustomed elsewhere. For we have learnt to see the natural and the supernatural not as two layers of being that have to be joined together, so much as two sets of language, man-language and God-language, in which it is possible to speak of the single cosmic process. In other words, what we are

[66] Alfred North Whitehead, *Process and Reality*, Cambridge University Press 1929, p.486.

[67] It is not, as Brian Hebblethwaite seems to suppose is being claimed, that contemporary *experience* 'refutes' the 'classical doctrine' of the two natures, let alone 'renders unintelligible the doctrine of the Incarnation' (id., 'The Appeal to Experience in Christology', in Sykes and Clayton (eds.), *Christ, Faith and History* pp.263–78). It is that this kind of language no longer succeeds in saying the same thing to us. I would deny entirely being among those concerned to 'justify reductionism', which he equates with 'rejecting the two nature doctrine' and opting for a 'purely human' Christ. These latter two are in any case not at all the same thing. Pannenberg makes the point very strongly (op. cit., pp.284f.) that the theory of the two natures is but *one* way of stating the *vere deus et vere homo* – and a way subject to grave scriptural and doctrinal (rather than experiential) objections.

talking about is not two storeys, but two stories.[68] The one is natural, scientific, descriptive. The other is supernatural, mythological and interpretative. The former views the course of events in the categories of an evolutionary cosmology, the latter in terms of 'moments' like the Creation, the Fall, the Incarnation, the Parousia.[69]

Thanks to the agonizing wrestlings of the past two hundred years (and particularly of the past hundred), there is now a substantial measure of agreement about how these two ways of speaking are to be related to each other. The 'events' in the latter series are not to be slotted into the former, as and when the supernatural penetrates or perforates the natural by special creations, interventions or acts of God. The supernatural is not a parallel, superior causal sequence, but an interpretation or unveiling (*re-velatio*), in terms of myth or a 'second' story, of the same process studied by science and history. The Creation and the Fall are not particular events in the historical past, but ways of giving theological expression to processes and experiences that are going on all the time. Similarly, we are beginning to realize that the Parousia or Second Coming is not a once-and-for-all event in the historical future, whether near or remote, but part of a myth designed to clarify what it means – as well as what it will mean – to see all things 'new' in the kingdom of God. It asserts that the reality depicted by the Fall, the truth of all things 'in Adam', is not the only or the final truth about the cosmic scene. In each case what the myth does is to focus and clarify in a single dramatized picture

[68] Cf. M. F. Wiles, 'Does Christology Rest on a Mistake?', *Religious Studies* XI, 1970, pp.69–76; reprinted in *Christ, Faith and History*, pp.3–12. I owe much in what follows to the stimulus of this essay, and my own contribution to the same volume, 'Need Jesus have been Perfect?' (pp.39–52), which, with permission, I largely reproduce here, arose directly out of it.

[69] Perhaps there is a parallel in what D. M. Mackay says about the physical world in his Eddington Memorial Lecture, *Freedom of Action in a Mechanistic Universe*, Cambridge University Press 1967. 'These two stories, one in "brain-talk" and the other in "mind-talk", are *correlates* of one another, they are not *translations* of one another, any more than a physicist's description of the electrical currents in a telephone line is a translation of what the speaker is saying' (p.28). One is about currents in the line, the other about the weather. One can be deterministic, the other indeterministic, without mutual contradiction (indeed with mutual corroboration). 'Although both relate in a sense to the same events, they are not making assertions about the same aspects of them' (p.29).

of black and white the realities obscured in the 'greys', the relativities and continuities, of the historical process.[70]

In order to ground these truths of interpretation, previous
generations have felt it necessary to assert that there must be
decisive events in the natural sequence to correspond to the
moments in the supernatural – some original day of creation,
some special insertion of the soul of man, some datable fall, some
predictable end of the world. If there were not this correspondence,
then the reality of the theological affirmations seemed to be
weakened or imperilled. We now see, however, that the demand
for such a 1:1 correspondence stems from a category confusion.
Indeed, the events in the two series or stories are strictly incom-
parable. In the historico-scientific series we are dealing with a
continuum where all things are relative and interconnected,
shading into each other by differences of degree, confused and
'grey'. In the mythological series we are concerned with discrete
'acts of God', with the unique in kind and not merely in degree,
the perfect, once and for all, absolute and final. These latter categories are not those of 'the flesh', and to predicate them of that
order is to deny the flesh as flesh. They are there to *interpret* the
continuities and ambiguities of the flesh as the carrier of the Logos
or meaning of God.

This is already to introduce Christological language, which
indeed the New Testament insists cannot be excluded from any
part of the cosmic process.[71] But before proceeding to the
Incarnation proper, we may pause to watch this principle exempli-
fied in the other so-called acts of God in history, of which the
Exodus is viewed by the biblical writers as paradigmatic. To see
the Exodus as decisive for the interpretation of God's meaning for
history it is not necessary to affirm that in the historical series this
event is anything but confused, protracted, blurred at the edges
and generally uneventful. It need not have even the relative
decisiveness, say, of Creasy's *Fifteen Decisive Battles of the World*.

[70] Van Buren seems to be saying much the same in his latest book *The Edges of
Language*, SCM Press 1972, when he distinguishes between what can be said
within 'the solid, rule-governed area of speaking' and what has to be said, if it can
be said at all, on or beyond the fringe of language. The latter is wild, apocalyptic,
'God' talk.   [71] John 1.1–14; Col. 1.13–20.

To expect that it must be more 'eventful' if it is to be divine in significance is to confuse the categories of *kairos* and *chronos*,[72] to allow what is historic to determine what is historical – just as it would be, later, to say that that particular birth at Bethlehem (if indeed it even occurred at Bethlehem) *must* have been more 'eventful' than the rest.

Yet continuity in the processes of nature and history does not mean that there are no climacterics, no genuinely new mutations, no moments which are not of more 'importance', again to use Whitehead's term, than any others. To deny the need for 'special creations' to explain them does not mean that the first appearance of life on this planet and the emergence of *homo sapiens* are not points of determinative significance in the evolutionary process – however non-discrete, blurred and outwardly unremarkable these events may still in themselves have been. As Teilhard de Chardin put it, the uniqueness of the human spirit is not lessened by the fact that it emerges 'so scrupulously prepared over so long a time that nothing quivers when it appears in nature'.[73]

Similarly, in history there are climacterics. There are Rubicons – however insignificant the stream. The 'sea of reeds', which has become for us the Red Sea, may have been another such ditch or swamp. Yet if the Exodus proved to be a pure 'myth' in the popular sense, a non-event, something that never happened or changed anything, then it would be difficult, to say the least, to celebrate it as the supreme example of the mighty acts of God as Lord of history. That of which the interpretation is the interpretation must have sufficient validity in the man-language series if the God-talk is to be credible.

With these criteria let us look at the event called 'the Incarnation'. The word belongs to the mythological story, but it is of the essence of this story that the happening it interprets belongs equally to the historical series. Indeed, it is at this point above all that Christian theology has felt it necessary to insist on the 1:1 correspondence. There must also be within the latter sequence a

[72] Cf. my *In the End God*, Fontana Books [2]1968, ch. 6.
[73] Pierre Teilhard de Chardin, 'The Phenomenon of Spirituality' in id., *Human Energy*, Collins 1969, p.102.

once-and-for-all event, a person, unique in kind, discontinuous with the past, perfect, absolute and final. Anything less would be a denial of the decisive act of God.

Yet we must be careful here, much more careful than we have hitherto needed to be. For all these categories belong to the 'second' group. Can we predicate them of the flesh without destroying the flesh as flesh? This, of course, in another form is the question that dogged the whole Alexandrian school of Christology and represented its perennial temptation – to allow the divine to swamp the human and to end up in monophysitism or crypto-docetism. Yet we must ask it again, much more seriously – and that because of what we now know both about nature and about history.

Until about a hundred years ago it did not really matter in regard to the first man whether the scientific story was confused with the mythological. Then it became vitally important to distinguish (though not to separate). If this had not been done, the theological interpretation would have been discredited – whereas in fact it has been greatly enhanced. Similarly today, with regard to Jesus, it has become vitally important to discriminate between what we can say 'according to the flesh' and what we can say 'according to the spirit'. Previous generations may not have been forced to distinguish, but it is, I believe, imperative today to insist, for instance, that the virgin birth story is not there to give information about gynaecology any more than the story of the Fall is there to give information about primitive anthropology. Its primary intention, as we have seen (though the New Testament writers were compelled to no such conscious antithesis), is not to assert discontinuity in the biological series (thus setting it directly against the genealogies that accompany it), but to make a positive statement at the level of spirit – to affirm the entire *genesis* of Jesus Christ as the act and initiative of God. In this the minute and often murky continuities of heredity and environment are not abrogated.

And it is an essential part of the 'offence' of Jesus for the New Testament writers that this can be so. His origin does not by-pass the ambiguities and relativities of history. He comes 'out of

Nazareth',[74] from Galilee,[75] a setting from which (as everyone knows) 'prophets do not come'.[76] But the real offence is that he has a traceable origin at all – the Christ should be above these things. 'We know where this man comes from, but when the Messiah appears no one is to know where he comes from':[77] that is what religion would like to believe. But of Jesus it is possible to say: 'Is not this . . . the son of Mary, the brother of James and Joseph and Judas and Simon? And are not his sisters here with us?'[78] He has a *patris*, a local origin, which has to be accepted with him,[79] a home background from which he cannot be detached. It is part of the possibility of offence, and *therefore of faith*, that the continuities and the ordinariness are not swept away. As Brunner puts it:

> The Son of God in whom we are to be able to believe must be such a one that it is possible to mistake him for an ordinary man. To break through the ordinary limitations of humanity would be to break through the possibility of faith.[80]

The fact that he is 'called of God' does not deny that he is also 'taken from among men':[81] the initiative 'from above' does not cancel the solidarity 'from below'. To know where Jesus 'comes from' physically is entirely compatible with his having his origin in 'the Father'.[82]

Nevertheless, there has been a perennial tendency in Christian theology to regard these emphases as antithetical. Christologies that stress the 'taken from among men' are thought to threaten the dimension of the divine. Equally, those that insist on starting from the Logos have tended to view the continuities and ambiguities of the flesh as expendable. An either/or has been set up in the popular mind. As a neighbour of mine once put it to me with complete simplicity, 'If Jesus was the Son of God, he *couldn't* have been the son of Joseph, could he?' Or there has been a blurring of

---

[74] John 1.46. For reflection on the significance of this cf. Geoffrey Ainger, *Jesus our Contemporary*, SCM Press 1967, ch. 6.
[75] John 7.41.   [76] John 7.52.   [77] John 7.27.   [78] Mark 6.3.
[79] Mark 6.1–6 = Matt. 13.53–58; Luke 4.16–30; John 4.44.
[80] Brunner, *The Mediator*, p.341. Brunner is here echoing Kierkegaard.
[81] Heb. 5.1–10.   [82] John 7.27–29.

the two, particularly by way of a 'spill-over' from the second language to the first: 'If Jesus really was God, he *must* have known that Judas would betray him.' But there is no direct or necessary transposition from the judgment of faith to statements of history.

In other words, we must in our own day and our own way insist with the Chalcedonian Definition that 'the difference of the natures' is 'in no way removed because of the union', but rather that 'the properties of each nature' are 'preserved'; or with Cyril (however much we may judge that he departed from his own canon) that 'neither has the nature of the Word deviated into that of the flesh, nor that of the flesh into that of the Word; each continues and is recognized by its own natural character'.[83] The flesh, the history, remains blurred, messy, ambiguous. Yet Christians have been too ready simply to transfer to it the categories of the absolute, unique, perfect, once-and-for-all and final. And it is particularly important to be wary of doing this in an age marked by the third change we noted in the first chapter, 'the dissolution of the absolute'. For these categories do not today represent a natural language, any more than that of Jewish mythology or Greek ontology, for trying to describe the 'ultimate' significance of the historical. If we confuse the categories (as the ancients were in constant danger of confusing the natures) and appear to be asserting that the Christian history itself *has* these characteristics and therefore *as history* is unlike any other history, then we shall be in worse case still. Today it is more vital than ever to stress with Leo that 'just as the Word does not retire from equality with the Father's glory, so neither does the flesh abandon the nature of our race'.[84]

The necessity to acknowledge more freely than we have done the relativistic character of the flesh, with its differences of degree rather than of kind, is closely related, too, to the fourth change we noted in the first chapter, which is demanded by the seriousness with which we must take historical criticism. Christians have

[83] *Ad Succens.* 2. The Antiochenes were still more insistent on preserving the differences in the properties of the natures against any kind of 'confusion', as were the Western Fathers (cf. Sellers, *The Council of Chalcedon*, pp. 194–203).
[84] *Tome* 4.

tended to apply terms like sinlessness and perfection, uniqueness and finality, to the Jesus of history and to the Christ of faith indiscriminately. But ignorance, if nothing else, forbids us making such absolute assertions of the former. And we should be careful to avoid theological judgments that imply historical statements we cannot substantiate. There is, for instance, a cluster of the latter in the classic challenge that if Jesus claimed to be God – in itself exceedingly doubtful – then he must either *be* God or be mad or bad[85] – the implication being that the latter two can self-evidently be ruled out. But the evidence is not so unambiguous. We must boldly say that nothing finally depends on the 1:1 correspondence. For we cannot substantiate it in any case.

Yet between the theological judgment and the statement of history the credibility gap cannot be too great. (This is the modern equivalent of the opposite error which Chalcedon condemned, that of 'separating' the natures to the extent of ending up with two Christs.) The Jesus of history must have been sufficient to have evoked and sustained the response, 'You are the Messiah, the Son of the living God'.[86] The relative must have been such as to point through to the absolute, so that men could actually conclude that to have seen him *was* to have seen the Father. And there can be no question but that in Jesus men did sense what can only be described as a breakthrough. The entire evidence of the gospels shouts aloud that here was, in their judgment, a new development, which could not be contained within the skin of the old: 'What is this? A new kind of teaching! He speaks with authority.'[87] 'No man ever spoke as this man speaks.'[88] Clearly here was no

[85] *Aut Deus aut homo non bonus*. Frequently revived in popular apologetic (e.g. C. S. Lewis, *Mere Christianity*, Fontana Books 1955, pp.51f.), this dilemma formed the heart of Liddon's Bampton Lectures, *The Divinity of our Lord and Saviour Jesus Christ*, of which J. M. Creed was to say, 'Against his will, Liddon has proved how very differently situated we are today, and how great a change is necessary if the doctrine of Christ's divinity is to have meaning in our age' (op. cit., p.79). Gore, who, for all his differences from Liddon, accepted the cogency of the argument in his own Bamptons five years later (*The Incarnation of the Son of God*, pp.16f.), wrote, 'Dr Liddon did not himself know, and I cannot ascertain, the source of the epigrammatic summary' (p.238). (In substance he traces it back to the fourth century, to Victorinus Afer, writing against Candidus the Arian, *De Gener.* 1.) For all its familiarity it does not appear in *The Oxford Dictionary of Quotations*.
[86] Matt. 16.16.   [87] Mark 1.27.   [88] John 7.46.

ordinary man – in the sense that there was nothing extraordinary about him. Yet, whatever the judgment of faith as to what *God* might be doing through him (and there was no ceiling they could place on that), there is nothing in the response of contemporaries, whether negative or positive, to suggest that the man or the events themselves were different *in kind* from what they met around them elsewhere. His miracles were not such as others did not[89] or could not[90] do; and even after one of the most remarkable, the raising of the widow's son at Nain, the reaction, however awesome, is expressed in categories like: 'A great prophet has arisen among us' and 'God has shown his care for his people'.[91]

We have already seen that the gospels make no exaggerated or absolutist claims for the perfection of Jesus, in the sense that he had or was everything a human being could have or be. Indeed, there are instances in all the gospels (and not least in the Fourth Gospel, where the 'second' language appears so dominant) to suggest that both Jesus' goodness and mental balance seriously caused men to question whether he could even be a 'man of God', let alone anything more:

'This fellow is no man of God; he does not keep the Sabbath.' Others said, 'How could such signs come from a sinful man?'[92]

'He is possessed, he is raving. Why listen to him?' Others said, 'No one possessed by an evil spirit could speak like this. Could an evil spirit open blind men's eyes?'[93]

Yet the correspondence must have been sufficient. 'To whom else shall we go?,'[94] asks Peter on behalf of the infant church. If Jesus had really thought of himself as a poached egg, or had a police record at Nazareth as long as your arm, or even been just another Zealot,[95] there are other candidates who come to mind.

---

[89] Matt. 12.27 = Luke 11.19.
[90] Matt. 10.8; Mark 9.14–29; John 14.12; Acts 3.1–16; 9.32–42; 19.11–17; 20.7–12; etc.; II Cor. 12.12.
[91] Luke 7.16f.   [92] John 9.16; cf. 7.12; 9.24; 10.33.
[93] John 10.20f.; cf. 7.20; 8.48, 52.   [94] John 6.68.
[95] I cannot here go into all the ramifications of *this* issue or the growing literature on it. I must simply refer to a forthcoming symposium, to which I have

Again, if it could really be shown that he never lived, or was too insignificant a character to have originated anything, it would be difficult, if not impossible, to sustain the judgment of faith that in this man took place the decisive act of God in world history.

The risk of historicity

To that extent the judgment of faith is ultimately vulnerable to the verdict of the historian. And this is a risk that the Christian faith can never escape if it is to take the flesh as seriously as the Logos. It represents 'the soft under-belly' (to use Winston Churchill's phrase) of the Word made flesh. And yet there has been an extraordinary reluctance to admit this vulnerability. Tillich, for instance, held that there was a sharp difference between the existential risk of faith and that of accepting uncertain historical facts.[96] Yet if one pins one's faith on a man who turns out historically to have had feet of clay, is not this existentially disillusioning?

In this Tillich was much influenced by Martin Kähler, his professor at Halle (whose *The So-called Historical Jesus and the Historic, Biblical Christ* was to set the terms of the German debate for the next two generations) and, like everyone else, by Kierkegaard.[97] He had sharpened the question, raised by Lessing, How can the *certainty* of salvation be made dependent on the *probability* of historical statements?[98] Under the impact of German biblical criticism, which threatened to leave no *locus standi* for the believer or the preacher, it was felt intolerable that the Word of God should be bound by the deliverances of the latest academic. And there was not a little logical confusion, born of the fear that if one

contributed, C. F. D. Moule and E. Bammel (eds.), *The Zealots and Jesus*, Cambridge University Press 1973 (?).

[96] Paul Tillich, *Systematic Theology* II, p.134. Cf. John P. Clayton's valuable critique, 'Is Jesus Necessary for Christology? An Antinomy in Tillich's Theological Method', in *Christ, Faith and History*, pp.147–63, and the literature there cited.

[97] The influence of Kierkegaard at this point on Barth, Brunner and Bultmann is well illustrated by McIntyre, op. cit., pp.119–23. For Kierkegaard's Christology, cf. P. Sponheim, *Kierkegaard on Christ and Christian Coherence*, SCM Press 1968.

[98] Søren Kierkegaard, *Philosophical Fragments* (1844), revised ed., Princeton University Press 1962.

conceded that the *kerygma* or preaching was in any way liable to
the verdict of the historian, one was saying that it owed its origin
to him. So immunity from the critics was bought at the price of
cutting the dependence of the Christian of faith on the Jesus of
history (except for his bare existence and death on the cross).[99]
The result has been a dangerous dichotomy which is in peril not
merely of producing a split mind in the critical believer, but of
reintroducing a docetic Christ-figure impervious to history
because untouched by it.[100]

   The proper relationship between the Logos and the flesh in this
matter of knowledge is important to establish. Clearly there is not
a 1:1 correspondence such as uncritical piety has demanded
between the Christ of faith and the Jesus of history. Neither must
one confuse the two languages, so as to make the judgment of
faith reducible to historical knowledge. But that the judgment of
faith is dependent on, in the sense of being vulnerable to, the facts
of history is surely inescapable for any historical religion such as
Christianity. And between the two there is not an all-or-nothing
relationship. Just as the conservatives have felt impelled to
'absolutize' the flesh to make it meet for the Logos, so the other
side has believed it necessary to insist that the assurance of faith
must be 'absolutely secure and certain', immune to any mere
assessments of probability, however high.[101] But the act of faith
is a constant dialogue with doubt. And the real threat to it is not,
I believe, an ultimate theoretical possibility that something might

[99] For a summary and critique of Bultmann's position at this point, cf. among
many others, Zahrnt, *The Historical Jesus*, ch. 6; W. Marxsen, *The Beginning of
Christology: A Study in its Problems*, Fortress Press, Philadelphia 1969, ch.1; and
Leander E. Keck, *A Future for the Historical Jesus*, SCM Press 1972, pp.50–8.
[100] Cf. Barbour, op. cit., pp.19–25, who shows how exclusive use by New
Testament critics of the criterion of 'dissimilarity' (by which only that is clearly
attributable to Jesus which is not to be paralleled either in late Judaism or in the
early church) isolates him from his background and continuities in a docetic
manner. 'The picture of Jesus has, so to speak, no depth in time – and consequently a curious lack of variegation in other respects too' (pp.23f.).
[101] Cf., e.g., John Knox, *The Church and the Reality of Christ*, Collins 1963, p.16.
For the best short survey I know of the possible positions and permutations here,
cf. H. K. McArthur, 'From the Historical Jesus to Christology', *Interpretation*
XXIII, April 1969, pp.190–206, who distinguishes three schools of thought: 'the
historical-certainty', 'the historical-risk' and 'the immune-from-historical-
research'. His own conclusion differs somewhat from mine.

be discovered that would knock out everything, from which it can, and must, logically be protected,[102] but 'the death of a thousand qualifications'.[103] There comes a point somewhere along the line where one ceases to be able to say of *such* a man, 'My Lord and my God'; and that is a matter of degree for each particular believer.

This is indeed a tangled jungle, but the following statement on the limits and relevance of the historical method would seem to me to get the balance which English writers have often succeeded in preserving:

> Its cutting edge is not verification but falsification. It cannot prove the truth of the Christian proclamation. It could conceivably provide disproof. Here lies its critical importance for belief. . . . If it be objected that such an admission leaves us with an intolerable uncertainty, the only answer that can be returned is that in Jesus God has put himself at risk, and that he who cannot abide that risk has failed to plumb either the nature of revelation or the nature of the certitude of faith.[104]

The test of the resurrection

But let us return from the 'uncertainty principle' in any faith-judgment about history to the status of the history itself. We have argued that there are no 'absolute' events or persons, different in kind from those around them, unaffected by the ambiguities, the continuities, the greys, which pertain to the flesh as flesh. Yet it is precisely such absoluteness that has been claimed by traditional

---

[102] Cf. Peter F. Carnley, 'The Poverty of Historical Scepticism', in *Christ, Faith and History*, p.188: 'The ghostly possibility that future discoveries may be made which would count against an historical assertion can, with conclusive evidence, be laid to rest.' Even if one accepts this as logically demonstrable, there are other much less ghostly possibilities.

[103] A. G. N. Flew, 'Theology and Falsification', in A. G. N. Flew and A. MacIntyre (eds.), *New Essays in Philosophical Theology*, SCM Press 1955, p.97.

[104] Neville Clark, *Interpreting the Resurrection*, SCM Press 1967, p.95. Cf. Bonhoeffer, *Christology*, p.76: 'Concealment in historicity is part of Christ's humiliation' – though from this he draws the conclusion that historical criticism 'never leads to a weakening of faith but rather to its strengthening', which is surely an exaggeration. But he makes the good remark that 'verbal inspiration is a bad surrogate for the resurrection'.

Christian theology for the total Christ-event that faith calls, under its different aspects, the Incarnation, the Atonement, the Resurrection. In the 'second' story these are seen as unique, once-and-for-all transactions which have changed irreversibly the course of history, so that (as in the case of the Fall) the situation is no longer what it was. They are not just occurrences among others of the same sort, but divine acts of an utterly different order. But how far is the Christian committed to seeing any such decisiveness or finality in the actual history itself? Let us concentrate on what on any reckoning is the hinge-event – the Resurrection.[105]

The very term *the* resurrection (*hē anastasis*) itself signifies the uniqueness, the finality with which it is seen in the 'second' series. Originally this term is part of the myth of the End and refers to the resurrection at the last day, and it is always so used in the gospels.[106] Its subsequent application to what *we* call 'the resurrection' on the third day (and to no other raisings from the dead) implies the theological conviction, found throughout the New Testament, that this was indeed 'the beginning of the end'. Here

[105] I cannot here go in detail into the massive historical and theological questions raised by this subject. I would refer to my article 'Resurrection in the New Testament' in *The Interpreter's Dictionary of the Bible*, Abingdon Press, Nashville 1962, IV, pp.43–53. To the bibliography there add, in order of publication W. Künneth, *The Theology of the Resurrection*, SCM Press 1965; H. F. von Campenhausen, 'The Events of Easter and the Empty Tomb', in: id., *Tradition and Life in the Church*, Collins 1968, ch.3; H. Grass, *Ostergeschehen und Osterberichte*, Göttingen ³1964; M. C. Perry, *The Easter Enigma*, Faber 1959; Hugh Anderson, *Jesus and Christian Origins*, Oxford University Press 1964, ch.5; W. Pannenberg, *Jesus: God and Man*, ch. 3; J. McLeman, *Resurrection Then and Now*, Hodder and Stoughton 1965; Jürgen Moltmann, *Theology of Hope*, ch.3; C. E. Braaten, *History and Hermeneutics*, Lutterworth Press 1966, ch.4; G. W. H. Lampe and D. M. MacKinnon, *The Resurrection: A Dialogue between two Cambridge Professors in a Secular Age*, Mowbrays 1966; Neville Clark, *Interpreting the Resurrection*, SCM Press 1967; S. H. Hooke, *The Resurrection of Christ as History and Experience*, Darton, Longman and Todd 1967; C. F. D. Moule (ed.), *The Significance of the Message of the Resurrection for Faith in Jesus Christ*, SCM Press 1968; P. Benoit, *The Passion and Resurrection of Jesus Christ*, Darton, Longman and Todd 1969; W. Marxsen, *The Resurrection of Jesus of Nazareth*, SCM Press 1970; C. F. Evans, *Resurrection and the New Testament*, SCM Press 1970; J. Jeremias, *New Testament Theology* I, ch.7; R. H. Fuller, *The Formation of the Resurrection Narratives*, SPCK 1972; D. H. van Daalen, *The Real Resurrection*, Collins 1972.

[106] Mark 12.18–27 par.; Luke 14.14; John 5.29; 11.24. Cf. Mark 9.9–11, where the puzzled objection that Elijah must come first before the Son of Man's 'rising from the dead' suggests that if there were any resurrection predictions in the teaching of Jesus they would have been understood to refer to the last day.

was the new act of creation, the start of the new humanity, the birth of the second Adam. The theological finality is not at issue. The question is whether this momentous 'act of God' requires on the other scale a 'special creation' comparable to that which traditionally was deemed necessary to mark the emergence of the first man.

In the historical series the most notable fact about the resurrection narratives in the canonical gospels, as opposed to the apocryphal,[107] is that nothing is described as happening. This reticence should make us wary of demanding instant 1:1 correspondence. But there is no doubt that the consequences of the resurrection of Christ as recorded in the New Testament – the empty tomb, the appearances, the transformation of the disciples – suggest, and have been taken to imply, a unique divine intervention (extending to a total molecular transformation) still more discontinuous with the ordinary processes of nature than the biological break felt to be required to match the theological significance of his birth.

But if we are concerned here as much as anywhere else to discern what is really being said at the two levels, we must be more discriminating. Or we shall be requiring of the historical series statements for which there is no evidence and which are in danger of denying the flesh as flesh. Equally, however, we must be aware of the other credibility gap – that of failing to provide sufficient historical cause to account for the theological judgment.

Let us start from the latter end. Any reconstruction of the history of the first century must stand condemned that fails to account not only for the initial transformation of the original disciples, but for the continuing and all-controlling conviction of Christ as a life-giving presence in the Spirit indwelling those who had never 'seen the Lord', let alone viewed the tomb.[108] That there was no such new spiritual reality, that nothing was altered, that it all rested on self-delusion or deceit, is to say that the unprecedented step of taking an element from the myth of the last things

---

[107] Notably *The Gospel of Peter* 35–42.
[108] This is how Paul sees the risen Christ in Rom. 8.1–11 and it is closely parallel to the conception of John 14.15–20. Cf. Gal. 2.19f.; Col. 3.1–4.

and transferring its 'finality' to a moment *within* history was purely arbitrary. Christianity would never have started, let alone survived, if the credibility gap had been that wide.

Equally, it seems to me, if the so-called 'appearances' had been purely subjective hallucinations (the equivalent of seeing pink rats) or purely private, it is incredible that Paul and others could have rested so much on them – especially when he sits so light to his own 'visions'.[109] That there were in the period immediately following Jesus' death genuine, shared psychic experiences, with whatever degree of materialization (and the accounts vary), which were at least *thought* to be veridical, seems necessary to explain the first dawning of the spiritual conviction that was subsequently independent of them. In form, these appearances should probably be classified as 'objectively projected' hallucinations,[110] not essentially different from other such phenomena. But they would have signified 'resurrection' (as opposed to the temporary survival of an individual loved one) only if in content a radically new spiritual awareness had communicated itself through them.

In his *Systematic Theology*, Gordon Kaufman takes the view that the appearances were naturally interpreted by the disciples to mean that Jesus was personally reawakened from death. Yet,

the theologically important fact both for the first Christians and for us . . . was not that this *finite man* as such lives again, but that *God's act begun in him* was a *genuine historical act* which *still continues*, that the love, mercy, and forgiveness present in their midst with Jesus, and brought to a burning focus with his self-sacrificial death, was still present with them

in the new community which *was* Christ just as much as previously the historical Jesus had been.[111] He appeals for this to the use of 'Christ' in the New Testament to mean not simply the person of Jesus but the whole of God's act consummated in the new corporeity the real form of his 'bodily' resurrection.[112]

[109] II Cor. 12.1–10; cf. Künneth, op. cit., pp.82–91.
[110] Perry, *The Easter Enigma*. This is an important but neglected study, starting from a fairly conservative critical position.   [111] Kaufman, op. cit., p.429.
[112] Cf. John Knox, *Jesus: Lord and Christ*, Harper and Brothers, New York 1958, pp.205–8. See especially Col. 2.9.

The finite objective historical reality correlative to faith was not in fact the reawakened Jesus of Nazareth but *the new community of love and forgiveness*, recreated and recognized under the impact of the resurrection appearances. Because of this actually present historical reality, the disciples' interpretation of the hallucinations as in fact the very act of God was not sheer subjective fancy; it was rooted in the experienced new quality of community, a quality they could attribute only to God's creativity, not to themselves.[113]

Kaufman's position is compatible with the phenomena being at their own level as elusive and inconclusive as those supervening upon the death of many another human being and proving in themselves no more and no less. Indeed, he is content to speak of them as hallucinations in the sense of a 'non-public but privately *extremely significant experience*'.[114] Yet psychologically they served as a necessary occasion, under the existing historical and epistemological conditions, for the breakthrough of the great divine reality that created and constituted the new covenant, 'the new being in Christ'.

What of the empty tomb? Again the credibility gap seems to me to rule out deliberate deceit by the disciples,[115] or that the women went to the wrong tomb and no one bothered to check,[116] or that Jesus never really died,[117] or that his body was not buried but thrown into a lime-pit (the burial is one of the earliest and best-attested facts about Jesus, being recorded in I Corinthians[118] as well as in all four gospels[119] and, for what it is worth, in the Acts *kerygma*).[120] More plausible is the oft-repeated thesis that the subsequent belief in the resurrection *created* the empty tomb story

[113] Kaufman, op. cit., p.430.
[114] Kaufman, op. cit., p.425. Italics his throughout.
[115] As suggested by the Jews according to Matt. 28.13–15 and in contrast with allegations about his birth decisively repudiated.
[116] Especially in the light of Mark 15.47.
[117] Denial of this appears to be behind the special stress on eye-witness in John 19.32–35. In any case, if Jesus did not die then, what happened to him? That he could simply have gone into hiding and disappeared stretches credulity.
[118] I Cor. 15.4.
[119] Matt. 27.57–61; Mark 15.42–47; Luke 23.50–56; John 19.38–42.
[120] Acts 13.29.

because this is what the Jewish hope would have pointed to. But what it pointed to was a rising at the last day for the final judgment. Prior to that, the most that could have been expected would have been either a temporary resuscitation (like that of Jairus' daughter) or a return in spirit (e.g. of Elijah and, perhaps, of 'John the Baptist raised from the dead'), with neither of which is the noun 'resurrection' ever associated.[121] *No one* expected to find a grave empty in the middle of history, nor if they had would they have associated it with 'the resurrection'. They would have associated it with bewilderment and probably with foul play – which is precisely what we find in the gospels.[122] Only in one verse in the Fourth Gospel[123] is one man reading back in faith represented as putting the two together.

If the empty tomb story had really been created subsequently to convince doubters, the church could surely have made a better job of it. It rested it entirely on the testimony of women (which in Jewish law was not binding and whose visions[124] do not even rate inclusion in the Pauline list),[125] and it did not involve the apostles.[126] As Lampe says, summarizing the synoptic evidence:

> Either the women did not tell them (Mark),[127] or they did tell them but they disbelieved the report (Luke),[128] or (in Matthew)[129] the women told them they should go to Galilee and the disciples therefore went on there without taking any action about the tomb.[130]

I cannot, however, follow him in thinking that the fact that the message was not passed on or was dismissed suggests that the

[121] Cf. C. F. D. Moule, in *The Significance of the Message of the Resurrection for Faith in Jesus Christ*, pp.8f.

[122] Mark 16.8; Luke 24.4, 11f.; and especially John 20.1f., 10–15.

[123] John 20.9.

[124] Matt. 28.9f.; John 20.14–18; [Mark] 16.9; Luke dissociates the appearances from the tomb altogether (24.24).   [125] I Cor. 15.5–8.

[126] The Jewish objector in Origen, *Contra Celsum* 2.55, mockingly fastens on this weakness.   [127] Mark 16.8.

[128] Luke 24.9–11. Verse 12 is usually taken to be secondary and inserted into the text under the influence of John 20.6. Even if we accept it, with A. R. C. Leaney, *St Luke*, A. and C. Black 1958, pp.28–31, and Jeremias, *New Testament Theology* I, p.305 (and it is only missing in one Greek manuscript), Peter remains completely mystified.   [129] Matt. 28.8–10.   [130] Lampe, op. cit., p.52.

evangelists (in their critical wisdom?) knew that the story 'was not part of the original Easter proclamation and had only developed at a relatively late stage in the tradition'.[131] You do not develop – or even include – stories merely to throw away their point. On the contrary, I would agree with Dodd's latest assessment:

> It looks as if they [the evangelists] had on their hands a solid piece of tradition, which they were bound to respect because it came down to them from the first witnesses, though it did not add much cogency to the message they wished to convey, and they hardly knew what use to make of it.[132]

The evidence suggests indeed that it was very early tradition. It is, after all, squarely in Mark, and shows no sign of being his creation but rather 'tradition with a long history behind it'.[133] Moreover, Paul's words in I Cor. 15.4 that Jesus 'was buried' and that 'he was raised to life on the third day' seem to presuppose some connection between resurrection and the tomb (and not merely the appearances) as part of what he received at his first instruction as a Christian and of what was universally believed by the apostles. Künneth, who takes this view very strongly, quotes Bornhäuser as saying:

> It should never have come to the point that in spite of the *etaphē*, 'he was buried', of I Cor. 15.3f. the phrase 'he was raised again the third day' was understood in any other way than as a raising from the tomb.[134]

Yet we must be careful not to jump to conclusions. As R. H. Fuller says, who also accepts (more tentatively) the connection with the tomb from the earliest times, this does not of itself imply any kind of transformation of the old corpse in order to return to earth, but translation into a new, eschatological mode of existence, in which Christ might be seen, if at all, in 'glory'.[135] Moreover,

---

[131] Ibid., p.48; cf. p.49.
[132] Dodd, *The Founder of Christianity*, p.167.   [133] Fuller, op. cit., p.171.
[134] K. Bornhäuser, *Die Gebeine der Toten*, Gütersloh 1921; quoted by Künneth, op. cit., p.94.   [135] Fuller, op. cit., pp.48f., 170.

Bornhäuser makes the important point that for Jewish thought the restoration of the whole personality in resurrection was quite independent of the fate of the dead bones. To create a 'new man' God did not require either their presence *or their absence*: for the old was not the 'matter' out of which the new was made. While, therefore, Künneth believes that Paul accepted the common apostolic tradition of the empty tomb,

> The fact of the tomb as such . . . does not have any power to prove the resurrection, since the latter in itself is wholly independent of any substratum of a material kind, so that Paul too, like the rest of the New Testament, does not adduce the fact of the empty tomb as a specific argument.[136]

Indeed the really significant thing is that he makes *nothing* of it. This scarcely suggests a strong motivation in the early church to create or elaborate it. He never uses the precedent of Jesus, as one might expect he would, in his subsequent discussion in the latter half of I Cor. 15 of the relation of the natural body to the spiritual. Indeed the one thing he says of Christ's relation to believers is that he is the 'firstfruits' (*aparchē*),[137] a word which (as he insists elsewhere)[138] means a genuinely representative sample. His expectation of resurrection for all Christians is the same as that for Christ, and he can argue directly, backwards and forwards, from the one hope to the other.[139] Yet if Jesus' body, unlike ours,[140] was not 'sown in corruption',[141] then his solidarity with the mass of mankind would be undercut. As Lampe puts it:

> If his body was transformed after death into something different, in such a way that it was annihilated, then he did not experience the whole of our human destiny. His entry into life

---

[136] Künneth, op. cit., pp.94f.   [137] I Cor. 15.20,23.   [138] Rom. 11.16.
[139] I Cor. 15.12–32; cf. Kaufman, op. cit., p.418.   [140] II Cor. 4.16–5.5.
[141] I Cor. 15.42–44. The testimonium from Ps. 16.10 to show that Jesus' body did not 'suffer corruption', placed in Acts 2.25–31 in the mouth of Peter on the day of Pentecost in Jerusalem, depends for its force, as C. F. Evans points out, *Resurrection and the New Testament*, pp.12f., on the use of the LXX text in a Greek-speaking community. The identical interpretation given to it on the lips of Paul in Acts 13.34–37 precludes us from regarding it as independent evidence either for Petrine or Pauline thinking.

beyond the grave was different from what we may hope to be our own.[142]

But whether we press Paul's logic at this point or not, it is clear that his fervent belief in the resurrection, on which his whole gospel hinged, did not *depend* in any way on the empty tomb or on anything exceptional having happened to the flesh-body of Jesus. Nor is there any hint, either in the Epistles or in Acts, that the form in which he 'saw the Lord' was directly connected with it.

The evidence, therefore, would suggest that, while the finding of the grave empty was not invented by the early church, it neither created belief in the resurrection nor was created by it. It was simply part of what was indelibly remembered to have happened. *Why* it was empty admits historically of no certain explanation, whether natural or supernatural. We must be content to suspend judgment. 'They' have 'taken him away'[143] is the first and obvious thought in what Jeremias is now convinced, interestingly enough, is the most primitive form of the story – that embedded in the Johannine account.[144] Perhaps it was grave-robbers – a not unreasonable suspicion since, as he says, 'it was unusual for the governor to release the body of a man executed for high treason, and fanatics could have remedied this decision by taking the corpse under cover of night to one of the criminals' graves.[145] This is not to imply that Jeremias himself thinks this is the explanation. Like most biblical theologians, he commits himself to no view as to what actually happened – though at least he thinks this is a legitimate and, unlike Bultmann, an important question.[146] It is simply that it is a supposition that

[142] Lampe, op. cit., p.59.   [143] John 20.2,13.

[144] Jeremias, op. cit., p.304, following what he calls the 'pioneering article' by P. Benoit, 'Marie-Madeleine et les disciples au tombeau selon Jean 20.1–18', in W. Eltester (ed.), *Judentum, Urchristentum, Kirche*, pp.141–52. Cf. also Benoit, *The Passion and Resurrection of Jesus Christ*, ch. 10.

[145] Jeremias, op. cit., p.305. He cites *Sanh.* 6.5–6.

[146] To say that 'the question, "What really happened?" is as misplaced as asking how creation occurred *ex nihilo* and as speculating on how the end will occur' (Keck, op. cit., p.239) is to forfeit the claim to say that the resurrection in any sense is an event within history.

I have the same difficulty with Fuller's statement, op. cit., p.23, that the resurrection was not a historical, but a 'meta-historical' event: 'By this we do not mean to suggest that nothing transpired between God and Jesus, but rather that what

cannot be ruled out as physically or psychologically improbable, especially in a political situation (not unfamiliar in the Middle East) of rival nationalist factions, with extremist groups only too ready to take justice into their own hands.

The point is often made[147] that the description of the grave-clothes in John 20.5–7 is deliberately intended by the evangelist to discount robbery and to convey the impression that the body had been spirited out of them, leaving them undisturbed. But his Greek is so ambiguous as almost to suggest the opposite.[148] It could perfectly naturally (if not most naturally) mean that the linen bands were 'lying about' and that the cloth that was 'over' (not round) the head[149] had been 'rolled up' (or bundled together) '*into* one place'. This certainly would not *rule out* human interference. Clearly John does not intend the evidence to point this way, and it is the more significant, therefore, that he does not say,

took place between God and Jesus took place at the boundary between history and meta-history, between this age and the age to come. As such the resurrection leaves only a negative mark within history: "He is not here" (Mark 16.6).' Yet the negative mark, by which he evidently means not simply that there was nothing to show for it but that there was *nothing* to show for it (i.e., an empty tomb) *is* 'within history' and must therefore be patient of historical enquiry. But I would of course fully agree that this is not to be *equated with* 'the resurrection'.

Equally, it is surely playing with words to say with Moltmann that the resurrection is 'a "historical phenomenon" only in relation to its future: it has its time still ahead of it' (*Theology of Hope*, p.191; cf. p.181).

Even Barth, who strongly criticizes Bultmann's position (CD III 2, pp.443–7), is extraordinarily equivocal when pressed on questions of historicity. He has no doubt that the resurrection was a historical event (as well, of course, as being much more). Yet the stories are describing 'an event beyond the reach of historical research or depiction. Hence we have no right to try to analyse or harmonise them' (p.452). What matters is that we accept the empty tomb – 'even as a legend' (p.453). He is equally evasive on the virgin birth, which, he says, belongs in 'indispensable connexion' with the empty tomb as 'a single sign' (CD I 2, pp.182f.). But if, as he grants, this is something 'undeniably taking place in the sphere of biological enquiry' (p.184), then it is impossible to silence the enquiry. It is not good enough to appeal to a seventeenth-century writer for the view that the mode of operation '*mirari deceat, non scrutari*'. He even holds that John of Damascus was 'essentially right' in describing 'Mary's ear as the bodily organ of the miraculous conception' (p.201)! But this is only a picturesque way of saying, with Paul, that 'faith is awakened by the message, and the message that awakens it comes through the word' (Rom. 10.17). It is to say nothing of what happened.

147 Classically by H. Latham, *The Risen Master*, Bell 1901, ch.3, and more recently by von Campenhausen, op. cit., pp.66–68; Benoit, op. cit., p.255; etc.

148 Even Latham confesses, 'I ought to tell the reader that the Greek words on which my notion rests are of uncertain interpretation' (op. cit., p.89).

149 Contrast the very precise description of Lazarus in John 11.44.

as Marxsen makes him say (!), that the clothes were 'neatly rolled together' and 'folded in an orderly fashion'.[150]

Yet the vagueness of the 'they have taken him away' and of the supposition 'if it is you, sir, who removed him'[151] is appropriate. What precisely happened to the old body will never be cleared up. The mystery, still unexplained, is subsequently interpreted (and this is the recognized function of angelic messengers),[152] not as the disaster it first appeared, but as a confirmatory sign of the action of God.[153] But unless there had been the new transforming reality of life in the Spirit, combined with the psychic phenomena, the physical evidence could not have been so construed (let alone constructed).

Every reconstruction of the history is a matter of weighing probabilities. Others will assess the credibility gap differently.[154] But I believe we must be *free* (as Ronald Gregor Smith insisted) to say that the bones of Jesus may still be lying around somewhere in Palestine.[155] Belief in the resurrection does not depend on –

---

[150] Marxsen, op. cit., pp.58, 60.   [151] John 20.15.

[152] Mark 16.5–7 par.; cf. Matt. 1.20–23; Acts 1.10f.

[153] So U. Wilckens, in C. F. D. Moule (ed.), *The Significance of the Message of the Resurrection* . . ., pp.73f.; and Fuller, op. cit., p.171.

[154] Despite many points on which I would differ, von Campenhausen perhaps comes nearest to my own conclusion, combining a high estimate of the empty tomb tradition ('If we test what is capable of being tested, we cannot, in my opinion, shake the story of the empty tomb and its early discovery. There is much that tells in its favour, and nothing definite or significant against it. It is, therefore, probably historical', op. cit., p.77), with a refusal to regard this bare fact, or that of the visions, as *requiring* supernatural explanation (pp.86–89). Cf. Hamilton, *The New Essence of Christianity*, p.112: 'I find myself in fairly strenuous opposition to that tradition in contemporary theology which denies the resurrection as an ordinary event on the one hand, while giving it a profound existential meaning on the other. . . . The empty tomb tradition at least, seems to me to contain historical material of a high degree of probability. The historical texture of this event is not equivalent to its meaning for faith, but there can be no meaning for faith, I am sure, without this historical texture.' I would agree. The word 'texture' allows for the kind of looseness which is appropriate.

[155] Ronald Gregor Smith, *Secular Christianity*, Collins 1966, pp.103–6. Clark, op. cit., pp.97f., who takes a more conservative position, says precisely the same thing: 'If a man would rest his belief upon the factuality of the Empty Tomb, then to such a man it must be answered that it is ultimately a matter of indifference as to whether or not the bones of Jesus lie somewhere in Palestine.' But he goes on: 'But if a man rests his faith where the New Testament rests it, to him there is given a signpost that points towards the Empty Tomb. What he will find there is neither a foundation for his faith nor a confirmation of it, but an irreplaceable indication of what it means' (p.98).

let alone consist of – the fact that they do not, for we cannot be sure. As Bonhoeffer said, 'Even here we cannot evade the realm of ambiguity.... Even as the Risen One, he does not break through his incognito.'[156] We can, and must, be able to make the affirmation of faith without being committed to a spill-over from the absoluteness of the interpretative language into statements about the history which would destroy the ambiguity and the greyness which properly pertain to it.

If in order to assert the absoluteness, the Christ, the Son of God, the seamless robe of the 'flesh' *has* to be torn, something has gone wrong. There has been a (not unnatural) tendency to believe that if Jesus had a human father, that if he was a fallible human being, that if his bones do lie around in Palestine, then he *could* not be the Son of God – *and vice versa*. But we must contend for the *possibility* of seeing the Logos in the flesh without the *necessity* of suspending its ordinariness and continuities. Yet it is equally important to insist that this does not involve the *necessity* of seeing (otherwise there would be no 'offence') or deny the *possibility* of suspension or interruption.

For nothing I have said should be taken to mean that I am therefore dogmatically excluding the possibility of virgin birth or physical resurrection or indeed of any radical discontinuity or novelty in the historical process. We cannot use the supposed requirements of theology or 'science' or 'the modern world-view' to dictate what is possible or impossible in the empirical series. I want rather to argue for retaining the possibility of ambiguity and openness, and therefore for agnosticism rather than dogmatism. I wish to rule out nothing – except what is excessively improbable on historical or psychological grounds. I certainly would not deny the possibility of total molecular transformation. But equally I do not think that the doctrine requires it – let alone substantiates it.

To indicate that what I have just said is not merely a theoretical concession, which if seriously admitted would undermine the entire thesis for which I have been arguing, I should perhaps try to show what openness to the possibility of total molecular trans-

---

[156] Bonhoeffer, *Christology*, p.117.

formation and of a tomb empty for non-external reasons might mean. I say 'might', because I have no personal experience on which to latch such an explanation and no way within my own competence of testing whether it is meaningful. But there is enough evidence to suggest that here, as in the whole area of paranormal phenomena, an open rather than a closed mind is appropriate – however critical and sceptical it should also properly be. For the power of spirit over matter is still so marginally understood that it would be dogmatic to discount the possibility that 'the next development in man' might be in the direction of the transformation of material energy, and therefore material substance, into spiritual. There are accounts, for instance, of rare but recently attested examples of Buddhist holy men who have achieved such control over the body that their physical energies and resources are so absorbed and transmuted that what is left behind after death is not the hulk of an old corpse but simply nails and hair.[157] An empty tomb would thus be the logical conclusion and symbol of the complete victory of spirit over matter.

Moule has suggested[158] that this is the kind of process Paul has

[157] Cf. Chögyam Trungpa, *Born in Tibet*, Allen and Unwin 1966, pp.95f.: 'We had been told the story of a very saintly man who had died there the previous year [1953]. . . . Just before his death the old man said, "When I die you must not move my body for a week; this is all that I desire". They wrapped his dead body in old clothes and called in lamas and monks to recite and chant. The body was carried into a small room, little bigger than a cupboard, and it was noted that though the old man had been tall the body appeared to have become smaller; at the same time a rainbow was seen over the house. On the sixth day on looking into the room the family saw that it had grown still smaller. A funeral service was arranged for the morning of the eighth day and men came to take the body to the cemetery; when they undid the coverings there was nothing inside except nails and hair. The villagers were astounded, for it would have been impossible for anyone to have come into the room, the door was always kept locked and the window of the little resting place was much too small. The family reported the event to the authorities and also went to ask Chentze Rinpoche about the meaning of it. He told them that such a happening had been reported several times in the past and that the body of the saintly man had been absorbed into the Light. They showed me the nails and the hair and the small room where they had kept the body. We had heard of such things happening, but never at first hand, so we went round the village to ask for further information. Everyone had seen the rainbow and knew that the body had disappeared.' I owe this reference to Sogyal Lakar Rinpoche, a student of mine and formerly pupil of Chentze Rinpoche mentioned above.

[158] C. F. D. Moule, 'St Paul and Dualism', *New Testament Studies* XII, 1966, pp.118–23.

in mind in II Cor. 4–5, as the perishable substance of the old order, the external or natural man, is exchanged and transformed by obedience to become the 'matter' of an invisible, spiritual humanity which death cannot touch: the new body is built up within *and out of* the old. In none of *us* is the material of the 'outer man' thus used up without remainder. The residue, as it were, returns to the pool to await the final resurrection and transformation of all matter. But Jesus was a forestalment of the end. His obedience was so complete that there was nothing left over that was not surrendered. Hence the empty tomb.

I personally am doubtful of this exegesis, attractive as it is, because the decay and dissolution to which Paul sees 'the flesh' as heir is not in itself, I think, viewed by him so positively. Above all, neither in this passage nor, where one might expect it, in I Cor. 15, does he draw the parallel with Jesus or even suggest it as an interpretation of the empty tomb or of the relation between the body of his humiliation and of his glory. But what he does do, as I said, is to insist on the principle that Christ is a genuine sample of the whole. If therefore such transformation without remainder *is* to be affirmed of him, it cannot be because he is an exceptional anomaly, but because he is a typical representative. In this respect, to be sure, he is typical not of the old level of humanity, which is to be comprehended within the categories of biology and psychology, but as the leading shoot of a coming, spiritual humanity, in which we shall all share as much as we have done in the order that links us with the evolutionary past.[159] If, then, one were to view the empty tomb as a sign and sacrament of this future, it would not be because uniquely and unrepeatably it severs the familiar continuities, but because as a further mutation within them it foreshadows a new breakthrough, of which one should *expect* to see signs elsewhere. But I should want to stress, once again, that the evidence does not demand such an interpretation. All that can – and I think must – be said is that this interpretation is perfectly compatible with such fragmentary hints as we have both from history and experience. In other words, we can be as

[159] I Cor. 15.45–48. On the interpretation of this passage, see below pp. 166–9.

free to say that the bones of Jesus do *not* lie around Palestine as we can be free to say that they do.

Conclusion

What I have been pleading for in this chapter, and shall go on to do in what follows, is the highest possible Christology in relation *both* to the humanity *and* to the divinity of Christ. But what does it mean to have the highest possible view of Christ's humanity? Let me focus the question by a simple illustration from two Christmas hymns:

> The little Lord Jesus no crying he makes.
> Tears and smiles like us he knew.

Which is the higher Christology? It is the latter, I suggest, that takes the humanity more seriously. Yet for most of its history the church would have opted for the former. And particularly throughout the patristic and medieval period, to honour Christ meant not to bring him 'deeper into the flesh', but to push things as far as possible in a monophysite direction.

As a final test of our own presuppositions, let me end with a rather remarkable passage from the book of Wisdom. The speaker is Solomon.

> I too am a mortal man like all the rest, descended from the first man, who was made of dust, and in my mother's womb I was wrought into flesh during a ten-months space, compacted in blood from the seed of her husband and the pleasure that is joined with sleep. When I was born, I breathed the common air and was laid on the earth that all men tread; and the first sound I uttered, as all do, was a cry; they wrapped me up and nursed me and cared for me. No king begins life in any other way; for all come into life by a single path, and by a single path go out again.[160]

The question I would ask is this: What do we need to affirm in order to say that 'a greater than Solomon is here'?[161] In the middle

---

[160] Wisd. 7.1–6. [161] Matt. 12.42 = Luke 11.31.

section there is clearly nothing that any Christian would wish to dispute of Jesus. 'When I was born, I breathed the common air and was laid on the earth that all men tread': the manger story[162] and Jesus' own words about the Son of Man having nowhere to lay his head[163] are fully in line with that. Clearly, too, as he himself understood it, to exceed 'Solomon in all his glory'[164] meant not having more splendid, supernatural robes but the unsurpassable beauty of nature. It is, however, at the beginning and end of the story that the pressures to modification have been felt. All Christians have wanted to say of Jesus with John that 'he came from God and went to God'.[165] In other words, his birth was due not simply to the forces of heredity and environment but to the purpose and initiative of God, and his life ran out not into nothingness and defeat but into God's resurrection order. That is not here at issue. All that is in question is whether in order to affirm these things we *have* to say that the *way* he came into this world and went out again was *not* the path of any other king. I am not persuaded that the earliest Christian witness commits us to saying that. It does not prevent us saying it. But we can have as high a Christology without it – and indeed, I believe, a higher.

[162] Luke 2.7.   [163] Matt. 8.20 = Luke 9.58.
[164] Matt. 6.28–29 = Luke 12.27.   [165] John 13.3.

FIVE

GOD'S MAN

Humanity and pre-existence

We have moved now in our argument from *a* man to *the* man, and from *the* man to Jesus as a man of whom 'God' language can also be predicated without his ceasing to be, in every sense, a human being like the rest of us. But there is a further step – corresponding to the first – from *a* man of God to *the* man of God. How, as Christian doctrine has wished to assert, can he be 'God's man', in the sense of a divinely commissioned 'man from heaven' 'sent' to earth 'for us men and our salvation'? Such language, of which the New Testament is full, would appear to carry the same threat to all we sought to establish in the last chapter as the need to see Jesus as *the* man has posed to his genuineness as *a* man.

For we have been insisting that, whatever *more* may need to be said of Jesus as the Christ, nothing must be said that in any way *detracts from* a humanity, as the Epistle to the Hebrews put it, '*at all points*' like our own. There could indeed be no more traditionally orthodox demand than that. Yet there is also an entire range of statements about Jesus as the Christ (and nowhere more than in the Epistle to the Hebrews) which appears to undermine this requirement *at source*. These cluster around the concept of pre-existence – of an eternal, heavenly being who enters the conditions of our history and humanity to dwell within it from the outside. This, too, is apparently so fundamental a statement of Christian doctrine as virtually to be a definition of what 'the Incarnation' means.

Yet Knox, writing both as a New Testament scholar and as a Christian, has recently made the outright judgment:

> We can have the humanity without the pre-existence and we can have the pre-existence without the humanity. There is absolutely no way of having both.[1]

If that is really true, it appears to pose an irreconcilable contradiction or an ultimate choice for a modern Christology.

It may be that we shall have to agree that pre-existence is a way of speaking that, like the language of virgin birth, can no longer be taken literally or descriptively and is so misleading as to be unusable today. But since it is so deeply embedded in the New Testament presentation of Christ – far more deeply than that of virgin birth – it is at least worth asking what the New Testament writers really had in mind when they used it and whether they saw it as the threat to humanity that we do – and if not, why not. This will involve spending virtually the whole of this chapter in a New Testament study – trying to see things through their eyes rather than ours. But it is basic, too, to the understanding of how they saw *God* in Christ, to which we must go on next. And it focusses inescapably what really is being asserted by incarnation.

Before going further, it may be useful, since we have made the comparison, to distinguish between the concepts of virgin birth and pre-existence. These have become combined and indeed fused in Christian teaching. But originally they were separate and *alternative* ways of giving expression, in terms of the 'second' story, to the divine significance of Jesus. The New Testament writers who speak most of pre-existence (Paul, John and the author to the Hebrews) say nothing of virgin birth, while the virgin birth story as such says nothing of pre-existence. On the contrary, it presupposes that Christ is brought into existence as son of Mary and Son of God simultaneously by the creative act of the Holy Spirit.[2] His link to God at the beginning is established not by pre-existence but by the line of human descent.[3] Pannen-

---

[1] Knox, *The Humanity and Divinity of Christ*, p.106.
[2] Luke 1.35: 'the holy child to be born will be called "Son of God".'
[3] Luke 3.38: '. . . son of Seth, son of Adam, son of God.'

berg goes so far as to say that the two concepts stand in 'irreconcilable contradiction'.[4] This is clearly an exaggeration. They have been harmonized so successfully (as the miraculous insertion into history of the pre-existent Son) that most people are unaware of any contradiction. Even Barth's profound and extended treatment of the virgin birth appears to show no consciousness of it.[5]

But the parallel between the two may serve as a starting-point. We have already seen that the New Testament writers combined, in a way that seems to us extraordinary, the story of the virgin birth (which presupposes no human father) and the genealogies (which presuppose Joseph as father), and held them together apparently without tension. And we find the same phenomenon with the pre-existence and humanity of Christ. The two are set side by side, seemingly without any sense of the antithesis which Knox articulates so acutely.

In the cases of Paul and John it is possible to reduce, if not to resolve, the dilemma. With Paul one *can* say that he had so little interest in the historical Jesus that he never really felt the problem. With John one *can* say – as Knox himself does[6] – that, whatever the evangelist's intentions, he does in fact present a quasi-docetic Christ whose humanity is little more than a veil. I personally do not accept either of these assessments. But what is quite clear is that there is no comparable escape route in the case of the author to the Hebrews. Everyone agrees that he stresses *both* the divinity *and* the humanity of Christ more unequivocally than any other New Testament writer. And his stress on the humanity is such that any hint that Jesus was not completely and utterly of our clay, 'a man of like passions with ourselves'[7] (sin only excepted), would be fatal to the theological interest which impels him to his insistence on it.

Yet neither Paul nor John nor the author to the Hebrews is a naïve writer. Indeed they are the three most sophisticated

[4] Pannenberg, op. cit., p.143.
[5] But the point is recognized by Brunner, *The Christian Doctrine of Creation and Redemption*, p.143.
[6] Knox, op. cit., p.62.
[7] This phrase is actually used in the New Testament only of Elijah (James 5.17), but is already being applied to Christ by the time of Justin (*Dial.* 48.3). Its suitability for Jesus was surely suggested by the Epistle to the Hebrews.

theologians in the New Testament. How, then, can they not have felt the dilemma we feel? The usual answer has been that they are content simply to hold both affirmations together, as equally vital to the faith, but to produce no theory to co-ordinate them. They laid the foundations of New Testament Christology (to use the title of R. H. Fuller's book[8]): it was left to others to build the superstructure.

Yet I have long felt this position (it would be wrong to call it a solution) unsatisfying. In the Epistle to the Hebrews, in particular, there is such a stark combination of opposites, of divinity and humanity, of pre-existence and adoptionism, of being and becoming, that it has seemed to me very hard to credit that a writer of such subtlety and sensitivity should not apparently have shown any sign of appreciating the tension, let alone the contradiction, between the diverse statements he makes – especially as I would agree with Knox in sensing that he *is* aware of the tension, if not the contradiction, between genuine temptation and complete sinlessness.[9] I have felt that there must be some other explanation, and that our dilemma did not exist for the New Testament writers because, in some way, we are attributing to them presuppositions which they did not share. But in what way?

Light came from an unexpected, and perhaps ultimately irrelevant source. But it was for me the by-product of one of those new encounters in dialogue which have the great asset of making us look at familiar problems in fresh matrices. I was talking with a Buddhist monk on the difference between Hindu and Buddhist understandings of reincarnation. If I have understood the difference aright, the Hindu concept (which is basically the same as the Pythagorean, which has entered Western thinking through Platonism) is that of a continuity of individual substance, or soul, which re-enters the world in a new body (whether of an animal or a man), retaining its identity and theoretically its memory of its previous state. The Buddhist concept of incarnation (rather than reincarnation) is different. Buddhism sees the individual as

---

[8] R. H. Fuller, *The Foundations of New Testament Christology*, Lutterworth Press 1965.
[9] Knox, op. cit., pp.44–9.

negated and dispersed by death – there is no continuity of that individual soul any more than there is of that individual body. Yet the spirit is no more destroyed than the matter: it is reunited with its source, and emanations of it are released into all the world to reappear in new configurations or individuals, with such additions or changes as have been wrought upon it by the holiness or otherwise of the particular bearer of it. Thus, the Buddha can be incarnate in, and the source of enlightenment to, countless other individuals, and a lama can become incarnate in a particular successor, not in the sense that his soul-substance is exclusively reborn in that one individual, but in the sense that a special portion of his spirit, as it were, finds embodiment in the one designated, and discerned by revelation, to be the inheritor of it.

This concept, as the phrase 'a portion of his spirit' indicates, is not alien from the biblical notion of the spirit of Elijah resting upon Elisha[10] or of John the Baptist being Elijah *redivivus* – not in the sense that he was literally his reincarnation but in the sense that 'in the spirit and power of Elijah'[11] he embodied his role. One could even say that this is how Paul and John see the spirit of Christ released by the death of the individual Jesus to become incorporate, as his *alter ego*, in the body of his followers. Of course, there are very real differences too. The Hebraic tradition, and particularly the Christian, has seen eternal life not in the negation of the individual in an impersonal *nirvana* but in the transcendence of the individual in the supra-personal network of the communion of saints. No doubt this distinction, as traditionally formulated by Christians, does not do justice to the difference between Christianity and Buddhism. But that is not the difference with which we are here concerned. Rather, it is the difference between a way of thinking about incarnation which finds expression in Hinduism (and through Pythagoreanism in Platonism) and a way of thinking about incarnation which finds expression in Buddhism. Is what is pre-existent and takes flesh 'an individual substance of a rational nature' (to use the later definition of a person)? Or is it that a life, power or activity (whether divine or spiritual) which is not as such a person comes to embodiment and expression

---

[10] II Kings 2.9–15.   [11] Luke 1.17.

(whether partial or total) in an individual human being? My contention is that the understanding of pre-existence in late Judaism and early Christianity has more in common with the latter way of thinking than with the former.

Clearly it would be false to place in any single, water-tight compartment such a thoroughly complex phenomenon as Hellenistic Judaism, to which in some form or other the Jewish wisdom literature, Philo, Paul, John and the Epistle to the Hebrews must all be assigned. It spans two world-views and has affinities both backwards and forwards. I am merely asking whether, if we look at what the writers of the first century have to say about pre-existence and incarnation with the latter set of presuppositions mentioned above, they may not make better sense. In particular, I would ask whether the kind of tension which we find it so difficult to think that the apostolic writers could not sense may not be the product of reading what they wrote with assumptions which they did not share. This is an issue that cannot be settled *a priori*. We do not know precisely how they thought. But if by trying another key we find that the difficulties from which we started begin to disappear, we are justified in supposing that partly at least these may be of our making, and that, though we can never prove it, the men of the first century were not thinking as we do and as the church was to do very soon afterwards.

According to the presuppositions that were to determine the theology of the patristic period, and which became explicit in the doctrine of *anhypostasia*, pre-existence meant the prior existence in heaven of an individual *hypostasis* or *persona* who was in the fullness of time to become the subject of the human nature taken from the virgin Mary. The Logos was already in the fullest sense a person (of the Trinity). At the Incarnation, he did not become an individual; he became human – without, of course, ceasing to be divine. He was *a* being, who did not start like us but was *made like* us by sharing our life. And it is this concept which it is so difficult (if not impossible) to combine with Jesus being, with the rest of us, a genuine product of the evolutionary process.

In late Judaism

Now it is generally agreed that this hypostatization of the Logos in ontological terms stemmed directly, if only in part, from the personification in late Judaism of the Word of God in mythological terms – along with similar personifications of the Wisdom of God and the Spirit of God. It would be tempting to jump to the conclusion that the shift in presuppositions I have spoken of is to be located at the point of transition from the mythological categories of Jewish thought to the ontological categories of Greek thought. But this transposition, however important, I believe merely consolidated a change that had already occurred *within* late Judaism, from the more functional and historical way of thinking characteristic of the prophets and early apocalyptic to the more mythological and speculative thought-forms of later apocalyptic, mysticism and philosophy. It is no part of our purpose here to go into the historical question of just when and how this change occurred (even if that could be answered with precision). It will be sufficient to set down examples of the sort of literature which belongs, in my judgment, on each side of the divide and to note the characteristic differences. Let us call them 'before' and 'after', though the chronological sequence is neither clear-cut nor decisive:

Before	After
Daniel	I Enoch, 37–71 (The Similitudes)
Wisdom of Solomon	II Baruch
Psalms of Solomon	IV Ezra
Dead Sea Scrolls[12]	III Enoch.

An illustration of the difference is to be seen in the treatment of the figure of the Son of Man in Daniel 7 and in the Similitudes of Enoch. In the former we are dealing with a representation

---

[12] With greater diffidence I should be prepared to add the Odes of Solomon. See especially Odes 12 and 16; and cf. J. H. Bernard, *The Odes of Solomon*, Texts and Studies VIII, Cambridge University Press 1912, pp.28–31; and J. H. Charlesworth, 'Qumran, John and the Odes of Solomon', in id. *John and Qumran*, Geoffrey Chapman 1972, pp.106–36, who has a new edition in preparation.

('one like a son of man', i.e., a human as opposed to an animal figure) standing for 'the saints of the most high'. There is no suggestion that he is an individual heavenly person with a proper name or an independent existence. But it is precisely this that we find in I Enoch and later apocalyptic. And the same is true of the Elect One, the Messiah, the Son of God. Originally these titles were applied to Israel, or to historical representatives of Israel, who embodied or would embody certain callings or functions of God. Some individual (or group) might *be* the Messiah or the Servant or even the Son of Yahweh in so far as he (or it) embodied the function or fulfilled the calling in question. But these figures were not thought of as existent or pre-existent beings with a life of their own. And we find the same kind of change that here meets us in apocalyptic in the transition, in the more philosophical field, from the Book of Wisdom to Philo, or, in the mystical, from parts of the Qumran literature to III Enoch. The end-term of all these trends – visionary, speculative and religious – is what we call Gnosticism, whose roots and origins in Judaism are, as we said earlier, increasingly being recognized. But it is, I think, better to keep that term for the full-blown phenomenon of the second and third centuries AD: anything we encounter in the first century is best labelled 'pre-Gnostic'.[13] But for our purposes the important question is on which side of the divide the main New Testament writers are to be placed, and in particular Paul, John and the author to the Hebrews.

Purely chronologically, the transition is probably to be dated towards the end of the first century AD–the Similitudes of I Enoch, with the continued absence of that section of the book from the Qumran fragments, looking less and less likely to have been current at the time of Jesus or to have exercised an influence.[14] I personally would put not only Paul but Hebrews and John early; but in any case the chronological argument cannot be decisive. It is a matter of testing their presuppositions *a posteriori*,

[13] Cf. Bo Reicke, 'Traces of Gnosticism in the Dead Sea Scrolls?', *New Testament Studies* I, 1955, pp.137–41.

[14] For a recent assessment in relation to the vexed question of 'the Son of Man', cf. R. N. Longenecker, *The Christology of Early Jewish Christianity*, SCM Press 1970, pp.82–93.

by judging which hypothesis yields the best interpretation of what they have written.

I shall argue that the clue to understanding what they say about pre-existence and incarnation, and in particular to their unaware-ness of the contradiction we feel, is to be found by regarding them as sharing the earlier rather than the later set of presuppositions. In other words, I think the New Testament evidence can best be read if we do not bring to it the assumption that in the Judaism in which these writers were nurtured the notion of pre-existence already involved the hypostatization of an individual heavenly person. It may be perfectly true, as Knox says, that what has usually been meant by 'pre-existence' is (when applied to Christ) that 'Jesus as the particular individual he was had existed before all worlds'[15] or that his 'existence as a man was in some self-conscious way continuous with his earlier existence as a heavenly being';[16] and I would fully agree with him that this – let alone the consciousness of it[17] – is incompatible with genuine humanity. I would question merely whether this was the assumption behind the New Testament writers. I suggest, rather, that it was in essence something much nearer to what Knox says must be our under-standing of pre-existence if we use it today; namely, that:

> God, the Father Almighty, Maker of the heavens and the earth, was back of, present in, and acting through the whole event of which the human life of Jesus was the centre. . . . But just because a human career, any human career, is an integral part of an entire cosmic process, we cannot say this about the career of Jesus without implying that God was creating him, *and creating him for his supreme redemptive purpose*, from the beginning of that process – that Jesus was 'appointed' to his high office 'before the foundation of the world'.[18]

---

[15] Knox, op. cit., p.61.   [16] Ibid., p.106.

[17] *If* the claim to be the Son of Man or the Messiah means to be conscious of oneself as a divine being at the right hand of God, then I agree with Knox that this is not compatible with normal human sanity (*The Death of Christ*, pp.68–72). But I would dispute the protasis and remain open to the considerable evidence that Jesus did identify himself with the Son of Man.

[18] Knox, op. cit., pp.107f. Cf. Kaufman, op. cit., p.205, who says that the myth of pre-existence expresses the conviction that 'it is *God* with whom we have

But this is to anticipate. To ground this conclusion in the evidence, it is necessary to start further back. We may begin with the wisdom literature, from which there can be no doubt that so much of the New Testament language in this area is derived. In the classic presentations of Prov. 8.22-31; Wisd. 7.22—8.1 or Ecclus. 24.1-22, we find *Wisdom* personified as God's constant companion and agent in creation, a pure reflection of the glory of the Almighty, who 'tabernacles'[19] among God's people and in age after age enters into holy souls, making them prophets and friends of God. There is no suggestion that this indwelling in any sense threatens their common humanity or connections with the human race. Indeed, Solomon begins his meditation on his gift of the 'spirit of wisdom' by saying of himself in the passage we have already quoted, 'I too am a mortal man like all the rest'.[20] Nor, of course, is it ever implied that those – prophets and priests, kings and craftsmen – to whom the *Word* of the Lord came or upon whom his *Spirit* descended were not completely normal human beings. The personification of all these functions, attributes or activities of God, which, of course, were eternal like himself, constituted no problem. And when John says in his prologue that the Logos gradually found expression first in nature, then in a people and then in a person, we are still in the same world of discourse.[21] In Jesus the pre-existent Word became embodied in a

to do in Jesus' and not that, in Barth's words, 'the man Jesus already was even before he was' (CD III 2, p.464), whom he accuses here of 'logical nonsense' and 'the theological error of docetism'. I am very conscious at this point of 'the peril of modernizing Jesus' and adapting the biblical writers' view of pre-existence to one that we can find acceptable. This does come through, for instance, in the otherwise very similar expression of its significance by Bethune-Baker, back in 1921 ('Jesus as Both Human and Divine', p.299), who introduces evolutionary concepts. But I do not think that this is true of Knox's statement, which indeed reinterprets pre-existence in terms of the earlier 'fore-ordination' language out of which I believe it grew. In any case the test lies in the detailed exegesis.

[19] Cf. Ecclus. 24.8 LXX with John 1.14.

[20] Wisd. 7.1; cf. p. 141 above.

[21] John 1.1-14. Still in the second century Justin presupposes this way of thinking in discussion with the Jew Trypho: 'I shall give you another testimony . . . from the Scriptures, that God begat before all creatures a Beginning (or, in the beginning, before all creatures], a certain rational power [or spiritual force, *logikē dynamis*] from himself, who is called by the Holy Spirit, now the Glory of the Lord, now the Son, again Wisdom, again an Angel, then God, and then Lord and Logos' (*Dial.* 61; Ante-Nicene Christian Library II, T. and T. Clark 1867;

single human individual who was so faithful a reproduction of it as to be its complete reflection and incarnation. But there is no suggestion that this individual was not a man in every sense of the word.

This man is also described as the *Son* of God, and as such is seen as filling a role which, like those of the Word and Wisdom of God, goes right back to the beginning. Again, however, it is important that we should not read back Nicene categories into first-century Hellenistic Judaism. Just as the Word and Wisdom, like the Spirit of God, were personified as agents of his relationship to the world, so the Son of God stands in Jewish thinking for the representative of his will and character, the one who truly embodies what he is and does, and in whom his authority is vested. God's 'son' is not an individual superhuman being of pre-existent substance but whoever stands, or rather is called to stand, in that relationship. For the embodiment, whether it be in his people[22] or its monarch[23] or the faithful Israelite,[24] God's true man,[25] is always less than complete or faithful.[26] God's son, like his *shekinah* or presence, waits to be fully incarnate among men; the role waits to be filled by a true representative. It is this function, this prepared position, that the gospels present Jesus as occupying. He is marked out at his baptism[27] and tested in the wilderness[28] as the true son that the old Israel was called – and failed – to be. In contrast with the prophets, who were sent as God's servants,[29] he is the son in whom all is

cf. *Apol.* II.10). It is noteworthy that 'the Son' is still included as a variant name of this 'power of God'. In *The Shepherd of Hermas*, Sim. 5.5f., we have a survival of the same presuppositions. On this passage Grillmeier, op. cit., pp.92f., comments: 'The *pneuma* [spirit] which God makes to dwell in the flesh of Jesus is regarded not as a divine person, but as a divine power, in some way analogous to the biblical *Sophia* [Wisdom], with the result that a similarity has also been concluded between it and the [Qumran] *Manual of Discipline* (J. P. Audet).' For a suggestive attempt to rehabilitate a 'Spirit-Christology' today, cf. G. W. H. Lampe, 'The Holy Spirit and the Person of Christ', in *Christ, Faith and History*, pp.111–30.

[22] Exod. 4.22f.; Jer. 3.19; 31.9,20; Hos. 11.1; Wisd. 18.13.
[23] II Sam. 7.14; I Chron. 17.13; 22.10; 28.6.
[24] Deut. 14.1; Isa. 43.6; Hos. 1.10; Ecclus. 4.10.
[25] So that 'son of God' and 'son of man' are virtually interchangeable; cf. Ps. 80.15 (Heb.) and 17.
[26] Isa. 1.2; 30.1; Jer. 3.22; Mal. 1.6.   [27] Mark 1.11 par.; cf. John 1.34.
[28] Matt. 4.1–11 = Luke 4.1–13.
[29] II Kings 17.13,23; Jer. 7.25; 25.4; 29.19; 35.15; etc.

vested,[30] the representative who stands in and acts for God himself.

In this capacity Christ is seen throughout the New Testament as the expression and agent of God's purpose from the start. He fills a role prepared for him from the foundation of the world[31] – though in this respect he is no different from the elect in general.[32] But as Son he is uniquely the reflection of God's person and character.[33] As such he occupies the place of the Wisdom of God.[34] Consequently it is a matter of indifference whether he is represented as saying, with Luke,[35] 'The Wisdom of God said, "I will send them prophets and messengers",' or, with Matthew,[36] 'I send you . . . prophets, sages, and teachers'. For in issuing the invitation, 'Come to me . . . and I will give you rest',[37] he is echoing the call of God[38] and his Wisdom[39]. It is thus entirely natural that Paul should see in Christ the pre-existent wisdom and image of God, with primacy over all created things, and the power of nature and history.[40] Natural, too, that John should view him as the creative Logos who was from the beginning with God and was God,[41] and portray him as speaking as one who was before Abraham,[42] and indeed shared the Father's glory before the foundation of the world.[43]

But none of these affirmations, however exalted, is intended to suggest that Jesus was not fundamentally *a man*, with all the antecedents of every other man, who was yet called from the womb to embody this unique role. *Qua* Son, indeed, he is not *of* this world and does not have his origin in space or time, where anyone can know or locate it.[44] And yet, as we have seen, as the man from Nazareth he is born and bred completely within the local human situation, with a parentage that is open to anyone's inspection – and insinuation.[45]

[30] Mark 12.1–12 par.; Matt. 11.27 = Luke 10.22; John 3.35; 8.35f.; 13.3; 15.15; Heb. 1.1f.
[31] John 17.24; I Peter 1.20.   [32] Matt. 25.34; Eph. 1.4; Rev. 13.8; 17.8.
[33] Heb. 1.3.   [34] Wisd. 7.25f.   [35] Luke 11.49.   [36] Matt. 23.34.
[37] Matt. 11.28–30. In the previous verse he speaks as 'the Son'.
[38] Exod. 33.14, 'My presence will go with you, and I will give you rest'.
[39] Ecclus. 24.19; 51.23–27.   [40] I Cor. 1.24; 10.4; II Cor. 4.4; Col. 1.15–20.
[41] John 1.1–3.   [42] John 8.58.   [43] John 17.5.   [44] John 8.14,23.
[45] John 1.45f.; 6.42; 7.27,40–42; 8.41.

That is the paradox as expressed in Johannine terms, and to these expressions I shall come back. But as a test of the pre-suppositions with which the New Testament writers were working, let us turn first to the Epistle to the Hebrews, where the contrasts are starkest and the language least ambiguous. The Fourth Gospel is so full of irony and double meanings that it is difficult to know always at what level or levels the author means his statements to be taken. But the author to the Hebrews is much more severely, almost humourlessly, determined that there shall be no misunderstanding. Whereas the Fourth Gospel lays itself wide open to being taken up – as indeed it was – as a Gnostic, docetic document (however much, to judge from the evidence of the Johannine Epistles, the writer retorts that to take it so is very anti-Christ),[46] it is impossible so to misconstrue the Epistle to the Hebrews. His Jesus – and no one uses the simple, human name so baldly[47] – is unequivocally flesh of our flesh and bone of our bone. Or is he?

In the Epistle to the Hebrews

The Epistle begins with the most stupendous affirmation of Christ, in contrast with all previous and partial revelations of God, as Son,

> who is the effulgence of God's splendour and the stamp of God's very being and sustains the universe by his word of power (1.3).

He is the complete representative and plenipotentiary of God, the agent of his purpose alike in creation and redemption. Yet if we ask who it is that fills this role, the whole point of the argument of the first chapter is that it is no angelic being but a *man*. Indeed, as I shall be arguing later of the 'form' (*morphē*) of God in Phil. 2.6, the language here is almost certainly intended to have reference not to a divine or semi-divine being but to the biblical account of the nature and glory of man. For to be the stamp (*charactēr*) of God's very being is truly to be in his image. Thus Philo says of the

46 I John 4.2f.   47 Heb. 2.9; 3.1; 4.14; 6.20; 7.22; 10.19; 12.2, 24; 13.12.

heavenly man that he was 'stamped with the image of God'.[48] Again, the word *apaugasma* should probably be translated the 'reflection' (rather than 'radiance') of his glory,[49] as the other metaphors of Wisd. 7.26 (from which it evidently derives) would suggest: 'the *apaugasma* of everlasting light, the flawless mirror of the active power of God and the image of his goodness'.[50] As we shall see subsequently in connection with John 1.14, the ideas of reflection, glory and image are fused in late Judaism and the New Testament to describe the mirror relationship in which a true son should stand to his father. Moreover, the language of Heb. 1.1–3 is also remarkably reminiscent of the parable of the Wicked Husbandmen in Mark.[51] Whereas the previous messengers, the prophets, were servitors, like Moses,[52] God has now finally spoken through a son,[53] who is heir of everything and set over his household.[54] There is no more suggestion in Hebrews than in Mark that the servants and the son are not equally human: it is the relationship, the function, that is decisively different.

Furthermore, in the midst of all this pre-existence language we get the apparently 'adoptionist' term 'made heir'.[55] And this is characteristic of the whole Epistle. Nowhere, in fact, in the New Testament more than in Hebrews do we find such a wealth of expressions that would support what looks like an adoptionist Christology – of a Jesus who becomes the Christ. Apart from that which we have just quoted, we have:

> Jesus has *become* superior to the angels, as the title he has *inherited* is superior to theirs (1.4).

---

[48] *De opif.* 69.

[49] It can have an active or a passive sense according to context (cf. W. F. Arndt and F. W. Gingrich, *A Greek-English Lexicon of the New Testament*, Cambridge University Press 1957, p.81). The majority of the Greek Fathers (for obvious theological reasons) took it here as active, but no doubt missed the overtones of its Jewish background.

[50] Cf. II Cor. 3.18: 'We all reflect as in a mirror the splendour of the Lord; thus we are transfigured into his likeness, from splendour to splendour.'

[51] Mark 12.1–12.   [52] Heb. 3.5.

[53] I would judge that this author's distinctive use of *huios* without the article never quite loses touch with the fact that it is first introduced as a metaphor from human relationships (cf. also the simile in 3.6). We shall notice the same phenomenon in John.

[54] Heb. 3.6.   [55] Heb. 1.2.

Because he has loved right and hated wrong, *therefore* God, his God, has *anointed* him (*echrisen*, 'made him Christ'?) above his fellows (1.9).

He has been *made to sit* at God's right hand (1.13). He has been *crowned* with glory and honour *because* he suffered death (2.9).

In Christ God *takes to himself* the sons of Abraham (2.16).

Out of the midst of the congregation Jesus *keeps his trust* fixed on God (2.12f.).

Like Moses, he is faithful to him who *appointed* him, but has been *deemed worthy* of greater honour than Moses (3.2f.).

As every high priest is *taken* from among men and *appointed* their representative before God, so Christ did not confer upon himself the glory of *becoming* high priest; it was *granted* by God, who said to him, 'Thou art my son; *today* have I *begotten* thee' (5.1–6).

He is *named* by God high priest in the succession of Melchizedek (5.10), and *becomes* this at his entry beyond the veil (6.20).

For he has first to be *made perfect* through suffering (2.10), and by *learning* obedience from it (5.8).

It is the Son thus made perfect whom the word of God's oath *appoints* priest for ever (7.28).

All this is astonishing language[56] for one who stresses the eternal pre-existence (and of course post-existence[57]) of Christ more than any other New Testament writer. Adoptionism and incarnationism are usually held to be opposite extremes in Christology. How is it, then, that our author holds them so constantly together without apparently any sense of discomfort or discrepancy? Only, I think, because he is starting from a different set of presuppositions from those which prevailed later.

[56] It is no less astonishing how it is overlooked. Cullmann, for instance, never alludes to it in his *Christology of the New Testament*, nor F. Hahn in *The Titles of Jesus in Christology*, Lutterworth Press 1969.
[57] Heb. 5.6; 6.20; 7.3,16f.,21,24,28; 9.24,28; 10.12–14.

A good test of this is the interpretation placed upon 2.17: 'Therefore he had to be made like (*homoiothēnai*) these brothers of his in every way.' Later doctrine took this to mean that the Logos had to be made like men from having been something very different (a heavenly, divine being). I believe that the whole context of his argument shows that our writer intended no such thing. Jesus was never anything but like his brothers. For it is essential that a consecrating priest and those whom he consecrates should be all 'of one stock' (2.11). 'The children of a family share the same flesh and blood; and so he too shared ours' (2.14). What was necessary was that the likeness (which was not in doubt) should be seen through to the end *in every respect*, 'so that he might *become* merciful and faithful as their high priest before God' (2.17). 'For since he himself has passed through the test of suffering, he is able to help those who are meeting their test now' (2.18). 'For ours is not a high priest unable to sympathize with our weaknesses, but one who, *because* of his likeness to us, has been tested *every* way' (4.15).

This is crucial also to the interpretation of the key passage in 5.7–9:

> In the days of his earthly life [that is when he was not yet a priest,[58] but was, as it were, preparing for the priesthood to be bestowed on him the other side of death][59] he offered up prayers and petitions, with loud cries and tears, to God who was able to deliver him from the grave. Because of his humble submission [or, more probably, out of his fear][60] his prayer was heard: son though he was, he learned obedience in the school of suffering, and, once perfected, became the source of eternal salvation for all who obey him.

On the presupposition of a heavenly figure coming in from the outside, this is interpreted to mean that, despite the fact that Christ was the Son of God, he condescended to be put through it like every other human being. On the presupposition with which I

---

[58] Heb. 7.13f.; 8.4.   [59] Heb. 5.10; 6.20; 7.27f.
[60] Cf. Montefiore, op. cit., p.98, who takes this to mean: 'being heard he was set free from fear'.

believe our author is working, it means that Jesus' call to the unique role of living as God's son or personal representative did not exempt him from having to go through it to the end: precisely the contrary, it required this of him without remission.

The difference might be stated in terms of the analogy which has often been used of the Incarnation (for instance, by Weston)[61] of the king's son becoming one of his father's workers. He chooses to live completely like them, sharing their lot in every respect – yet ultimately he is not (and cannot be) of the same blood. Our author seems to be working with exactly the opposite analogy, of the worker who is raised above his comrades (1.9) and is summoned to live as the king's son. But this does not allow him relief (as, humanly speaking, one might expect) from any of the solidarity he shares with them. Precisely the opposite: it is only by maintaining his identification with them to the limit that, as their leader or foreman (2.10), he can be made perfect and thus enable them, in all their numbers, to become partners (3.14) in his relation of sonship.

The notion that Jesus started from a superior position, came down for a time to men's level and was once more exalted above them, is commonly assumed to be asserted in 2.9, where we read: 'In Jesus . . . we . . . see one who *for a short while* was made lower than the angels, crowned *now* with glory and honour.' But the temporal contrast is not in the Greek (*ton de brachy ti par' angelous ēllattōmenon blepomen Iēsoun . . . estephanōmenon*), and the interpretation of *brachy ti* to mean 'for a short while' (which is a predominantly modern one)[62] comes not from the context but from reading in our presuppositions. In Ps. 8.6, from which it is quoted, it must mean that man's status is so exalted as to be 'little lower than the angels', and when our author first uses it in 2.7 of man in general it is difficult to see how he can mean anything else.[63] For mankind has not been lower than the angels for a short

[61] Weston, op. cit., pp.182f.

[62] RV marg., RSV, NEB, Weymouth marg., Moffatt, Smith and Goodspeed, the Jerusalem Bible, *Good News for Modern Man* and, among the commentators, M. Dods (Expositor's Greek Testament), J. Moffatt (ICC), O. Michel (Meyer Kommentar), C. Spicq, W. Manson, J. Héring and H. Montefiore.

[63] Cf. B. F. Westcott, *The Epistle to the Hebrews*, Macmillan 1889, p.44:

time: this has always been so. And when he comes to speak of
Jesus, his point of contrast is not that he (unlike other men)
started higher than the angels but that in him (and as yet in no
other man) we see fulfilled the ultimate *destiny* of man. Indeed he
has already said that Christ *became* superior to the angels 'when
he . . . took his seat at the right hand of Majesty on high' (1.3f.).

As a final test of our author's presuppositions it is instructive to
look at the combination of apparent opposites in ch. 7. He begins
by observing of Melchizedek that 'he has no father, no mother,
no lineage; his years have no beginning, his life no end. He is like
the Son of God' (7.3). This could suggest that he envisaged Christ
as an eternal divine being inserted disconnectedly into the human
scene, not only without father but even without mother. This
would indeed be an eccentric Christology by any New Testament
standard. But it is clear from what he goes on to say that he
envisages no such thing. He speaks of the levitical priests as being
descendants of Abraham (7.5); indeed, they could even be said
to exist in his loins when Melchizedek met him and received tithe
of him (7.10). Now Jesus was not of that stock. But this does not
mean that he was of no stock. On the contrary, our author
accepts as incontestable the fact that Jesus stemmed from Judah
(7.14) and belonged to his tribe (7.13).[64] That this, as we remarked
earlier, is a theological liability for him rather than an asset (as it is
for the other New Testament writers, who wish to present Christ
as a royal rather than a priestly Messiah) makes it the more impressive. He could have passed it over in silence. But it was a given
and vital part of Jesus' continuity with the stream of human
heredity and environment. And this was in no way threatened or
complicated by the fact that, like Israel whose vocation he embodied, he was also 'brought into the world' as God's 'first-

---

'*brachy ti* is used here of degree and not of time. The Hebrew is unambiguous;
and there is no reason to depart from the meaning of the original either in this
place or in v. 7. So the Vulgate, AV, RV and Weymouth. J. B. Phillips recognizes
the difficulty by translating 'a little' in v.7 and 'temporarily' in v.9; but this is
quite arbitrary.

[64] He uses the same word (*meteschēken*) as he uses in 2.14 of Jesus belonging to
our flesh and blood, which reinforces the view that it cannot there be interpreted
as coming to share in something that he previously did not have.

born'[65] His 'begetting' as son does not cut across or contradict his being 'taken' from among men.[66]

I have analysed the Epistle to the Hebrews in some detail because its writer is so admirably explicit. But if I am right about his presuppositions, it may shed light also on the thinking of Paul and John.

In Paul

It is noticeable that in Paul, too, we find the conjunction that theoretically should not be, of high pre-existence language and apparent adoptionism. Thus, in Rom. 1.3f. he speaks of the gospel of God,

> announced beforehand in sacred scriptures through his prophets. It is about his Son: on the human level he was born of David's stock, but on the level of the spirit – the Holy Spirit – he was declared [or designated, *horisthentos*] Son of God by a mighty act in that he rose from the dead.

Here we have the same paradox of the predestined Son, in succession to the prophets, who is yet a man, with all his human background, installed in power by virtue of the resurrection. It is not a heavenly being who becomes human, so much as a man who enters into the office of Son of God marked out for him from all eternity. From the point of view of God, the Son, God's 'own' or only one, waits to be sent to his people: that role of perfect obedience and representation stands ready to be revealed until he for whom it is prepared is due to be born. From the point of view of man, the faithful one waits to be brought forth, by human seed, from within the womb of Israel. It is with these presuppositions, I believe, that we should read such typical Pauline statements as Gal. 4.4, 'God sent his own Son, born of a woman, born under the law'; and Rom. 8.3, 'What the law could never do . . . God has done: by sending his own Son in a form like that of our own sinful nature.' The picture is not of a divine being arriving to look like a

[65] Heb. 1.6; cf. Exod. 4.22; Jer. 31.9; IV Ezra 6.58; Ps. Sol.13.8; 18.4.
[66] Heb. 5.1–5.

man, but of a man born like the rest of us, from within the nexus of the flesh, law and sin, who nevertheless embodied the divine initiative and saving presence so completely that he was declared at his baptism and confirmed at his resurrection to be everything God himself was – his Son,[67] his power and his wisdom,[68] his image,[69] his fullness.[70]

The same can, I think, be shown to be true of the crucial passage in Phil. 2.5–11 which I quote, first, in the NEB version:

> Let your bearing towards one another arise out of your life in Christ Jesus. For the divine nature was his from the first; yet he did not think to snatch at equality with God, but made himself nothing, assuming the nature of a slave. Bearing the human likeness, revealed in human shape, he humbled himself, and in obedience accepted even death – death on a cross. Therefore God raised him to the heights and bestowed on him the name above all names, that at the name of Jesus every knee should bow – in heaven, on earth, and in the depths – and every tongue confess, 'Jesus Christ is Lord', to the glory of God the Father.

This has usually been seen as the *locus classicus* in the New Testament for the myth of a supernatural, heavenly Redeemer visiting this earth in the form of a human being. Such an interpretation certainly cannot be ruled out. For this myth entered the stock of Christian thinking somewhere, and this could be its point of entry. The one statement that can, I believe, be made with growing confidence is that this is not, as Bultmann[71] and others have asserted, a pagan myth which Paul (and John) Christianized,

---

[67] Behind Gal. 4.6, 'to prove that [*hoti: not* 'because', as in the AV, RV, RSV] you are sons, God has sent into our hearts the Spirit of his Son, crying "Abba! Father!" ' (cf. Rom. 8.15, 'a Spirit that makes us sons, enabling us to cry "Abba! Father!" ') may lie the tradition that Jesus, too, was declared Son of God at his baptism. Cf., just beforehand, Gal. 3.26f.: 'Through faith you are all sons of God in union with Christ Jesus. Baptized into union with him, you have all put on Christ.'

[68] I Cor. 1.24.

[69] II Cor. 4.4; Col. 1.15. I have not here gone into the exposition of Col. 1.15–20. I would interpret it along the same lines as Heb. 1.1–4 and as Phil. 2.5–11 discussed next.

[70] Col. 1.19; 2.9.

[71] E.g. in his *Theology of the New Testament* I, SCM Press 1952, p.175.

but a Gnosticizing version of the distinctively Christian message.[72] Indeed, in its developed form it is not present even in the newly discovered Gnostic texts of the second century.[73] If any pre-Christian myth lies behind Phil. 2 it is much more likely that of Adam, with whom Christ is fairly clearly being compared and contrasted.[74] In Jewish circles under the influence of Platonism, as we know from Philo,[75] the ideal Adam (or 'idea' of Man) was seen as a primal, uncreated, heavenly figure. Christ could be being identified with this celestial figure, but, as I shall argue later, I think it is more likely that Paul's conception of the spiritual or heavenly man is deliberately different: 'the spiritual does not come first'.[76] Rabbinic Judaism, which idealized Adam in a more earthy way (as indeed did Philo also), is the more plausible background for Phil. 2.5-11.[77]

It is presumptuous to attempt an exegesis of this pregnant passage in a few sentences, when whole books have been written on it.[78] Everything turns on what Paul means by his opening statement that Jesus was 'in the form of God'. I believe that Cullmann is essentially right in saying that this 'does not refer to Jesus' divine "nature", but rather to the image of God which he possessed from the beginning'.[79] He argues,[80] like others before him,[81] that *morphē* (form) and *eikōn* (image) represent variant

[72] Cf. E. Percy, *Untersuchungen über den Ursprung der johanneischen Theologie*, Lund 1959, pp.287-99, and the discussion in R. P. Martin, *Carmen Christi: Philippians 2.5-11 in Recent Interpretation and in the Setting of Early Christian Worship*, Cambridge University Press 1967, p.121-8; Keck, op. cit., pp.112-19, 144-51.
[73] Cf. F. L. Cross (ed.), *The Jung Codex*, Mowbrays 1955, p.78; Wilson, *The Gnostic Problem*, pp.75,98,218-27.
[74] Cf. Martin, op. cit., pp.120-33,161-4.   [75] *Leg. alleg.* 1.31.
[76] I Cor. 15.46. See below, p.167.
[77] Cf. W. D. Davies, *Paul and Rabbinic Judaism*, SPCK 1948, pp.45-9.
[78] Cf. especially the exhaustive study by R. P. Martin, *Carmen Christi*, and the bibliography there cited; and, subsequently, C. F. D. Moule, 'Further Reflexions on Philippians 2.5-11', in W. W. Gasque and R. P. Martin (eds.), *Apostolic History and the Gospel*, Paternoster Press 1970, pp.264-76; J. Carmignac, 'L'importance de la place d'une négation (Phil. 2.6)', *New Testament Studies* XVIII, 1972, pp.131-66.
[79] Cullmann, op. cit., p.176.
[80] Comparing Phil. 2.6-8; 3.21; Rom. 8.29; 12.2; I Cor. 15.49; II Cor. 3.18; 4.4; and Col. 3.10.
[81] Especially J. Héring, *Le Royaume de Dieu*, Paris and Neuchâtel ²1959, pp.146ff. Cf. A. M. Hunter, *Paul and his Predecessors*, SCM Press 1940; F. W.

renderings of the idea that goes back to Gen. 1.26 of man being made in the image of God. Jesus, as the 'proper' man,[82] is the exact image or true son of God that Adam was created to be.[83] As such, he could have enjoyed as of right all the divine glory[84] of which humanity since the Fall has been deprived.[85] Yet, no more than the son of the Epistle to the Hebrews, did he think equality with God, which sonship implies,[86] to mean self-assertion.[87] On the contrary, he beggared himself of all his wealth, that through his poverty we might share his riches.[88] By utter self-negation (*heauton ekenōsen*), he took the form of humanity that properly belongs not to a son but to a slave. Observe that Paul does not say that he became a man (from having been something else) but that he shared the lot of *men*, becoming totally obedient to the human condition (*en homoiōmati anthrōpōn genomenos*). Though he might have enjoyed for himself mankind's true state of glory, he preferred for his brothers' sake to be conformed to its present state of dishonour.

The subsequent words, 'being found (*heuretheis*) in fashion (*schēmati*) as a man [wearing, that is, our common clay] he humiliated himself (*etapeinōsen heauton*)', must, I believe, be interpreted in terms of their reversal in the following chapter, where

---

Eltester, *Eikon im neuen Testament*, Berlin 1958, p.10; J. Jervell, *Imago Dei*, Göttingen 1960, p.228. See further Martin, op. cit., pp. 102–19.

[82] Cullmann interprets this of the Heavenly Man and says that the *kenosis* consisted in the fact that '*the* Man became *a* man' (op. cit., p.178). But this is surely to read later categories into it.

[83] Cf. Luke 3.38.

[84] J. Behm, '*Morphē*', in Kittel, *Theological Dictionary of the New Testament* (= TDNT) IV, Eerdmans, Grand Rapids, Michigan 1964–, writes: ' "The form of God" in which the pre-existent Christ was is simply the divine "glory"; Paul's "being in the form of God" corresponds exactly to John 17.5: "The glory which I had with me before the world was".' See the literature cited there. So, earlier, Johannes Weiss, *The History of Primitive Christianity*, Macmillan 1937, p.478, and subsequently Vincent Taylor, *The Person of Christ in New Testament Teaching*, Macmillan 1959, p.75. Cf. II Cor. 4.4,6, 'the glory of Christ, who is the very image of God' and 'the glory of God in the face of Jesus Christ'; also, as we saw, Heb. 1.3, 'the reflection of God's glory and the stamp (*charactēr*) of his very being'.

[85] Rom. 3.23. For the fantastic glory of Adam before the Fall in Jewish speculation, cf. Davies, op. cit., pp.45f.

[86] Cf. John 5.18.

[87] So Moule, op. cit., pp.226–8, 271–6.

[88] II Cor. 8.9.

Paul speaks in very similar terms of himself having forfeited everything, that he might be 'found (*heurethō*) in him . . . being conformed (*summorphizomenos*) to his death, . . . who will refashion (*metaschēmatisei*) the body of our humiliation (*tapeinōseōs*) to be conformed (*summorphon*) to the body of his glory'.[89] That is to say, as Christ shared the *schēma* of our humiliation, so we shall share the *morphē* of his glory as the image or son of God. For the state of being in the form of God is just as human as that of our present dishonour – in fact far more truly and richly so. For both Paul and John, the whole purpose of Christ's work can be described as communicating to his own the glory which belongs to him as the true son of the Father[90] – a glory which he enjoys not in virtue of his sole divine substance but in virtue of his uniquely normal humanity. Later on, Luther, though having the insight to see that 'the form of God' applied not to Christ's divine essence but to his manhood,[91] held that no one who *was* not God could have the right to this divine style of life. Yet it is precisely this reflection of God's glory, which is Christ's by nature (*hyparchōn*) – in contrast with the divine title of 'Lord' subsequently given to him – that all God's children, as Christ's fellow-heirs, are destined to share by being 'glorified together' with him.[92]

But this is to anticipate. For Paul has not yet plumbed the depths of Christ's identification with us. So far from asserting or

[89] Phil. 3.7–11,20f. It is remarkable that in the voluminous discussion of Christ's humiliation in Phil. 2.6–8, summarized by Martin, op. cit., pp.134–228, the relevance of Phil. 3 is never even mentioned.

[90] Rom. 8.29f.: 'God . . . ordained that they should be conformed (*summorphous*) to the image (*eikonos*) of his Son, that he might be the eldest among a large family of brothers . . ., to whom he has also given his splendour'; I Cor. 15.43,49; 'Sown in dishonour, it is raised in glory . . . As we have worn the image of the man made of dust, so we shall wear the image of the heavenly man'; II Cor. 3.18: 'We are being transformed (*metamorphoumetha*) into the same image (*tēn autēn eikona*) from glory to glory' (my translations). Similarly, John 17.22: 'The glory which thou gavest me I have given to them'; 17.24: 'Father, I desire that these men . . . may be with me where I am, so that they may look upon my glory, which thou hast given me because thou didst love me before the world began' (cf. 17.5).

[91] WA 17/II 238f. This was the first recognition of this since the phrase had been appropriated by orthodoxy against the Arians to refute Christ's subordination to God; cf. Athanasius, *Or. contra Ar.* 1.37f.; Victorinus, *adv. Ar.* 1.9.13 and 23.

[92] Rom. 8.17.

'pleasing' himself,[93] Jesus filled the role of a slave (who cannot even call his life his own) right through to its final term of death by crucifixion. '*Therefore* God highly exalted him and graciously bestowed on him (*echarisato*) the name above every name', so that henceforth the human name Jesus should be inseparably linked, at its every mention in worship, with the divine name, *kyrios*, Lord.[94] Once more, and supremely here, we have the combination of pre-existence and adoptionist language. The picture is not that of a celestial figure lowering himself to become a man, to be exalted still higher than he was before. Rather, it is that the entire fullness of God was enabled by divine grace and human obedience to find embodiment in one who was as completely one of us as any other physical descendant of Abraham.[95] Thereby he 'broke the barrier' between man and God. Jesus was not, I believe, for Paul, as he became for later dogmatics, a divine being veiled in flesh or one who stripped himself of superhuman attributes to become human; he was a man who by total surrender of his own gain or glory[96] was able to reveal or 'unveil'[97] the glory of God as utterly gracious, self-giving love.[98]

But there is one further Pauline passage which, as usually understood, would seem to suggest that the manhood of Christ, unlike ours, was 'spiritual' rather than 'natural', and had its origin not on earth but in heaven. This is I Cor. 15.45–47 (NEB):

> 'The first man, Adam, became an animate being', whereas the last Adam has become a life-giving spirit. . . . The first man was made 'of the dust of the earth': the second man is from heaven.

If the implications of this were pressed, we should have here an entirely eccentric, and indeed heretical, Christology – of a Christ-figure whose humanity as well as whose divinity was of a heavenly substance. But, as we have seen, Paul makes it absolutely clear elsewhere[99] that the Incarnation meant the complete identification of God in Christ with our earthly humanity of powerless, sinful

---

[93] Rom. 15.3.
[94] I find it difficult to see how Moule (op. cit., p.270) can hold that the name given to Christ (at his exaltation) was that of Jesus. He had *that* name before.
[95] Cf. Gal. 3.16.   [96] Cf. John 7.18; 8.50,54.   [97] Cf. II Cor. 3.12–18.
[98] Cf. Rom. 5.6–8.   [99] Rom. 8.3; II Cor. 5.21; Gal. 4.3f.

flesh. One way in which exegetes have tried to get round the difficulty is to interpret the 'becoming' not of his incarnation but of his glorification. That is to say, by virtue of the resurrection he *became* a life-giving spirit, from having been (like us) an animal being. But this contrast destroys the parallelism with Adam (where *egeneto eis* must mean 'was created as'), and it does not in any case account for the subsequent phrase that the second man is 'from heaven' *as opposed to* 'the dust of the earth'.

But in fact I am convinced that the reference in this passage, as the context shows, is not to Adam and to Jesus Christ as individuals, but to two different 'bodies' or conditions of humanity, *adam* and *anthrōpos* being ways, in Hebrew and Greek, of referring to 'man' with a capital M. Our primary manhood is that in which we share by virtue of the natural creation. This humanity may be comprehended entirely in physical and psychological categories; it is *choïkos* and *psychikos*. But the second can be comprehended only in spiritual or heavenly categories: it is *pneumatikos, epouranios*. It is spirit – *not* 'a spirit'[100] – and it is life – real life, in contrast with mere animation. For it is spirit alone that gives life, as John [101] and Paul [102] both insist. The first level of living Paul sees as having been initiated in Adam, the second as having been opened up through Christ. To that extent there is an irreversible historical sequence: 'The spiritual does not come first; the animal body comes first, and then the spiritual.'[103] It is 'in Christ', in the body of Christ, that all are 'made alive'[104] and that the 'law of the spirit of life'[105] operates. The last (or eschatological) Adam, the new man, which both has been created[106] and 'is being constantly renewed in the image of its Creator',[107] is the life-giving spiritual corporeity, which indeed *is* Christ:

> If Christ is dwelling within you, then although the body is a
> dead thing because you sinned, yet the spirit is life itself because

[100] Any more than God is 'a spirit' in John 4.24. Never, I think, does Paul say that Christ *is* 'a spirit' or 'the Spirit' – even in II Cor. 3.16–18, where I am convinced (with the NEB) that *ho kyrios* refers to the Lord of the Old Testament.
[101] John 6.63.   [102] II Cor. 3.6; Gal. 3.21.
[103] I Cor. 15.46. As has often been observed, Paul may here deliberately be reversing Philo's assertion of the priority of the heavenly man.
[104] I Cor. 15.22.   [105] Rom. 8.2.   [106] Eph. 4.24.   [107] Col. 3.10.

you have been justified. Moreover, if the Spirit of him who raised Jesus from the dead dwells within you, then the God who raised Christ Jesus from the dead will also give new life to your mortal bodies through his indwelling Spirit.[108]

Thus I believe the contrast in I Cor. 15.44–49, as in the whole of the previous paragraph,[109] is between the *sōma psychikon* (the natural body) and the *sōma pneumatikon* (the spiritual body), the two solidarities or states of humanity, *both* of which Jesus shared and both of which we shall therefore share:

> He died on the cross in weakness, but he lives by the power of God; and we who share his weakness shall by the power of God live with him.[110]

So Paul speaks in precisely the same language of the transformation of the human condition:

> Sown in humiliation it is raised in glory; sown in weakness, it is raised in power.[111]

The 'it' is the form of our humanity or manhood, and it is to the ultimate state of this, rather than to Jesus Christ as an individual, that the heavenly Man refers.[112] Just as 'the first man',[113] 'the old man',[114] 'the outer man',[115] 'the natural man'[116] are for Paul equivalent terms, so too are 'the second man',[117] 'the last man',[118] 'the new man',[119] 'the inner man',[120] 'the spiritual man'.[121] They refer to collectives in which the individual participates – as also does 'the perfect man'.[122] In the same way, 'the man from heaven'

---

[108] Rom. 8.10f. [109] I Cor. 15.33–44. [110] II Cor. 13.4. [111] I Cor. 15.43.
[112] Cf. A. E. J. Rawlinson, *The New Testament Doctrine of the Christ*, Longmans 1926, p.129: 'I believe that the true exegesis of the passage depends upon recognizing that the expanded quotation from Gen. 2.7 in I Cor. 15.45 is a parenthesis which should be printed in brackets and that vv. 44,46 should be read together as a continuous sentence. . . . The reference all through is to the antithesis between the "natural" and the "spiritual" body, not to the contrast between the "earthly" and the "heavenly" man.' It is surprising how rare this recognition is among commentators.
[113] I Cor. 15.45,47. [114] Rom. 6.6; Eph. 4.22; Col. 3.9. [115] II Cor. 4.16.
[116] I Cor. 15.46; cf. 2.14. [117] I Cor. 15.47. [118] I Cor. 15.45.
[119] Eph 2.15; 4.24; Col. 3.10; cf. II Cor. 5.17. [120] II Cor. 4.16; Eph. 3.16.
[121] I Cor. 15.46; cf. 2.15. [122] Eph. 4.13.

corresponds to 'the habitation from heaven' – the new corporeity.[123] But these equivalences have been hidden from our eyes largely through the scribal gloss (perpetuated in the Authorized Version), which goes back to Marcion: 'the second man, *the Lord* from heaven.' And this has provided scriptural anchorage for the Gnostic concept of a supernatural heavenly Man, not of our clay, who is celestial *as opposed to* earthly, spiritual *rather than* material.[124] It is difficult to believe that Paul entertained any such notion.

In John

But what, finally, of the Fourth Gospel? It is here that from the beginning men have seen the presentation of a celestial being walking this earth in the clothing of a humanity that is merely a disguise. This view has recently been asserted in singularly unqualified form by Ernst Käsemann. 'John is, to our knowledge,' he writes, 'the first Christian to use the earthly life of Jesus merely as a backdrop for the Son of God proceeding through the world of man and as the scene of the inbreaking of the heavenly glory.'[125] He classes the work as 'naïve docetism'[126] and even says that 'from the historical viewpoint, the Church committed an error when it declared the Gospel to be orthodox'.[127]

An American writer, E. L. Titus, takes the same line:

Although the prologue forthrightly asserts that the Logos became flesh (1.14), the picture of Jesus that the body of the Gospel presents makes a farce of Jesus' humanity. This picture

[123] I Cor. 15.47; II Cor. 5.2. There is throughout a close parallel between the argument of I Cor. 15 and that of II Cor. 3–5, with the themes in common of the 'earthly' and the 'heavenly' (I Cor. 15.40,47; II Cor. 5.1), of being 'changed' (I Cor. 15.51; II Cor. 3.18) from one 'glory' to another (I Cor. 15.40–43; II Cor. 3.18; 4.17), of 'putting on' (I Cor. 15.53f.; II Cor. 5.2–4) that which is not subject to 'corruption' (I Cor. 15.42, 50,53f.; II Cor. 3.16), of the 'mortal' being 'swallowed up' (I Cor. 15.54; II Cor. 5.4), and death being vanquished in life (I Cor. 15.54–57; II Cor. 4.10–12). Both passages are concerned with entry upon the new corporeity, the new man, which is the body of Christ (cf. Col. 3.10f.; Rom. 13.14; Gal. 3.27), the building from God (I Cor. 3.9; II Cor. 5.1; Eph. 2.20–22).

[124] It is not surprising that Apollinarius found support in this text for his view of Christ's humanity (*Ep. ad Dionys.* 1.10; cf. H. Lietzmann, *Apollinaris von Laodicea und seine Schule*, Tübingen 1904, p.261).

[125] Ernst Käsemann, *The Testament of Jesus*, SCM Press 1968, p.13.

[126] Käsemann, op. cit., p.26.   [127] Ibid., p.76.

does not support a true doctrine of the incarnation. John's Jesus is a god who dips into history but scarcely touches it; he is in history but not of it.[128]

Yet he is compelled to recognize that this is not the whole story. There is also another very different picture, what he calls 'the historical "given" with which John operates' and which 'in a very general way . . . corresponds to "that which happened" '.[129]

> In effect two Jesus figures appear in the Fourth Gospel. There is the Jesus who appears as a god, whom we have described above. Then there is the Jesus of the Jews. The latter stands in sharp contrast to John's Logos-Christ: he is a Galilean Jew (1.45f.; 7.41, 52); his father's name is Joseph (1.45; 6.42); he is a Sabbath breaker (5.16); he is a revolutionary (7.12); he is an unlettered man (7.15); he is demon possessed (7.20; 8.48; 10.20); his origin is known (7.27); he is a sinner (9.24); he makes blasphemous claims (10.33); he is subject to arrest (7.44f.; 11.57) and to punishment by death (11.53); his reply to the high priest is considered insolent (18.22); he is an evildoer (18.30).[130]

How John manages to hold these two pictures together Titus never explains. It seems to me that we should begin by crediting the evangelist with being neither naïve, stupid nor schizophrenic, and ask whether it is not *we* who have introduced such a polarization.

First, let us recognize that there is a difference between John's portrait and that of the Epistle to the Hebrews, and even of Paul. There is none of the more obviously 'adoptionist' language; nor is there any suggestion that Jesus himself grows in awareness. There is no hint that he develops or learns from the things that he suffers – merely a waiting for his 'hour' to come and his 'time' to ripen.[131] Whereas in Hebrews it is he who is subject to *teleiōsis*

---

[128] E. L. Titus, 'The Fourth Gospel and the Historical Jesus', in F. T. Trotter (ed.), *Jesus and the Historian: Written in Honor of Ernest Cadman Colwell*, Westminster Press, Philadelphia 1968, p.104.
[129] Titus, op. cit., p.111.
[130] Ibid., p.105. I have corrected the references, several being obviously wrong.
[131] John 2.4; 7.6,8,30; 8.20; 12.23; 13.1; 17.1.

or maturation, there is nothing of this in the *tetelestai*, 'it is finished', of John. If, as I have argued elsewhere,[132] we apply the standards of psychological verisimilitude rather than of theological verity, then not only does this gospel *look* docetic, static and unhistorical: it is docetic. And it is not in the least surprising that this has been the charge it has invited from the beginning. Yet we should do the author the justice of accepting that such a judgment is in his eyes a fearful misunderstanding. For this point of view is not that from which it (or for that matter the portraits of any of the other evangelists) should be judged: for this is to regard things 'superficially',[133] 'by worldly standards',[134] rather than with true discernment.

The whole message of the gospel, and the source of its distinctive depth and irony, is that there are two levels at which everything about Jesus can and must be judged. It is not that one is true *or* the other, or that one is real at the expense of the other. If both were not equally valid there would be no misunderstanding, no offence and therefore no faith. It is possible at one level to know completely where Jesus comes from and yet at another to know nothing.[135] Yet both sources of origin – his earthly father and his heavenly father – are equally real. To suggest that the former is merely a sham is to destroy the whole tension and texture of the gospel.

For John there is no contradiction between coming or being sent from God and being utterly and genuinely a man. No other gospel uses the word 'man' anything like as much of Jesus.[136] It is employed of him exactly as it is of John the Baptist: 'a man . . . whose name was John' (1.6) and 'the man called Jesus' (9.11).

---

[132] John A. T. Robinson, 'The Use of the Fourth Gospel for Christology Today', in B. Lindars and S. S. Smalley, *Christ and Spirit in the New Testament: Studies in Honour of Professor C. F. D. Moule*, Cambridge University Press 1973. I have reproduced some sentences from this essay in summary form in this paragraph.

[133] John 7.24.   [134] John 8.15.

[135] John 6.41–44; 7.15–18,27–29; 8.14–19,21–25; 9.29–31. Note especially the contrast in 7.27, 'We know where this man comes from', and 9.29, 'As for this fellow, we do not know where he comes from'.

[136] The figures are: for *anthrōpos*, Matthew 1; Mark 1; Luke 6 (the Matthean and Markan parallels, plus four times on the lips of Pilate); John 16; for *anēr*, Luke 1; John 1.

The Baptist says of Jesus in comparison with himself, 'A man can only have what God gives him'(3.27). Indeed, when he first introduces Jesus it is in terms of 'after me a man *(anēr)* is coming who takes rank before me', and his manhood is not in question because it can *also* be said of him, in explanation of his precedence, 'for before I was born, he already was' (1.30). No more, later, does the charge 'You, a mere man, claim to be a god' (10.33) imply that, really, he was *not* a mere man. On the contrary, as we shall see, the argument of the passage presupposes that he was no less and no more of a man than those to whom the word of God came in the Old Testament.[137]

It is characteristic of this evangelist that, for all his stress on Jesus' otherness, the language he uses to designate Christ in his profoundest relationship to the Father is the *same* language that he applies in a weaker and more general sense to men in general. If Jesus is unique, it is *not* because he does not share the human origin and condition or the relationship to God open potentially to all the other men.

To substantiate this linguistically involves, inevitably, a somewhat close study of the text. Those who prefer to accept it as read can take up the argument again at p. 175.

Thus, to 'come into the world', which might suggest some special kind of supernatural entry, is used identically of Jesus,[138] of 'the prophet',[139] of the Messiah,[140] and indeed (if this is the right punctuation) of 'every man'.[141] It is the equivalent of being 'born' (18.37) or being 'born into the world' (16.21), which again is applied indifferently to Jesus and to any woman's child. Similarly, not only Jesus but John the Baptist is a man 'sent from God' (1.6; cf. 3.28); and even Nicodemus acknowledges Jesus as a teacher 'come from God' (3.2) – for no one, he admits, could do such signs unless God were 'with him' – the very phrase, however weak on his lips, which is also used by Jesus himself to describe his most intimate union with the Father.[142] Yet this intimate union itself is grounded in a moral affinity potentially open to any man.[143]

[137] John 10.34–36.   [138] John 9.39; 12.46; 16.28; 18.37.
[139] John 6.14.   [140] John 11.27; cf. 4.25; 7.27,31,41f.
[141] John 1.9.   [142] John 8.29; 16.32.   [143] John 8.29; 15.10.

Similarly, the estimate of Jesus as 'a man of God' (*para theou*, 9.16,33), which in its general sense is equated with 'a prophet' (9.17), and indeed with 'anyone who is devout and obeys his will' (9.31), is precisely the expression that Jesus employs to designate his own unique relationship to God: 'He who has come from God (*para tou theou*) has seen the Father, and he alone.'[144] Yet this revelation of 'what I saw in my Father's presence' (8.38) can be described by Jesus himself as the work of '*a man* who told you the truth as I heard it from God' (8.40).

There is a continuum, too, between the very distinctive language which John uses to describe Jesus' sonship and that which ought to apply to every man. To have God as father is what should be true of the Jews, as they themselves claim (8.41). But morally they have forfeited that claim, for 'he who has God for his father listens to the words of God. You are not God's children; that is why you do not listen.'[145] Consequently, it is not superhuman presumption for Jesus to claim sonship of God. 'Those are called gods,' he points out, quoting Ps. 82.6, 'to whom the word of God was delivered – and Scripture cannot be set aside. Then why do you charge me with blasphemy because I, consecrated and sent into the world by the Father, said, "I am a son of God"?' (10.35f., my translation of the last clause; there are no articles in the Greek). The only thing that could impugn that claim is failure to show God's character: 'If I am not acting as my Father would, do not believe me. But if I am, accept the evidence of my deeds . . . so that you may recognize and know that *the Father is in me, and I in the Father*' (10.37f.). Yet this last apparently exclusive union of mutual indwelling is that to which the disciples also are called.[146] For even though the normative filial relationship is not fulfilled in

---

[144] John 6.46; cf. 7.29; 16.27; 17.8; etc. C. H. Dodd has argued, *The Interpretation of the Fourth Gospel*, Cambridge University Press 1953, pp.259f., that whereas *para tou theou* and *apo tou theou* do indeed have wider reference, the phrase *ek tou theou* carries the sense of unique origination in the being of God 'applicable to no prophet or messenger'. Yet the prepositions in the parallel expressions in 16.27 (*para*), 28 (*ek*; if indeed this is the right reading) and 30 (*apo*) appear to be no more than synonymous variations. Above all, being *ek tou theou*, which is applied to Jesus in 8.42, is in 8.47 applied to any man, and should apply even to the Jews.

[145] John 8.47; cf. the whole dialogue of 8.27–55.

[146] John 15.5–10; 17.21–23, 26.

all, or indeed in any – and consequently in John only Jesus is designated 'son', while others are God's 'children'[147] – yet to be 'the offspring of God himself' is every believer's rightful destiny.[148]

Similarly, to be 'consecrated' and 'sent' into the world is true not simply of Jesus in his unique sonship: it is something that believers are to share with him,[149] just as he shared it with the prophets before him. Thus God said to Jeremiah, 'Before you were born I consecrated you. . . . You shall go to whatever people I send you and say whatever I tell you to say.'[150] In exactly the same way, Jesus has to listen to the Father and be taught by him what he is to say.[151] And again it is stressed that in this pupil's status he is in the same position as everyone else. Indeed he himself is made to say: 'It is written in the prophets: "And they shall all be taught by God." Everyone who has listened to the Father and learned from him comes to me' (6.45).

Yet immediately these words are followed by the most uncompromising statement of his unique position: 'I do not mean that anyone has seen the Father. He who has come from God has seen the Father, and he alone' (6.46). But if we ask *why* for this writer 'no one has ever seen God' (1.18), it is again apparently (at any rate in part) for moral rather than for metaphysical reasons. Jesus says to the Jews, 'You never heard his voice, or saw his form' (5.37). Yet, it is implied, they *should* have done: 'But his word has found no home in you, for you do not believe the one whom he sent' (5.38).

Jesus is indeed for John the unique revealer and mediator of God. As 'the only son',[152] or even 'the only one, who is himself God', he alone has 'made him known'.[153] Again, 'no one ever went up into heaven except the one who came down from heaven, the Son of Man';[154] and it is this Son of Man alone who can give

---

[147] Paul uses 'sons' of Christians, but makes it clear that their sonship is by 'adoption' into that of Christ.
[148] John 1.13; cf. I John 2.29–3.2; 3.9f;. 4.7; 5.1–3, 18f.
[149] John 17.17–19; cf. 20.21.
[150] Jer. 1.5,7.
[151] John 7.16; 8.26,28,40; 12.49f.; 14.10; 15.15; 17.8.
[152] John 1.14; 3.16,18.
[153] John 1.18, accepting the harder but best-attested reading; cf. 1.1.
[154] John 3.13. But the subsequent phrase, 'who is in heaven' – even, as it was

and sustain eternal life (6.27–58). Jesus is and Jesus does what no other man can be or do. Yet in order to be this and to do this, he is not other than a man in complete continuity with all other men. There is no suggestion in this gospel, unlike the first and third, that he enters this world in any other way. 'Not born of any human stock, or by the fleshly desire of a human father, but the offspring of God himself' is for John a description not of Jesus but of believers (1.13). Of course, it is also true at this level of Jesus: he is *par excellence* the one who is 'from above' (3.31), who 'comes down from heaven' – yet not in a way to deny the physical links (6.42) or to separate him from others.

The real difference in this gospel is that the 'designatory' language found in the other writers, which appears, by subsequent standards, so 'adoptionist', is placed by John firmly at the beginning, thus avoiding any impression, so properly repudiated in later doctrine, of God lighting upon Jesus as an afterthought. As the predestinarian terms that accompany it in Hebrews and Paul make clear, this is a false impression there also. But John is careful to give it no handle. In this gospel Jesus is indeed 'sealed' (6.27) and 'consecrated' (10.36) by God, in language not unreminiscent of the Epistle to the Hebrews, where too the Son is a 'priest appointed by the words of an oath'.[155] Yet in Hebrews, as we have seen, this takes place only after he is 'made perfect'. In John it happens from the start. True, its finishing[156] has to await the moment of his glorification[157] and exaltation.[158] Yet both of these are seen as a *return* to what obtained before.[159] And it is this that gives the counter-impression, which I believe is equally false, that for John (unlike the author to the Hebrews) Jesus was not a real man. He was just as real. But if this man *was*, as Hebrews says, 'the reflection of God's glory and the stamp of his very being', then, as John sees it, the glory and the being, or what he epitomizes as 'the

later taken to imply, during the Incarnation (e.g. Augustine, *In Joan. hom.* 27.4; 61.2) – is almost certainly no part of the true text.
[155] Heb. 7.28.
[156] John 4.34; 17.4; 19.30.
[157] John 7.39; 12.16,23,28; 13.31f.; 17.4f.
[158] John 3.14; 8.28; 12.32,34.
[159] John 3.13f.; 6.62; 17.5. This is also the main difference between the Johannine and the Synoptic 'Son of Man' sayings.

name',[160] must have been 'given'[161] to him from the beginning.

The reason why language that is eternally true of God can be applied to Jesus without measure[162] or qualification is not because he is not a man but because, unlike other men, *all* that the Father has is his (5.19f.). Everything has been entrusted to him,[163] including authority over all men for life and death.[164] He has been sent as the Father's personal representative[165] or plenipotentiary, who is given his seal of authority[166] and the credentials to act in his name.[167] And this, as in the parable of the Wicked Husbandman[168] and in Hebrews,[169] is the crucial difference between a servant and a son: there is nothing to which the son of the house has not free access.[170] John never implies, any more than the writer of Hebrews, that because Jesus is son he does not stand in the same human relationship to God as every other man. On the contrary, it is because he is the one completely obedient man, who 'always' does his Father's will, right 'to the end',[171] that he is the perfect reflection or representation of God, in the way that an only son may be said to be the very image of his father.[172] Consequently, anyone who has seen *this man* has seen the Father.[173]

Yet the impression still lingers that this is not truly a human story. If it is an erroneous impression, it is one that the author has not wholly succeeded in dispelling. And this, indeed, is not accidental. It is integral to his whole method. For he is deliberately telling two stories, two histories, at once – and superimposing them on each other.

[160] John 17.6,11f.,26; cf. 12.28.

[161] John 17.11f. (where the harder and better-attested reading, referring to the name rather than the disciples, must be preferred), 22,24; cf. 5.26, where the Father 'gave' the Son to 'have life in himself'.

[162] Cf. John 3.34.

[163] John 3.34f.; 13.3. This is why everything the Spirit is to make known will be drawn from him (16.14f.).

[164] John 5.21–29; 17.2.

[165] John 13.20; 14.21; 15.23.

[166] John 6.27.

[167] John 5.43; 10.25.

[168] Mark 12.2–7 par.

[169] Heb. 3.5f.

[170] John 8.35f. Cf. the parable of the Prodigal Son (Luke 15.31), where too the son is 'always' at home (as in John 8.35), and 'everything the father has is his' (precisely the wording in John 17.10).

[171] John 4.34; 5.30,36; 6.38; 8.29; 10.17; 17.4. Cf. the corollary in 11.42, 'thou always hearest me'.

[172] John 1.14. On the interpretation of this see below, p.p.1.87f

[173] John 12.45; 14.9.

The first is the story of the Logos, the history of the wisdom and light and love of God. This history comes to its climax in Jesus and is so totally incarnate in him that he can speak directly in the name of God and utter the divine 'I am'. In this, indeed, John is saying nothing different from the Synoptists.[174] What he does is to draw out the depths and significance of this fact. Such a voice can only come from 'the world above' (8.23). Its source and ground are not 'of this world'[175] but 'with God'.[176] Indeed it *is* God speaking and acting. Consequently, its *archē* or origin is not just the moment of Jesus' birth, but is before Abraham (8.58), before the world (17.5,24), and indeed at the beginning of all things (1.1f.). As the embodiment of this 'I am', Jesus does not speak 'of himself'.[177] It is no wonder, therefore, that he sometimes sounds like a ventriloquist's dummy.

Yet this does not mean that it is *not* himself speaking. For the gospel is also telling another story, the history of a human being who comes from nowhere more exalted than Nazareth in Galilee and whose connections are known to all. There is no mystery about his origin, and it is absurd to say of this historical individual that he is pre-existent. To mix up the stories, to confuse the categories, as the Jews do, is to make nonsense of everything, as crudely as when Nicodemus confuses birth from above with being born again here below.[178] Yet the possibility, and indeed the inevitability, of misunderstanding is for John an essential part of the whole. To write it out of the story, or to make things so plain that faith is not needed in order to discern, is to falsify. We may indeed wish that he had made clearer what is to be taken as theology and what as history or psychology or any other part of the 'first' story. For in our age it has become important to discriminate, if the humanity is not to be threatened by the pre-existence. Yet it is integral to his purpose that statements shall be able to be taken *both* ways, at two levels. He does not, as we might like and as commentators have often claimed, distinguish the different levels, of 'seeing' for instance, by different words: he

---

[174] Cf. most notably the 'I' of the Sermon on the Mount (Matt. 5.17–48; etc.). I shall return to this in the next chapter.

[175] John 8.23; 17.14,16; 18.36.

[176] John 1.1,18.

[177] John 5.19,30; 7.16–18,28; 12.49.

[178] John 3.3–12.

uses the same words[179] for each at different times. Or again, it is impossible to be certain, when Jesus says of himself 'I am', if this is charged with divine significance or if it is simply an indication of human identity.[180] The scene at the arrest is typical:

> 'Who is it you want?' 'Jesus of Nazareth', they answered. Jesus said, 'I am he'. . . . When he said, 'I am he', they drew back and fell to the ground. Again, Jesus asked, 'Who is it you want?'. 'Jesus of Nazareth', they answered. Then Jesus said, 'I have told you that I am he' (18.4–8).

The risk of misrepresentation is openly courted. Yet it would be an even greater misrepresentation to say of either story that it was merely a guise.

What John is doing is, as it were, to show us two series of colour transparencies. At the beginning we can watch how each of them starts:

> When all things began, the Word already was . . . (1.1)
> There appeared a man named John. . . . (1.6)

But very soon the slides of both are deliberately projected together, the one over the other. It is possible to see only one or the other – or the two hopelessly confused. But with the eye of faith, by 'the true light' (1.9), it is possible to view both in focus – and then to see the glory incarnate (1.14). There *is*, he is saying, a way of having the languages both of 'pre-existence' and of 'humanity', if we can understand what each is doing 'without separation' and 'without confusion'.[181] But, by deliberately superimposing them rather than laying them side by side (as the author to the Hebrews tends to do), he risks all to gain all.[182]

---

[179] *Blepein, theōrein, horān.*

[180] E.g. John 4.26; 6.20 (cf. Mark 6.50); 8.24,28; 13.19; cf. 9.9 (of the blind man).

[181] For how John thus holds them together and how we should interpret him today, I must again refer to my essay 'The Use of the Fourth Gospel for Christology Today'.

[182] Since writing this chapter I have re-read G. B. Caird's essay, 'The Development of the Doctrine of Christ in the New Testament', *Christ for Us Today*, pp.66–80, and am happy to discover how strongly he supports the line I have taken at so many points, especially from his much greater knowledge of the apocryphal literature. He writes: 'The Jews had believed only in the pre-existence of a personification. Wisdom was a personification, either of a divine attribute

This is not, of course, to say that *we* are committed to the language of pre-existence. Even if it were still for us a natural way of speaking, it is probably by now too much identified, as Knox says, with presuppositions that *are* destructive of humanity to be rescued to say what I have argued the biblical writers were meaning by it. For, whether or not I am right in my interpretation of them (and I would not wish to be dogmatic at any point), there is no doubt that either in New Testament times or soon afterwards the transition from one set of presuppositions to another did take place. And thereby Christian doctrine became committed to an understanding of incarnation that involved the veiling in flesh of a heavenly being.

The sole question is whether this is the only or indeed the original understanding of what incarnation means. I believe that the word can just as truly and just as biblically (in fact more truly and more biblically) be applied to another way of understanding it. This is: that one who was totally and utterly a man – and had never been anything other than a man or more than a man – so completely embodied what was from the beginning the meaning and purpose of God's self-expression (whether conceived in terms of his Spirit, his Wisdom, his Word, or the intimately personal relationship of Sonship) that it could be said, and had to be said, of that man, 'He was God's man', or 'God was in Christ', or even that he *was* 'God for us'. This way of putting it clearly involves no whit less of a stupendous claim. And it is that claim to which we must now go on.

or of a divine purpose, but never a person. . . . Neither the Fourth Gospel nor Hebrews ever speaks of the eternal Word or Wisdom of God in terms which compel us to regard it as a person. If we are in the habit of crediting them with such a belief in a pre-existent person, and not just a pre-existent purpose, it is because we read them in the light of Paul's theology' (p.79). As will have become clear, I do not regard Paul as an exception. I believe he appears to be so only because we read *him* in the light of later theology.

SIX

GOD FOR US

The essential identity

How can Christ *be* God for us – without ceasing truly to be man? This is the ultimate question for Christology, the question of the *vere deus*, of which the iota of difference between *homoousios* (of one substance) with the Father and *homoiousios* (of like substance) was at a historic moment the touchstone.

Before becoming involved in the details we may find it useful to clarify what in principle is at stake. Whether or not Jesus *can* sustain such a claim for him is not at this point the issue. The question is what is really being asserted in saying, as Nicaea and Chalcedon said, that he is 'very God of very God'. At heart it is what John Hick has perhaps not very felicitously called the 'numerical identity' between his love and God's love – that he is *homoagapē*, of one love, with the Father.[1] In other words, what Jesus was and did was the direct expression and implementation of

---

[1] John Hick, 'Christology at the Cross Roads', in F. G. Healey (ed.), *Prospect for Theology: Essays in Honour of H. H. Farmer*, Nisbet 1966, ch. 6. Norman Pittenger, *Christology Reconsidered*, p.18, criticizes Hick on the ground that his phrase could mean that God's love replaces Jesus' human love, just as in Apollinarianism the Logos usurps the place of the human mind. But (to use Sölle's distinction to which we shall be referring later) Hick is clearly intending to assert representation not replacement, identification rather than equation. Pittenger himself is surely meaning the same thing when he writes in *The Word Incarnate*, pp.121f.: 'To say that Jesus Christ is the embodiment of God's love or of the divine goodness, if it is to go deep enough to make any difference, must at the same time point to the fact that that which in Jesus Christ we call divinity is not only a *quality* attaching to his human life, but that it is the very *being* of God himself here active in human life.'

God in action; not simply, in Austin Farrer's phrase, a man doing 'human things divinely' but a man doing 'divine things humanly'.[2] That is to say, in what he was and what he did we do not merely see a love of the same quality, such a perfect reproduction that we could infer, 'This is what God must be like', because it was 'so amazing, so divine'. Nor are we dealing just with a man reporting, however accurately, what he believed God said to him, as the prophets declared to their contemporaries 'Thus saith the Lord'. Nor are we concerned with the validity of this man's experience of God, his God-consciousness, as Schleiermacher called it, which may indeed have been intimate and revealing beyond parallel. We are concerned with whether it can be said of this man's life and death that 'God was in Christ reconciling the world to himself'.[3] Does what we see in Jesus actually bring us into contact with God at work, so that to have seen him, met him and been judged by him is to have seen, met and been judged by God?

Such a requirement does not imply that God is exclusively at work in this man or even that there is a difference in kind rather than degree between his action here and elsewhere. Indeed, if it is *God* who is revealed in action here, he is by definition the one who is 'behind' everything that ever happens and in everyone who has ever lived. To claim, however, of someone that he is the Christ is to claim that here we see the *clue* to God's action and presence everywhere else, because (to use absurdly anthropomorphic language) God 'put himself into' this event in a way that was uniquely or specially revealing. If this event does not disclose the initiative, the involvement, of God to a unique degree, *as well* as the human response to it, then something less is being claimed. The Word, in Pittenger's paraphrase again, was 'the

---

[2] Austin Farrer, *Saving Belief*, Hodder and Stoughton 1964, p.75.
[3] II Cor. 5.19. Whether we translate it thus or (with the NEB margin) 'God was reconciling the world to himself by Christ' makes no difference to the centrality of the agency of God. Baillie recognized its crucial significance for Christology by taking it as the title of his great book. It is scarcely possible to credit that it is not even mentioned in the four largest studies of the subject since: Cullmann, *The Christology of the New Testament*; Hahn, *The Titles of Jesus in Christology*; Fuller, *The Foundations of New Testament Christology*; and Pannenberg, *Jesus: God and Man*.

Self-expression of God':[4] it '*was* God' addressing himself to men. Or, to say the same thing without using 'God' terminology, if Jesus is the Christ, he must tell us something not merely about human nature, but about all nature, about the very grain of the universe itself, about how things are at the heart and ground of being. This is what was at stake in the *homoousios* debate.

I have stressed this so heavily for two reasons. The first is that there is an inevitable psychological tendency to assume that unqualified stress on the *vere homo* must lead to qualified stress on the *vere deus* – just as in practice, though not in intention, it happened the other way round. Secondly, I wish to distinguish this fundamental affirmation from certain ways in which it has been expressed that have come to be regarded so much as part of it that to question the latter looks like questioning the former. But to stress the 'numerical identity' or, as the Fourth Gospel puts it, to say that Jesus and the Father are 'one thing',[5] that 'what God was, the Word was',[6] is not to be committed to any particular way of representing it, however hallowed by tradition.

Three representations of reality

The way in which this reality is represented will depend on how we find it convincing to represent reality in general; and as a convenient schema we may return to the three ways I mentioned before,[7] in which van Peursen analyses how man has thought of his world and tried to express what is most real to him – the mythological, the ontological and the functional.

The *mythological* is epitomized in the kind of literature in late Judaism and early Christianity which we examined in the last chapter. It embraces both the divisions we there sought to distinguish because, as I argued, the change in presupposition about how it was *understood* did not coincide with the shift from mythological to ontological categories. The language of the visions of Daniel or I Enoch, of the Epistle to the Philippians or later Gnosticism, is

---

[4] Cf. *The Word Incarnate*, p.240; 'In trinitarian terminology, the Word is God Self-Expressive in the world, the Holy Spirit is God responding through the world.'

[5] John 10.30.   [6] John 1.1.   [7] See p.33 above.

equally mythological. In this representation of reality, the identity of God with the Christ-figure is expressed in terms of a personification of some aspect of his being or will. He is seen as a heavenly figure who is constantly with him in all he does. As his Word or Son he belongs at his side, but he visits this earth as his emissary in human form, subsequently to be reunited with him in glory and in judgment. Whatever the degree of hypostatization, the identity between the sender and the sent is not in doubt.

The second, *ontological* representation of reality translates this from poetic to philosophical categories. The unity of Christ with God is safeguarded by positing identity of substance between Father and Son. Christ is seen as a co-equal person of the Godhead himself, sharing his uncreated being, who assumes manhood without for one moment ceasing to *be* God. The doctrine of the two natures was framed to preserve the inexpungeable duality, while the single subject of action was guaranteed by making the divine *hypostasis* the ego also of the human nature of Jesus. There was a literal metaphysical continuity: Jesus *was* God under the form of flesh. The Son of God is translated as God the Son. As I said earlier, it looks to us as if this is a heightening of Christology – and indeed one could get no higher than that. But in fact this is more apparent than real. For,

> The highest place that heaven affords
> Is his, is his by right,

under the mythological way of thinking as well. There, too, he is given 'the name above every name', the title of *kyrios* or *adonai* that belongs to God himself. It is simply that the ontological categories 'feel' more substantial to us, nurtured as we are in the tradition of Platonic and Aristotelian philosophy.

In contrast the third, *functional*, way of representing reality *looks* as if it is saying much less than the other two, having neither the robust rotundity of personification nor the solidity of substance. Yet it is another, equally serious way of asserting identity – but in terms of verbs rather than substantives or substances. The Christ is the one who does what God does, who represents him.

He stands in the place of God, speaking and acting for him. The issue is not where he comes from or what he is made of. He is not a divine or semi-divine being who comes from the other side. He is a human figure raised up from among his brothers to be the instrument of God's decisive work and to stand in a relationship to him to which no other man is called. The issue is whether in seeing him men see the Father, whether, in mercy and judgment, he *functions* as God, whether he *is* God to and for them.

This way of thinking is both primitive and modern. It is much nearer the Hebrew prophetic tradition before it was influenced by the streams of thought that entered Judaism in the centuries immediately before and after the Christian era. It is also one that comes naturally to an empirical, scientifically trained generation. For we find it much more difficult to make our own the language of agencies or essences behind the scene. Van Peursen neatly illustrates the difference by comparing the way in which medieval man viewed the soul and modern man thinks of the intelligence quotient: 'An I.Q. is nothing in itself; it is not a hidden entity in our heads; it is merely the result of certain tests.'[8] Yet the reality it refers to is no less real for that.

With regard to Christ, the distinction between these ways of representing his divinity, or identity with God, can perhaps be brought out in terms of the human analogy by which in scripture it is most commonly expressed – that of royalty. The mythological and ontological stories of the Incarnation have used the image of the divine visitant, of the king who becomes a commoner. This has presupposed two orders of being. The king is a royal personage, *not* a commoner. He may enter upon the other estate, he may *become* in every respect a commoner, but, like the Japanese emperor, nothing can ever stop him *being* different. He remains a being of completely other blood.

But we can start from quite a different model of royalty – and the opposite extreme to the Japanese is the Swedish. Here the king *is* a commoner, who has a royal office. He embodies royalty,

[8] In Bowden and Richmond, *A Reader in Contemporary Theology*, p.121. For a 'functional' revaluation of 'soul' (which, without the article at least, has unexpectedly become a modern word again) cf. Hick, *Biology and the Soul*.

he exercises it, discloses it, wears it. He is part of the ordinary human scene. He does not have to come on to the scene or make a visitation: he has grown up within it. You may see him on the streets any day. There is nothing different to see – yet you have seen the king.

Similarly, we may view the Christ as a man who embodies divinity, or what the gospels call the kingly rule of God, who exercises it, discloses it, wears it – rather than a divine being who takes on humanity. He is a completely ordinary human being, a 'common man', born and bred, who is nevertheless the carrier of the divine disclosure – all that Barth magnificently expounds as 'the royal man'.[9]

The man who lived God

One cannot say that any one of these ways of representing the presence of God in his Son is *the* biblical one. All are traceable in the New Testament – though the ontological one less than the other two. The difficulty felt by the Fathers in requiring *homoousios* in the Creed – that it was not a biblical word – merely reflects the fact that this whole way of thinking is post-biblical, though none the worse for that. It is perhaps possible to see the beginnings of it in the Epistle to the Hebrews with its Platonic background and in the prologue to the Fourth Gospel (though not I think in its body).[10] But though we may read the Fourth Gospel in particular through the ontological spectacles of the Nicene Fathers, it is, as we have seen, highly mythological in its representation[11] (which is partly why the Gnostics seized on it as 'their' gospel);[12] and indeed its basic categories are often remarkably

[9] Barth, CD IV 2, pp.154–264. Cf. Norman Pittenger, *God in Process*, SCM Press 1967, p.32: 'As a man . . . he wore our humanity as a royal garment.'

[10] I believe the prologue, like the epilogue, to have been added, by the same author, at a later stage. See my article 'The Relation of the Prologue to the Gospel of St John', *New Testament Studies* IX, 1963, pp.120–9; reprinted in *The Authorship and Integrity of the New Testament*, SPCK 1965, pp.61–72.

[11] For examples: John 1.51; 3.13,31f.; 6.38,41f.,51,62; 8.23; 13.1,3,33; 16.28; 17.5,11,24; 20.17.

[12] The other reason, of course, is its appeal to individual inwardness, which soon won it the name of the 'spiritual gospel'.

'functional' precisely at the points where they look most ontological.[13]

This is especially true of the central terms of 'the Father' and 'the Son'.[14] In origin this is parabolic language, drawn, as in the Old Testament,[15] from human relationships: 'Is there a father among you who will offer his son a snake . . . ? How much more will the heavenly father. . . . ?'[16] We are used to thinking of 'king' as a parable for God but surprised to realize that 'father' is also. But Jeremias[17] has convincingly argued that, in the so-called 'Johannine thunderbolt' in the Q tradition,[18] the 'the' in the words 'no one knows the Son except the Father', which makes the saying sound so ontological, is really generic (as in 'the sower went forth to sow'[19] or 'who is the faithful and wise steward?').[20] English idiom requires the indefinite article: 'As only a father knows his son, so only a son knows his father.' The saying is a parable drawn from the intimate knowledge that a father and a son alone have of each other, which Jesus is using to describe the *abba* relationship to God that he is claiming for himself, and ideally for every child of man. This parabolic language is, of course, interpreted and allegorized in the gospel tradition – and correctly so – to designate Jesus in his unique relationship to God. In the same way, in the parable of the Wicked Husbandmen,[21] the son who is heir to the estate, in contrast with the servants, is clearly meant by the evangelists to refer to Jesus. Indeed, I believe it is inconceivable that Jesus himself did not intend it to be taken thus – the story having no point unless in some sense it is a picture of God's dealings with Israel through the prophets and now through

---

[13] This is recognized by van Buren, *The Secular Meaning of the Gospel*, pp.48–50. Cf. the whole section 'A Christology of "Call" and "Response"' (pp.47–55).

[14] For an expansion and closer documentation of the material in the next few pages I must refer again to my essay 'The Use of the Fourth Gospel for Christology Today'.

[15] E.g., Mal. 1.6, 'A son honours his father, and a slave goes in fear of his master. If I am a father, where is the honour due to me? If I am a master, where is the fear due to me?'; 3.17, 'I will spare them as a man spares the son who serves him'; cf. Deut. 1.31; 8.5; II Esd. 1.28f.   [16] Luke 11.11–13.

[17] Joachim Jeremias, *The Central Message of the New Testament*, SCM Press 1965, pp.23–6.

[18] Matt. 11.27 = Luke 10.22.

[19] Mark 4.3 par.   [20] Luke 12.42.   [21] Mark 12.1–12 par.

himself.[22] Thus 'the Father' and 'the Son' come to stand absolutely, in Mark[23] and Q[24] as in John, as proper names for God and Christ. But I believe it is in John that the original parabolic foundation of this language is still most clearly visible beneath the theological surface.

In fact, where it is first introduced, at the climax of the prologue, it is specifically in the form of a simile from human relationships: 'glory *as* of a father's only son' (*doxan hōs monogenous para patros*).[25] There are no articles in the Greek, and yet they are constantly supplied by translators and interpreters. The simile was already a familiar one for describing Israel in relation to God: 'Thy chastisement is upon us as upon a first-born, only son.'[26] I have not been able yet to find a precise parallel for an only son being called his father's 'glory'. But *doxa* (glory) and *eikōn* (image) were used as equivalents in late Judaism to mean 'reflection',[27] as by Paul in I Cor. 11.7: 'Man is the image of God, and the mirror of his glory, whereas woman reflects the glory of man.'[28] The idea behind John 1.14 is almost certainly, therefore, that the incarnate Christ is the exact counterpart or reflection of God, his very spit and image, like an only son of his father.[29] Indeed, the best exegesis of it I know is actually Montefiore's comment on Heb. 1.3: 'As a son may be said to reflect his father's character, so the Son is the refulgence of his Father's glory, and so the exact representation of God's being.'[30] In a letter Dodd has

[22] This is not, of course, to say that there is no pointing up and elaboration in the transmission. Indeed, Dodd's reconstruction of the original form of the story as telling of two servants followed by a son (Mark 12.5 being later expansion to fit the history of Israel) has since been strikingly vindicated by the version in the *Gospel of Thomas* 66.

[23] Mark 13.32.

[24] Matt. 11.27 = Luke 10.22.

[25] John 1.14.　　[26] Ps. Sol. 18.4; cf. 13.8.

[27] Cf. Jervell, op. cit., especially pp.174f., 180, 299f., 325f.; L. H. Brockington, 'The Septuagintal Background to the New Testament Use of *doxa*', in D. E. Nineham (ed.), *Studies in the Gospels: Essays in Memory of R. H. Lightfoot*, Blackwell 1955, pp.7f.; and Martin, op. cit., pp.102–19, and the extensive literature there cited.

[28] Cf. II Cor. 8.23 (NEB marg): 'They are delegates of our congregations; they reflect Christ (*doxa Christou*)'.

[29] Cf. Ecclus. 30.4, where it is said of a son: 'When the father dies, it is as if he were still alive, for he has left a copy of himself behind.'

[30] Montefiore, op. cit., p.35.

said to me: 'I think we should now agree that the true rendering is "a father's only son", the statement being, as in other similar passages, essentially a parable.' But what is introduced in v.14 as a simile from human relationships is already fully allegorized by v.18, especially if *monogenēs theos*, 'the only one who is himself God', is indeed the right reading.

Yet at other points in the gospel the original parabolic basis of the father–son language still shows through. Dodd has argued this of John 5.19f.,[31] where, again transposing from the definite to the indefinite article,[32] we have what he calls the parable of the Apprentice:

> A son can do nothing on his own;
> he does only what he sees his father doing:
> what father does, son does;
> for a father loves his son and shows him all his trade.[33]

There is also what must be recognized[34] as the parable of the Servant and the Son in John 8.35:

> A servant has no permanent standing in the household,[35]
> but a son belongs to it always.[36]

But, above all, nowhere in the New Testament are we closer than in the Fourth Gospel to the fundamental Hebraic use of sonship to designate not an absolute status or title but a functional relationship marked by character. This comes out very plainly in the dialogue that follows in 8.37–47. To be a son is to show the character, to reproduce the thought and action, of another, whether it be Abraham, or the Devil, or God. To claim, therefore, to be a son of God is a sign of fidelity, not of blasphemy as

[31] C. H. Dodd, 'A Hidden Parable in the Fourth Gospel', *More New Testament Studies*, Manchester University Press 1968, pp.30–40.

[32] For a parallel instance in Johannine usage, cf. John 12.24, '*the* grain of wheat remains solitary' where English demands an 'a'.

[33] For the analogy, cf. Phil. 2.22, 'He has been at my side . . . like a son working under his father'.

[34] Dodd, *Historical Tradition in the Fourth Gospel*, pp.380–2.

[35] Cf. John 15.15, 'A servant does not know what his master is about', which is clearly parabolic.

[36] Cf. Luke 15.19,31; and (with John 8.36) Matt. 17.25f.

the Jews suppose. Their Bible, says Jesus, in a passage to which we have already referred, should have taught them better:

> Is it not written in your own Law, 'I said: You are gods'? Those are called gods to whom the word of God was delivered – and Scripture cannot be set aside.[37] Then why do you charge me with blasphemy because I, consecrated and sent into the world by the Father, said 'I am a son of God' (*huios theou*)? If I am not acting as my Father would, do not believe me. But if I am, accept the evidence of my deeds, even if you do not believe me, so that you may recognize and know that the Father is in me, and I in the Father.[38]

This argument, which places Jesus on exactly the same metaphysical level as every other son of God, yet attests him *functionally* unique, because he alone 'always does what is acceptable to him',[39] could scarcely have been invented later, nor even, I believe, in a Greek-thinking milieu.[40] It presupposes a thoroughly Hebraic cast of mind.

All this, of course, is not to say that John has a low view of Jesus' sonship. Nothing could be further from the truth. Yet the highest and most intimate union with God is grounded in his utter faithfulness, his listening obedience. Indeed, Jesus can say in one and the same discourse that 'the Father is in me, and I in the Father' and 'my Father and I are one' *because* 'I am . . . acting as my Father would': 'my deeds done in my Father's name are my credentials'.[41] Again, in a later discourse, he says, 'Anyone who has seen me has seen the Father' because 'I am *not* myself the source of the words I speak to you: it is the Father who dwells in me doing his own work' (14.9f.). Christ is the very 'exegesis' of the Father (1.18), and indeed himself *theos* (1.1,18), because *as a*

---

[37] Not only in Ps. 82.6, which Jesus cites, but in Exod. 21.6; 22.8f., 28, the judge is called 'God'; for he represents him, as Jesus himself is claiming to do.
[38] John 10.34–38.   [39] John 8.29.
[40] Cf. J. H. Bernard, *St John*, International Critical Commentary, T. and T. Clark 1928, *ad loc*: 'The argument is one which would never have occurred to a Greek Christian, and its presence here reveals behind the narrative a genuine reminiscence of one who remembered how Jesus argued with the Rabbis on their own principles.'
[41] John 10.38,30,37,25.

man he is utterly transparent to *another*, who is greater than himself (14.28) and indeed than all (10.29). The paradox is staggering, and it is no wonder that this Christology later fell apart at the seams into a disastrous *antithesis* between moral unity and metaphysical union.[42]

I have deliberately expounded this theme from the Fourth Gospel, where 'sonship' is the dominant Christological category, because it is usually seen as the main support of the ontological construction and because no one could accuse John of not having a high Christology. But it is the same conception of filial obedience in terms of which the Synoptists represent Jesus as having his call.

The voice he hears at his baptism[43] (itself undertaken in response to the Baptist's summons to a purified Israel) is in terms of the relationship of sonship and servanthood prefigured in the Old Testament.[44] The temptations that follow reveal this to be understood in the light of the wilderness call of Israel to be God's son.[45] In each case the answer given by Jesus is a quotation from Deuteronomy and represents the faithful response which the old Israel had refused. '*If* you are the son of God,' says Satan, 'prove it by putting God to the test as Israel did: presume upon it and force God's hand.' 'No,' replies Jesus, 'sonship is to be proved by filial trust and obedience, for that is the only meaning, and therefore the only verification, of the relationship.' There is no suggestion that the essence of divine sonship is a second superhuman nature that can do and say and know things which the ordinary sons of men

---

[42] One of the few in the later history of Christology to grasp this paradox was characteristically Luther, who wrote of Christ that he 'accords everything to the Father as author; whatever he does or says, he always refers to the authorship of the Father: "As he commands, I do"; "What I hear from him, I say." He always attributes his divinity to the Father. . . . Thus, when I look upon his words, his blood, his tears, I see through him himself, and in him himself, into the will of the Father' (WA 40/II.254f.). In the sentences I have omitted, Luther expresses his preference for this functional way of putting the unity of Christ with the Father over the subsequent talk of the relation of the persons of the Trinity. The passage is quoted by Gogarten, op. cit., p.284, who himself writes: 'This constant repetition of "not from himself" has not only a negative, but above all an extraordinarily positive sense. One can perhaps express this best by saying that Jesus possesses the whole existence which God has given him in being sent by God' (p.70).
[43] Mark 1.11 par.; cf. John 1.34.   [44] Ps. 2.7 and perhaps Isa. 42.1 and 44.2.
[45] For a fuller exposition of this see my article 'The Temptations', *Twelve New Testament Studies*, pp.53–60.

cannot. Quite the reverse. The only power and knowledge are those that come from the intimate dependence on the Father in which the true son lives. As Zahrnt has well put it:

> The understanding of Jesus as Son of God involves nothing 'suprahistorical', 'supernatural', or even unnatural. . . . Jesus is the Son of God not through a special act of procreation, and thus through a special physical quality, but through his special attitude within history. Jesus Christ is the Son because he alone allows God really to be his Father.[46]

This conception of the one who allows God to show through, who is transparent to source and thus speaks of God because he does not speak of himself, is reflected in all Jesus is and does in the gospels. He is sensed to speak 'with authority', and 'not as the scribes',[47] because he has been 'there'. *His* words and deeds come from source, from the ground of being (*ex-ousia*). He is 'the man who lived God',[48] who dared to stand *in loco dei*, as his 'representative'.

The significance of this last, very pregnant category, has been brilliantly worked out by Dorothee Sölle in her book *Christ the Representative*,[49] which has the rare freshness in this field of a genuinely lay contribution. And it is a category which has the advantage of being as nearly grounded in history as we are likely to find. Ernst Fuchs sums up the results of the 'new quest' of the historical Jesus in these words: '[Jesus'] conduct is neither that of a prophet nor of a teacher of wisdom, but of a man who dares to act in God's stead.'[50] What Jesus claimed for himself in the way of titles – Son of God, Christ, Son of Man – is notoriously uncertain and much disputed.[51] He may indeed more truly be represented

---

[46] Zahrnt, *The Historical Jesus*, p.142. [47] Mark 1.22 par.
[48] The title of an article in *The Times*, 19 December 1970, by Bishop F. R. Barry, who attributes it to Austin Farrer.
[49] Especially Part 3, pp.99–152.
[50] Ernst Fuchs, *Studies of the Historical Jesus*, SCM Press 1964, p.22; cf. Brown, *Jesus, God and Man*, pp.96–8.
[51] Cf. among many others: Vincent Taylor, *The Names of Jesus*, Macmillan 1953; Cullmann, op. cit.; Hahn, op. cit.; Fuller, op. cit; Hans Conzelmann, *An Outline of the Theology of the New Testament*, SCM Press 1969, pp.127–39; Jeremias, *New Testament Theology* I, pp.257–76. I would agree with I. Howard Marshall, 'The Divine Sonship of Jesus', *Interpretation* XXI, January 1967, pp.

as claiming nothing for himself – but everything for what God was doing through him. He was condemned for blasphemy,[52] for 'making himself God'[53] – not, however, as far as we can now tell, for arrogating *to himself* the name of God,[54] but precisely for speaking without so much as a 'Thus saith the Lord'. As Bornkamm puts it:

> The reality of God and the authority of his will are always directly present, and are fulfilled in him. There is nothing in contemporary Judaism which corresponds to the immediacy with which he teaches.[55]

This is epitomized in his characteristic address 'Amen, I say to you' which, it has been well remarked, contains 'the whole of Christology *in nuce*'.[56] Citing this judgment, Fuller comments:

> Whereas the Jew concluded his prayer to God with Amen, thus expressing his faith that God would act, Jesus *prefaces* his words with an 'Amen', thus denoting that prior to his utterance there is his total engagement to the act of God, of which his words thus become the channel.[57]

In overruling and re-editing the law (with the astonishing contrast: 'You have heard that it was said *to* them [i.e. by God] . . . but I say to you'),[58] in forgiving sins,[59] in quelling the spirits and

---

87–103, that 'sonship is the supreme category of interpretation of the person of Jesus in the Gospels; and messiahship occupies a subordinate place' (p.99).

[52] Mark 14.63f. par.; John 19.7.   [53] John 10.33–36; cf. 5.18.

[54] Even in Mark 14.61f. I believe that the reply to the question 'Are you the Son of the Blessed One?' is originally more likely to have been 'You have said that I am'. See my *Jesus and his Coming*, pp.47–50. In the Matthean and Lukan parallels and in the reply to Pilate in all four gospels the answer is ambiguous.

[55] Günther Bornkamm, *Jesus of Nazareth*, Hodder and Stoughton 1960, p.57.

[56] H. Schlier, '*Amen*', in Kittel, TDNT I, p.338.

[57] R. H. Fuller, *The New Testament in Current Study*, SCM Press 1962, p.43.

[58] Matt. 5.21–48. Cf. Jeremias, op. cit. I, p.251: 'We may take it as quite certain . . . that we are hearing the words of Jesus himself . . . because this has neither Jewish nor early Christian parallels.' He compares Matt. 7.24–27 = Luke 6.47–49, 'the person who hears *my* words', with the contemporary Jewish saying, 'the person who hears the words of the *Torah* and does good works builds on firm ground'; and Mark 9.37, 'whoever receives me, receives not me but him who sent me', with 'the one who receives the scribes is like the one who receives the *shekinah*', adding: 'The emphatic *ego* indicates that the person who uses it is God's representative' (p.254).   [59] Mark 2.1–12 par.

the powers of nature,[60] he steps, in the eyes of his contemporaries, into the space reserved for God. He refuses to 'make room' for God. He invites men to come to him for life and rest – but always to himself as God's representative.[61] He says that men's attitude to him will decide God's attitude to them.[62] In his parables he justifies *his* conduct by the way *God* acts.[63] Indeed, he is there to be 'the parable of God'.[64] Just as 'the plot of the parables is secular; "God" is not one of their *dramatis personae*',[65] so Jesus speaks in parables because his whole life is to be the *persona* of God – to 'play' God in the human drama. 'Am I in the place of God?', asked Joseph.[66] No Jew could contemplate an affirmative to that question. But that is the question which the gospels present Jesus first as facing as an incredible possibility ('*If* you are the Son of God . . .') and then as *living out* the answer, Yes. All the talk about it may be secondary, but I believe it is impossible to make sense of the gospels, any of the gospels, without the presupposition that he went about, and was condemned for, acting as though he were God's vicegerent. 'Take away every hint of this,' as Gerald Downing has said, 'and you are left with a blank.'[67]

This is not, as Sölle so well distinguishes, a vocation to usurp or replace God – Jesus' utter dependence on the Father remains unquestioned,[68] and nowhere more than in the Fourth Gospel.[69] It is the vocation to represent him, the fearful calling to play God, to live God, to *be* him to men. And it is the more fearful because this does not mean what we mean by 'playing God', lording it

---

[60] Mark 1.21–27 par. and Mark 4.36–41. Both pose the question 'Who can do this?', which is answered in Ps. 65.7 (Heb.): God.

[61] Matt. 11.28–30; cf. Exod. 33.14; Ecclus. 51.23–27.

[62] Mark 8.38 par.; Matt. 10.33 = Luke 12.9; cf. John 14.21; 15.23.

[63] Jeremias, op. cit., p.254, instances the three parables of the lost things (Luke 15) and those of the generous employer (Matt. 20.1–15) and the two men at prayer (Luke 18.9–14), commenting again: 'He acts so to speak as God's representative'; cf. Eduard Schweizer, *Jesus*, SCM Press 1971, pp.28–30.

[64] Keck, op. cit., p.243–9.   [65] Ibid., p.243.   [66] Gen. 50.19.

[67] Downing, op. cit., p.45.   [68] E.g. Mark 14.36 par.

[69] For this emphasis, cf. J. E. Davey, *The Jesus of St John*, Lutterworth Press 1958. The essential difference between representation and replacement is well brought out in Acts 12.22f.: ' "It is a god speaking, not a man!" Instantly an angel of the Lord struck him down, because he had usurped the honour due to God.' Despite the Jews' failure to distinguish (John 5.18; 10.33), Jesus is never 'the voice of God and *not* a man'.

over others,[70] manipulating their lives. Precisely the opposite; it means to identify with them in suffering, serving love. It is to place oneself completely at their disposal – like the son in the parable, again, of the Wicked Husbandmen in whom all the patrimony is vested, and who therefore more than any other invites elimination: for he alone stands between men and God.[71] As John interprets it, there is no need to look beyond him: he who has seen him has seen the Father.[72] Or, as Bornkamm puts it, summarizing the Synoptic evidence. 'To make the reality of God present: this is the essential mystery of Jesus.'[73]

This is the 'high' language of verbs in which the New Testament speaks. The Father and Son are one, but not because the Son is more than a man. The Son speaks true of God, he is the Word of God, the embodiment of God – in fact he *is* God for us – without ever ceasing to be completely and totally a man. In Bonhoeffer's words, to say 'This man is God' does not 'add anything to his manhood':[74]

> One does not first look at a human nature and then beyond to a divine nature. One looks at the whole historical man Jesus and says of him, 'He is God'.[75]

Yet there is something in all of us, brought up in the way we have been, that is not content with this 'is'. Is this really what the *homoousios* debate was all about? And, of course, it was not. It was about Jesus being God in a much more literal, metaphysical sense. The church was not content with this 'primitive' functional conception of sonship, which it labelled 'adoptionism', and it went on

---

[70] Mark 10.42–45 par.   [71] Mark 12.6f. par.   [72] John 14.8–10.
[73] Bornkamm, op. cit., p.62.   [74] Bonhoeffer, *Christology*, p.107.
[75] Ibid., p.108. I have reversed the order of the two sentences in this quotation. At this point, as he acknowledges (p.81), he is following Luther, whom Gogarten (op. cit., p.290) also quotes as saying that belief in Christ is 'not to believe that Christ is a person who is God and man, for that is of no help to anybody; but that this person is Christ' (WA 17/I. 255.1). There is a strongly existentialist note in Luther's 'is'. Indeed, Tillich describes him as using the 'method of correlation' he himself advocated, quoting his remark; 'As somebody is in himself, so God is to him' (Paul Tillich, *A History of Christian Thought*, ed. C. E. Braaten, SCM Press 1968, p.249). With this should be compared the famous remark of Melanchthon: 'To know Christ is to know his benefits, not, as the schoolmen teach, to contemplate his natures and the modes of his incarnation' (*Loci Communes*, Preface).

to seek to re-express the truth of the identity of the Son with the Father in terms first of mythology and then of ontology, telling the story of Jesus as a pre-existent heavenly being who was 'with God' and who 'was' God in a way that no ordinary human being could be. But this, though it appears to us to be higher doctrine, is in fact only translation – translation into terms which enabled men to 'place' the mystery of the Christ where they located what to them was most real.

Both the mythological and the ontological stories use what I have called the supranaturalistic projection. In other words, they locate the most real in another realm above or beyond this world, from which it comes into this world, impinging upon it from without. The source, the origin, the *patris* of the Christ, is therefore elsewhere. This is in contrast to the Jewish prophetic way of thinking, which is much nearer the modern functional. Here the origin of the Christ is within Israel, the hope of every Jewish mother being that she might be the mother of the Messiah. He would be raised like any other boy, yet he would be the Lord's anointed, his chosen Son. This was not in any way to deny the working of God – absolutely the contrary: all was of God. Yet the way God was conceived as working was through history, the history which he had been guiding, correcting, drawing with the bands of his love, since the foundation of the world. The locus of reality, the place where his presence was to be sensed and his will responded to, was events; not beyond history but the process itself shot through with, and seen as, the meaning of God. And the clue to this meaning was the mystery of the Christ, the Logos, secretly at work within it, coming out rather than coming in.

The different representations are simply different ways of choosing expressing reality. We must choose whatever means most to us. In former times the mythological and the ontological made the mystery of the Christ, as they made the mystery of God, most real. Today, as I have said, the projection with which they work has, for very many at any rate, a displacement effect, actually making God less real rather than more real. And the same is true of Christology. The Christ becomes evacuated of reality – a remote, unreal, docetic figure, who can be God for us only at the expense of being a genuine human being. The mythology of the pre-existent person and the metaphysic of the two natures has very limited cash-value in our world – though their devotional and 'antique' value (as part of the 'poetry' of the old city) are not to be underestimated or despised. Psychologically, as Jung has shown, they can still be very potent. And, of course, there are vast numbers who still *prefer* their religion in the Authorized Version.

But what are we to put in the place of this currency for those for whom it has lost its purchasing power? Clearly it is not a question of digging up some yet more ancient coinage, with a different image and superscription, in characters of Hebrew, rather than Greek or Latin. If I have been appealing to an earlier way of putting things which I believe to be basic to both the Old and the New Testaments, it is not because we can simply make that way our own today. I have gone back to it partly because, as a biblical scholar, I am concerned to show that what may *appear* to be a reductionist Christology is in fact not so, and partly because this pattern of thinking, unlike the other two, is not *tied* to the supranaturalist projection (though it *can* be expressed in terms of it, as God from on high lighting upon and raising up a man). And this freedom is surely a strength today when that projection is so counter-productive of reality. But two things remain to be done. One is to defend it against the inadequacies which were sensed in it and which led to its being left behind by the church as a way of expressing its central conviction. And the second is to begin to show how it could be integrated into a contemporary, secular, scientific cosmology.

The fear and failure of adoptionism

The first task is simpler. The main objection has just been indicated – that it is mere 'adoptionism' – God from outside as it were 'taking up with' a man. This was something of which the Fathers had great fear and it is as well that we should expose it for ourselves, too. It lies at the root of why the *homoousios* was re-iterated at Chalcedon. Originally at Nicaea it had been put in to

rule out the Arian belief in a Christ who was *neither* fully human
nor fully divine but a sort of angelic compromise. It is fairly safe
to say that no one today consciously wishes to assert this of Jesus,
however much popular presentations of him as a kind of magic-
man may often imply it. Arianism as a considered theological
option is not a serious contemporary temptation. Those who do
not want him as God do not want him as an angel either. But the
homoousios was retained in the Chalcedonian Definition against
those 'who shamelessly pretend that he who was born of the holy
Mary was a *mere* man' (*psilon anthrōpon*). This phrase, though
vigorously denied by Nestorius against whom it was aimed,[76]
represented one of the persistent fears of the Cyrilline school. But
they had a tendency to smell out denial of divinity (a man *and
nothing else*) whenever insistence was laid on the fact that Jesus was
completely human, like everyone else.[77] (This reaction is not dead
yet. It couches in the ambiguity of the phrase 'a purely human
Christ'.) Nevertheless, the reaffirmation of divine substance in
Jesus stood against the view that he was just a God-like man, who
speaks to us only of man and man's God-consciousness. For on this
view there is no identity with the divine action: Jesus is not God at
work, God is not implicated in what he says and does. The
homoousios was there to assert the *vere deus*.

But this, as I hope I have sufficiently indicated, I have no concern to deny. I am wishing to affirm Jesus as the Son of God as the
New Testament speaks of him, as the one who was called at his
baptism and vindicated at his resurrection to *be* God's decisive
word to men, the embodiment of his nature and the enactment of
his will. The sole question is *how* to express this identity of the
divine with the human. Is it effected by God's joining a second
(human) nature to his own, or is it by his using, acting through, a
man? Is it, in a phrase, by taking manhood or by taking a man?

This was ultimately what divided the Alexandrian from the
Antiochene approaches to Christology. The position of the
latter is well stated by Theodore of Mopsuestia in his *Commentary on the Nicene Creed*:

[76] Cf. the references in Grillmeier, op. cit., p.319, n.3.
[77] Ibid., pp.254f.

In this they [our blessed Fathers] showed us the gift of his grace which they saw in the human race, and through which he assumed a man from us, was in him and dwelt in him, and they taught us that he endured and bore all according to human nature so that we might understand that he was not a man in appearance only, but that he was a real man;[78]

or by the *Tome* of the Council of Constantinople in 381 (reflecting the views of Diodore of Tarsus):

For the salvation of us men he took from us a complete man and dwelt in him.[79]

But this approach, strong though it was on the humanity of Christ, was full of danger to the Alexandrians. It seemed to smack of adoptionism and to threaten what Barth was to call the 'freedom' of God: it looked as if God were being made dependent on man. But let Cyril speak for himself:

It was not an ordinary man, who was first born of the holy Virgin, and upon whom afterwards the Word descended, but himself, united to humanity from the womb itself, is said to have undergone fleshly birth, as making his own the birth of his own flesh.[80]

To put it crudely, Jesus was not a divine 'pick up'. God did not hang around until someone appeared whom he could use and whom he *then* adopted as his instrument and agent. Adoptionism is objectionable because it derogates from the divine initiative. The Antiochenes, needless to say, denied this temporal succession, as if the Incarnation were in any respect an afterthought on God's part. They were as insistent as the others that the birth of Jesus was an act of the divine initiative from the moment of his conception (they, too, thought of him as a special creation through the virgin Mary). It was merely a question of *how* God was understood as functioning. The great fear of men like Athanasius and Cyril was that if you said that the Logos united himself to a

---

[78] *Comm. in Symb. Nic.* 7; ed. A. Mingana, Woodbrooke Studies V, Cambridge University Press 1932, p.73.
[79] Quoted by Grillmeier, op. cit., p.268.   [80] *Ep. Nest.* II.

man this was not incarnation but inspiration.[81] And so they insisted
that 'the Word became man and and did not come into a man',[82]
opposing the 'flesh-bearing God' (*theos sarkophoros*) to a 'God-
bearing man' (*anthrōpos theophoros*). But by so doing they erected
a false antithesis, which led to a double failure. They themselves,
for all their intention to the contrary, failed to do real justice to the
humanity of Christ. And they were prevented from understanding
that men like Theodore and Nestorius really were arguing (as we
can now see) for a genuine and deeply *personal* union of God and
man in Christ – however inadequate their vocabulary and however
distorted their problem in advance by having, as we said earlier,
to place two individual entities on one spot.

Translating into modern terms their concern for a union that
depended on moral volition rather than automatic substance,
Pittenger puts it like this:

> The *most complete*, the *fullest*, the *most organic and integrated*
> union of Godhead and manhood which is conceivable is
> precisely one in which by gracious indwelling of God in man
> and by manhood's free response in surrender and love, there
> is established a relationship which is neither accidental nor
> incidental, on the one hand, nor mechanical and physical on the
> other; but a full, free, gracious unity of the two in Jesus Christ,
> who is both the farthest reach of God the Word into the life of
> man and also (and by consequence) the richest response of man
> to God.[83]

There is no contradiction between a man 'living' God and God
'living' a man. For, as Nestorius put it, in words that St John would
have approved, to have 'the *prosōpon* of God' (or, as we should
say, to be the personal expression of God) 'is to will what God
wills, whose *prosōpon* he has'.[84] And for that, to be fully and

[81] Cf. the statement of Newman, p.105 above.

[82] Athanasius, *Or. contra Ar.* 3.30; Cyril, *Or. ad Dominas* 31; cf. Apollinarius, in
Ps-Felix, *frag.* 186 (Lietzmann, *Apollinaris*, p.318).

[83] Pittenger, *The Word Incarnate*, p.188.

[84] *The Bazaar of Heracleides*, p.592; quoted by R. A. Norris in his important
essay, 'The Image of God and the Prosopic Union in Nestorius' *Bazaar of Hera-
clides*', in Norris (ed.), *Lux in Lumine*, pp.46–61.

independently a man is an essential qualification, not a dis-
qualification.

But, deep down, the horror felt by Cyril that God should have
used or assumed a 'common man' (*anthrōpos koinos*) born in the
natural process of things – rather than a special creation endowed
with 'his own flesh' – reflects a view (shared in different degrees
by both sides) that the divine initiative must come as an external
exception to, rather than the supreme exemplification of, the
created order. Athanasius had already distorted the issue by asking,
'Is Jesus Christ a man like all other men, or is he God bearing
flesh?'[85] Consequently those who came later were confronted
with the false disjunction of God taking the initiative *or* accepting
a man who would have been born 'anyhow'.

Clearly the only view the biblical writers are prepared to consider
is that the Incarnation realizes a purpose initiated by God from start
to finish. As Paul van Buren paraphrases it in biblical terminology,

> Yahweh determined in his heart of hearts upon having his
> faithful son, Jesus, and through him a faithful creation. He
> created this world and called his people Israel for this purpose.
> He realized this purpose concretely in history when he called
> this man into a role in history upon which he had decided 'before
> the foundation of the world'.[86]
>
> The apostolic witness will not allow us to say of this decision
> that 'there was a time when it was not'.[87]

Yet this way of putting it is entirely compatible with Jesus
being in every way 'a man', a slow product of the species *homo
sapiens*, whom God 'raised up' through the normal processes of
heredity and environment and who would have existed 'anyhow',
if that word is understood, as it should be, to mean 'with God'
rather than 'apart from God'. Far from being either an afterthought
or an *ad hoc* creation, the Christ is prepared for and elected from a
progeny as countless as the sands of the sea.[88] He is indeed
selected, 'taken from among men', to be 'their representative
before God'. The fear of the Fathers, powerfully reiterated by

[85] *Or. contr. Ar.* 3.51.   [86] Van Buren, op. cit., pp.52f.
[87] Ibid., p.51.   [88] Cf. Gen. 22.27 and Gal. 3.

Barth, against which they both thought it necessary to insist on the doctrine that Jesus was not '*a* man', was to suppose that he existed or might have existed independently of God's purpose or Logos. But for the biblical writers, while he is totally human and therefore as independent of God as any other man, his whole life – and all that leads up to it and flows from it – is seen as the climax and fulfilment of a divine process going back to the beginning. His entire being is shaped and constituted by the destiny to be God's true man, the Son of his love, the very reflection and image of his person.[89]

Yet there has been a persistent tendency in the history of Christian doctrine – stretching again from the Fathers to Karl Barth – to assume that Jesus could not be *both* a genuine product of the process *and* the Word of God to it.[90] For one of the effects of

[89] Barth, as we have seen, does not deny Jesus' individuality, but he still believes it necessary to retain the doctrine of *anhypostasia* to guard against his being one man among many whom God could have taken: 'For this would necessarily mean either that the Son of God, surrendering His own existence as such, had changed Himself into this man, and was therefore no longer the Son of God . . . or that He did not exist as One, but in a duality, as the Son of God maintaining his own existence, and somewhere and somehow alongside this individual man. And if, as is not possible, we could and should accept one of these absurd alternatives, what would happen to all other men, side by side with the one man who is the Son of God in one or other of these curious senses? What significance could His existence, with its special determination, have for others? How far could God, in and with the adoption of this one man to unity with himself, adopt them all? How far could the one Son of God not be merely *a* son of man but *the* Son of Man, the man who could represent them all, who could plead with God for them all and with them all for God?' (CD IV 2, p.48).

But it is necessary to sift the truth from the error in this. Clearly, as we have insisted, it is essential to question the idea of Jesus' independent existence *if by that is implied* that he existed independently of the divine purpose. As van Buren paraphrases Barth's meaning, 'Jesus was indeed a man as we are men, but the fact that he existed as a man was totally dependent on the fact that God the Word, the eternal Logos, had called him into being to be the historical bearer of this divine Word' (op. cit., p.31). But this does not mean that he could not also be 'taken' out of countless millions. For he is elected not for exclusive privilege but for representative service. And when Barth says that the only way such a man could be the Son of God is by the 'absurd alternative' of the conversion of the Godhead into flesh or uneasy co-existence, we are bound to reply that, for once, Barth is not treating the question with sufficient theological seriousness. The Epistle to the Hebrews at any rate found it not impossible to see him as *both* 'Son' *and* in *every* sense of the word 'a man', and it is up to theologians to wrestle with the problem without discarding one of the factors in advance.

[90] Note the antitheses in Barth's language (italics mine): 'The existence of this man . . . is *not* the consequence of the series . . . but . . . the work of a new act of

the supranaturalist projection, which locates God outside the process and over against it, has been to confirm the impression that nothing that does not come into it from without can really express his initiative.

Emergent humanity and expressive deity

This leads us into the second question, of how we may today see the functional language of the Bible as part of a theology of the evolutionary and historical process which does justice to modern insights. I do not propose to develop this at length, because the lines of the sort of solution I would favour (though I do not pretend to follow all they say) have already been indicated by those who stand within the tradition of process philosophy, notably by Norman Pittenger whose study, *The Word Incarnate*, seems to me one of the great books in this field, supplemented more recently by his *Christology Reconsidered*.[91] And since his

God' (CD IV 2, p.37); 'Mankind itself has *not* produced Jesus Christ as the realization of one of its possibilities. . . . It was *not* itself the active subject in His becoming. . . . It was *only* there when He became' (p.45); 'As man He is also the creature of God. But even His existence as a creature is from *no* other source. . . . He derives *entirely* from His divine origin '(pp.90f.).

[91] Cf. also W. R. Matthews, *The Problem of Christ in the Twentieth Century*, pp.62–73; Rahner, 'Current Problems in Christology', *Theological Investigations* I, pp.164–7; id., 'Christology Within an Evolutionary View of the World', *Theological Investigations* V, pp.157–92; Dyson, *Who is Jesus Christ?*, ch.7; P. N. Hamilton, *The Living God and the Modern World*, Hodder and Stoughton 1967, chs. 6 and 7, and 'Some Proposals for a Modern Christology' in *Christ for Us Today*, ch.10; J. E. Barnhart, 'Incarnation and Process Philosophy', *Religious Studies* II, April 1967, pp.225–32; Schubert M. Ogden, *The Reality of God*, SCM Press 1967, especially chs. 6 and 7; D. Griffin, 'Schubert Ogden's Christology and the Possibilities of Process Philosophy', *The Christian Scholar* L, Fall 1967, pp.290–303; Daniel Day Williams, *The Spirit and the Forms of Love*, Nisbet 1968, especially chs. 8 and 9; D. A. Pailin, 'The Incarnation as a Continuing Reality', *Religious Studies* VI, December 1970, pp.303–27; J. B. Cobb, 'A Whiteheadian Christology', in D. Brown, R. E. James and G. Reeves (ed.), *Process Philosophy and Christian Thought*, Bobbs–Merrill, Indianapolis and New York 1971; L. S. Ford, 'The Resurrection as the Emergence of the Body of Christ', *Religion in Life* 42, 1973 (forthcoming).

For the assessment of a notable attempt of a previous generation to interpret the Incarnation in terms of a philosophy of organism, L. S. Thornton, *The Incarnate Lord*, Longmans 1938, see: Baillie, *God was in Christ*, pp.91–3; Smedes, *The Incarnation: Trends in Modern Anglican Thought*, pp.39–48; Pittenger, *The Word Incarnate*, pp.107–9. All agree in concluding that, in order to safeguard Christ's uniqueness, Thornton has postulated of him a humanity which turns out to be essentially different from ours.

earlier book was written, there is all the illumination shed by the publication of Teilhard de Chardin's writings, with their vision of Christification as the crown and climax of what Barry Wood, in his engaging book *The Magnificent Frolic*, has called this 'incarnating universe'. Indeed, as John Macquarrie has said, we may even be able to make use again of the old language of the two 'natures' of God and man if we remember that *in each case* the root meaning of *phy* in *physis* (nature) is 'emerging'.[92]

In my own *Exploration into God* I tried to indicate a perspective from which we might more easily see how the ultimate meaning of the process – the clue to the universe as personal – could be embodied in a man born and bred and evolved from within it, a product of it rather than an invader of it. In what I called the 'panentheistic' projection, love comes out not into, through not down. The 'seed' of the Logos (to use the old phrase) was there from the beginning; it is thrown up by the process, it surfaces, breaks out, expresses itself. There is eruption rather than inruption. The Incarnation does not mean insertion into the living stream, an intervention by God in the form of a man, but the embodiment, the realization of God in this man. The Word is seen, as in the Johannine prologue, as moulding the process from the beginning, drawing it onwards and upwards like light, immanent in it yet constantly transcending it, rather than as something transcendent that *became* immanent. There is a divine necessity about the flowering, a waiting to take flesh, to blossom and burst. Yet everything is dependent upon the human response. God, in Whitehead's phrase, is the chief cause, not the only cause. There is no overriding or overruling. Yet equally it is not simply a case of God waiting on the sidelines for an adequate man to turn up. The Christ has been in the process – yes, in process – from the start, and in this sense we may speak of the 'eternal generation of the Son'. His birth in Jesus is indeed a decisive moment – yet it is not sudden or discontinuous, incidental or accidental, any more than that of the first man. It is a new development in man, what Paul, as we have seen, signalizes as the difference between living

[92] John Macquarrie, *Principles of Christian Theology*, SCM Press 1966, pp. 273–5.

soul and life-giving spirit, between a humanity that can be understood within psychological categories and one which can only be
described in terms of spirit.[93] In the 'ascent towards the personal'
there is a breakthrough of cosmic consciousness, a 'moment' of
Christification which is still compatible with the continuities and
ambiguities of 'a universe in which', to quote Teilhard de
Chardin, 'nothing is produced and in which nothing appears
except by way of birth'.[94]

For Teilhard, Christ occupies the same place in the cosmic
process as for Jung he does in the psychic.[95] For Jung, the archetype of the self takes countless forms, images, symbols. These
'represent the prototypes of the Christ-figure that was slumbering
in man's unconscious and were then called awake by his actual
appearance in history'.[96] Hence Jesus is immediately interpreted
in terms of them (the stone and the fish are the best-known
examples): he is assimilated to the existing psychic matrix. But he
also gives the Christ-figure a new delineation, a new realization
in terms not of some inanimate or animal form, but of personal
obedience – 'humanly', as Ignatius put it,[97] 'as in a son', in Theodore's phrase.[98] Yet even he has to be perfected, has to achieve
completion, only through suffering and death.[99] Similarly, for
Teilhard, Christ is a decisive event in the maturation of the human
spirit and the integration of the universe out of increasing com-
plexification – the totally human figure around whom 'the perfect man', 'mature manhood'[100] comes, through sacrifice, to
identity and fulfilment.

It is vital to insist that, because in this projection the process is

---

[93] I Cor. 15.44–49.
    [94] Pierre Teilhard de Chardin, *Le coeur de la matière*, Paris 1950, p.30; quoted by
Dyson, op. cit., p.115.
    [95] I owe this point to my former pupil Kevin Maguire. Cf. Bernard Towers,
'Jung and Teilhard', in his *Concerning Teilhard and Other Writings on Science and
Religion*, Collins 1969, pp.54–64. But he does not mention Christology.
    [96] Jung, *Aion*, p.189.   [97] *Anthrōpinōs*, Ignatius, *ad Eph.* 19.3.
    [98] *Hōs en huiō(i)*; Theodore, *De Incarn.* 7; ed. H. B. Swete, *Theodore of Mopsu-
estia on the Minor Epistles of St Paul* II, Cambridge University Press 1882, p.296.
    [99] Cf. Jung, op. cit., p.69: 'The individual may strive after perfection (Matt.
5.48), but must suffer from the opposite of his intentions for the sake of his
completeness (Rom. 7.21). The Christ image fully corresponds to this situation:
Christ is the perfect man who is crucified.'   [100] Eph. 4.13.

not viewed supranaturalistically, it does not follow that God is discounted or that the Christ-event is seen (as Moule expresses the common fear) as 'simply "emerging" as by evolution' or as the result of 'human striving'. Indeed, I would borrow his own description of what he believes to be the New Testament position: it is 'given' – yet 'from within'.[101] *All* is of grace – yet *all* is of nature. Even the *physis* (nature) is the expression of *charis* (grace). And it is this claim that the Incarnation is the fruit of what Teilhard called a 'personalizing' purpose which, I believe we must recognize, lay behind the language on which the Antiochene theologians insisted for describing the relation of Christ to God.

When Theodore said that the union was not by 'being' (*ousia*) but by 'good pleasure' (*eudokia*),[102] it appeared to the Alexandrians that he was merely denying hypostatic, ontological union; and Nestorius' term *synapheia*[103] was seen as implying no more than moral affinity or mechanical conjunction. But the real point was that Christ's distinctiveness and indeed uniqueness depends on something more than nature. For, as Greer has said in interpretation of Theodore, '*ousia* is common to all, in that God is the ground of being for all creation. But God dwells in different men in different degrees by good pleasure.'[104] The decisive difference in Christ's case is that it was 'as in a son', and that the indwelling was by personal union and not just by intermittent grace. But by sticking to the biblical category of 'good-pleasure' (for which Raven suggests the modern equivalent might be 'love in action'), Theodore grounds the Incarnation in the personal purpose of God without sacrificing either the distinctiveness of Christ or his continuity with other men. He would have agreed with Augustine

---

[101] Moule, 'The Manhood of Jesus in the New Testament', *Christ, Faith and History*, p.107.

[102] Migne, PG vol. 66, 973.

[103] Defined by Pittenger, *Christology Reconsidered*, p.13, as 'intimate co-operative union in moral terms'.

[104] Greer, *Theodore of Mopsuestia*, p.57. On this most attractive patristic theologian cf. also Raven, *Apollinarianism*, ch.7, 'The Answer to Apollinarius'; F. A. Sullivan, *The Christology of Theodore of Mopsuestia*, Rome 1956; Norris, *Manhood and Christ: A Study of the Christology of Theodore*; Grillmeier, op. cit., pp.338–60. Theodore was not condemned for more than a century after his death, at the Fifth Ecumenical Council in 553, and that as an act of revenge by the Alexandrians for the condemnation of Origen ten years earlier.

when he boldly said, 'Every man, from the commencement of his
faith, becomes a Christian by the same grace by which *that* man
from his formation became Christ'.[105]

In similar vein the heretic Nestorius (whom we can now see to
have been no 'Nestorian') is defended by the Jesuit Grillmeier:

> It is because the very act of taking a human nature comes
> from above that Nestorius lays so much stress on its freedom
> and character of grace. The Incarnation is not a necessary natural
> fact, a *henōsis kata physin*, but a free disposal by the divine
> dispensation (*oikonomia*). Christ is therefore a *henōsis kat'*
> *oikonomian* or *kat' eudokian*, or *kata charin*. ... [These expressions]
> are not meant to loosen the unity in Christ; they merely stress
> the divine freedom in the work of the Incarnation.[106]

Yet this 'divine freedom' neither denies nor is denied by the
'chance' and 'necessity' of the cosmic process leading up to man.
There is no either/or here. Pittenger puts it thus:

> Emergent humanity is itself the instrument for expressive
> Deity; the Word is made flesh, in one of our own kind, our
> Brother, without over-riding or denying the humanity which
> is ours, but rather crowning and completing all that is implicit
> in humanity from its very beginning. The divine intention ... is
> ... 'enmanned' among us.[107]

Perhaps the contrast between the kind of perspective for which
I have been arguing and that of the mythological and ontological
representations of reality can best be brought out in relation to the
motif of *kenōsis* and *plērōsis*, self-emptying and fulfilment. The

---

[105] *De praedest. sanct.* 1.15; quoted by Baillie, op. cit., p.118, whose own
Christology also centres in this 'paradox of grace'.

[106] Grillmeier, op. cit., p.447. For his overall assessment of Nestorius cf. pp.
372–99; 433–52; 496–505. Cf. earlier J. F. Bethune-Baker, *Nestorius and his
Teaching*, Cambridge University Press 1908; F. Loofs, *Nestorius and his Place in
the History of Christian Doctrine*, Cambridge University Press 1914; and Driver
and Hodgson, *The Bazaar of Heracleides*.

[107] Pittenger, *The Word Incarnate*, p.131. Cf. p.168: 'It should be carefully
noted that the view which we have advocated does not *confuse* the divine and the
human, neither is it immanentist in tendency. It is *incarnational* in outlook, for it
safeguards the transcendence of deity while at the same time it insists on the continuous divine activity in the creation through the Word.'

development of kenotic Christologies in the latter half of the nineteenth century,[108] first in Germany[109] and later in England[110] and Russia,[111] was a response to the felt inadequacies of the static doctrine of the two natures with its presupposition of divine immutability and impassibility (still retained by such men as Newman and Liddon). Under the impact of historical studies and evolutionary theories, kenoticism performed a valuable function as 'a bridge from the past to the present',[112] particularly in what Forsyth called 'the moralizing of dogma'.

Its defect, as presented in supranaturalist terms, was that it presented Christ as stripping himself precisely of those qualities of transcendence which make him the revelation of God. The under-lying assumption was that his superhuman attributes must be shed or modified in order for him truly to live within a human frame. The theory was subjected to damaging criticisms from which it has not recovered.[113] Yet still, as Creed recognized,[114] it contains a vital truth, and there have been, and no doubt will be, attempts to reinstate it.[115] Nevertheless, as an exercise in showing how a divine person or semi-divine being or even a heavenly man could 'become' a man or 'experience life as a man' without

[108] For surveys cf. Bruce, op. cit., ch.4; Smedes, op. cit., ch.1; and particularly D. G. Dawe, *The Form of a Servant: A Historical Analysis of the Kenotic Motif*, Westminster Press, Philadelphia 1964.

[109] Notably by G. Thomasius, *Christi Person und Werk*, Erlangen ³1886–8.

[110] Notably by Charles Gore, 'The Holy Spirit and Inspiration', in id. (ed.), *Lux Mundi*, John Murray 1889, pp.313–62; id., *The Incarnation of the Son of God*; id., *Dissertations on Subjects Connected with the Incarnation*, John Murray 1895, pp.69–225; id., *Belief in Christ*. Cf. Forbes Robinson, *The Self-Limitation of the Word of God*; R. L. Ottley, *The Doctrine of the Incarnation*, Methuen 1896; Weston, *The One Christ*; Forsyth, *The Person and Place of Jesus Christ*; Mackintosh, *The Doctrine of the Person of Jesus Christ*.

[111] Cf. N. Gorodetsky, *The Humiliated Christ in Modern Russian Thought*, SPCK 1938, especially pp.128–74 on V. Soloviev, M. M. Tareev and S. N. Bulgakov.

[112] Bethune-Baker, 'Jesus as Both Human and Divine', p.291.

[113] Cf. Temple, *Christus Veritas*, pp.192f.; Baillie, *God was in Christ*, pp.94–8; Ramsey, *From Gore to Temple*, pp.30–43.

[114] J. M. Creed, 'Recent Tendencies in English Theology', in G. K. A. Bell and A. Deissmann (eds.), *Mysterium Christi*, Longmans 1930, p.136; id., *The Divinity of Jesus Christ*, p.79.

[115] E.g. O. C. Quick, *Doctrines of the Creed*, Nisbet 1938, pp.132–9, 178–83; Vincent Taylor, *The Person of Christ in New Testament Teaching*, chs. 19 and 21.

ceasing to be essentially other than a man, I believe it represents a fruitless expenditure of theological ingenuity.

But if it is used, as I think the New Testament uses it, to show how a man, and an utterly humiliated man, could nevertheless *be* the self-expression of the wisdom and the power, the freedom and the triumph, of the love that 'moves the sun and other stars', then it provides a marvellously rich vein for theological exploration. For it declares the profound truth that 'the form of a servant' is not a derogation from or even a modification of the glory of God, but precisely the fullest expression of that glory as love.[116] For of no other omnipotence than that of love could a man riveted in impotence be the supreme exemplification and chief declaration.[117] Equally, 'the chief end of man', his true glory, is by utterly generous obedience to be the transparency of that love, so that there is no 'interference', and nothing of self gets in the way. That is why, from both sides, the emptying is the fulfilling. As Moule puts it, faithfully, I believe, interpreting the New Testament:

> *Kenōsis* actually *is plerōsis*; which means that the human limitations of Jesus are seen as a positive expression of his divinity rather than as a curtailment of it: 'Jesus divinest when thou most art man'.[118]

Taking the complementary phrases in II Cor. 4.4 and 6, 'the glory of Christ, who is the image of God' and 'the glory of God in the face of Jesus Christ', Grillmeier makes the comment: '*God* himself becomes visible in Christ, his image.'[119] And this 'image' language, of which the New Testament is so full, is particularly fruitful. On the one hand, it is essentially 'man' language, being the classic description of Adam's true nature. There is no hint in it of any pressure towards modifying 'the glory of man' – quite the

---

[116] This was the great emphasis of Forsyth, op. cit., pp.313–16, which makes his book a lasting contribution.

[117] Cf. the words of the Collect for Trinity XI: 'O God, who declarest thy almighty power most chiefly in showing mercy and pity . . .'

[118] Moule, 'The Manhood of Jesus in the New Testament', p.98. The quotation is from F. W. H. Myers, *St Paul*, Macmillan 1902, p.16.

[119] Grillmeier, op. cit., p.25. Italics his.

opposite. On the other hand, it is God language. It speaks of *his* 'express image', of *God* making himself visible. It has been well said that the major contribution of Nestorius to Christology was precisely to explicate the *prosōpon*, the face or person, of God in Jesus Christ in terms of *eikōn* or image:[120]

> God dwells in Christ and perfectly reveals himself to men through him. Yet the two *prosōpa* are really one because *both the humanity and the divinity are the image of God.*[121]

One life speaks true both of God and man. For here he is reflected, defined and focused 'as in a son'. The partition between the servants' quarters and the master's part of the house is down. The veil is removed, the heavens opened, there is a point of transfiguration, a dwelling of the *Shekinah* among men, angels ascending and descending upon the Son of Man. In all these picturesque ways the New Testament writers seek to communicate the fact that in Jesus the transcendent has been for them uniquely visible 'from below', the meaning of the process has become translucent, luminous as sacrificial love. Here they have seen a window into God – at first hand: not just the love of human response but God coming through, not *homoioagapé* but *homoagapé*.

Yet the language of 'image' and 'focussing' allows us also to speak of this uniqueness in a way that sees in this man the *concentration* as in a burning-glass (to use Pittenger's phrase again)[122] of 'the true light' that enlightens 'every man'. There has been much discussion as to whether Jesus should properly be called unique in degree or kind.[123] If one had to choose, I should side with those who opt for a 'degree Christology'[124] – however enormous the

[120] As we have just seen, the two terms are already equivalent in II Cor. 4.4,6.
[121] R. A. Greer, 'The Image of God and the Prosopic Union in Nestorius' *Bazaar of Heracleides* in R. A. Norris (ed.), *Lux in Lumine*, p.50. Italics mine.
[122] Pittenger, *The Word Incarnate*, p.167; cf. Macquarrie, *Principles of Christian Theology*, pp.276–9, who sees in Christ 'the focus of being'.
[123] Cf. Hick, 'Christology at the Cross Roads'; Pittenger, *The Word Incarnate*, pp.236–44, and *Christology Reconsidered*, ch.6. I am always tempted at this point to reply with Temple, *Christus Veritas*, p.147: 'Is the difference of kind itself a difference of degree or a difference of kind?'
[124] Hick correctly poses the question whether there can be a 'non-Arian degree Christology', but then seems to imply that all degree Christologies are Arian by definition. This is palpably not true of Pittenger's position.

degree. For to speak of Jesus as different in kind from all other men is to threaten, if not to destroy, his total solidarity with all other men, which we have regarded as unexpendable. Yet the traditional 'liberal' degree Christology has tended to locate the difference by pointing to Jesus as having more of everything than all other men – more love, more insight, more courage, even more suffering. But this proves both too much and too little. No one would deny that there does meet us in the gospels a figure who is incomparably freer, more radically obedient, more compelling in his sheer goodness, than the run of mankind. Yet, as we have seen, we have not the evidence to demonstrate that Jesus was always loving, or even that he was braver in the face of death than Socrates or the Maccabean martyrs. Moreover, this is not the difference to which the New Testament writers are alluding when they make their claims for the uniqueness of Jesus Christ. In speaking of Jesus as God's 'only' Son, it is not his moral qualities they are exalting, but his unrepeatable relationship to the Father. 'According to the flesh', as far as the human story is concerned, he is absolutely one with us, and even as Son he 'does not shrink from calling men his brothers'.[125] Still less should we. The difference here indeed is *merely* one of degree. But 'according to the spirit', in the divine interpretative story, he is from within called to a unique response which is not simply that of the prophet to declare the word of God, but to *be* the word of God, to act and speak as *God for us*.

Van Buren seems to me to get the matter right when he interprets the biblical evidence of Jesus thus:

> This man . . . though fully man and in no sense 'more than a man', is not to be confused with other men. He stood apart from them for the very reason of his solidarity with them: he was the one man who truly existed for others. His calling was to be the one for the many, whereas the calling of all other men is to let him be that for them.[126]

This, to be sure, is a theological judgment, not an extrapolation from history. It demands no more of the history than that the

---

[125] Heb. 2.11.   [126] Van Buren, op. cit., p.54.

credibility gap be not too great. Yet it is saying of Jesus as *the* son of God (and perhaps the New Testament balance is best caught in English by underlining the 'the' and spelling 'son' with a small 's') that 'the structure of his existence', to use John Cobb's term,[127] though *totally* human, is *uniquely* constituted by God's vocation to him to be what none of us is called to be.

This still makes enormous claims in relation to other men which we must seek to clarify in the final chapter. But by way of summary of this chapter let me close with the words of a New Testament scholar whose position I have elsewhere had occasion to criticize:

> We do well to speak of the humanity and the divinity of Jesus. But by his 'humanity' we mean the whole nature of him who was 'made like his brethren in every respect' (Heb. 2.17). The 'divinity' was not half of his nature or a second nature, but was that purpose and activity of God which made the event which happened around him, but also in him and through him, the saving event it was. The divinity of Jesus was the deed of God. The uniqueness of Jesus was the absolute uniqueness of what God did in him.[128]

[127] I am much indebted to his book *The Structure of Christian Existence*, Hodder and Stoughton 1968, and to his article 'A Whiteheadian Christology', and to the trouble he has taken in correspondence to clarify his position to me.

[128] Knox, *The Death of Christ*, p.125.

SEVEN

MAN FOR ALL

The continuing representation

According to the New Testament Jesus is the man of God, the son of God, God for us, precisely as he is not the man for himself, but the man for others, the man for all: he is the representative man, who dies – and lives – for all.[1] He is the universal man, the final man, the man for all space and all time. In this last chapter I want to try to bring together and examine the vast range of issues that are included in this claim.

But first I would say that Christology in the Christian tradition suffers from having been too narrowly rather than too broadly conceived. I touched on this in the opening chapter. It has been confined to Jesus and his person. Its concern has been concentrated either on the timeless relation of this person to the Godhead as a whole or on the narrow span of time delimited as 'the Incarnation'. And the Incarnation has been viewed as a temporary visitation, like the trip of a being from another world, landing, staying for a time and then taking off again after finishing his work – 'Christ's comet' (to use Masefield's title) zooming to earth before receding once more into space (though there is the promise that it will come round again before the end of the world).

Obviously this is a caricature of the 'heavenly' story and a distortion of its meaning. But it can scarcely be disputed that this has been its effect, psychologically, in the popular mind. *The Christ goes out with Jesus.* During the life of Jesus of Nazareth the

[1] II Cor. 5.14f.

divine, mythological story is intertwined inextricably with the human, historical story, interpreting it, clarifying it, and charging it with eternal significance. This heavenly story does not, of course, stop with his death, resurrection and ascension – it continues timelessly beyond the veil – but it ceases at that point to be earthed in 'our' world of secular history. The two tales part, and continue their separate ways. Their intertwining seems to belong to a closed chapter of a fairy-story existence.

The drama of the myth has lost its connection with the ordinary experiences and hopes of human beings now. And so in relation to that existence, the real world for secular man, it is dead. The interpretative story banishes the Christ to other realms of being from those in which people live their daily lives. It thus effectively disincarnates him. The embodiment of the Logos, the clue to the universe as personal which John sees as going on from the beginning, is felt to have ceased rather than been intensified as the meaning of the Christ more and more takes flesh. Altizer's protest is, I believe, at this point correct.[2] Traditional orthodoxy has had the effect, though not the intention, of cutting short the process of incarnation, of the immanence of God with men coming out and coming through *until* he is all in all.

Another way of saying this is that it has conceived the uniqueness of Jesus Christ exclusively rather than inclusively, or, in Dorothee Sölle's terms, that it has only taken seriously half the understanding of Christ the representative to which Jesus' own language points.

We saw in the last chapter how fundamental to Jesus' vocation and how firmly grounded in the gospel tradition is his claim, not indeed to replace God, but to represent him, and that it is this relationship, rather than any divine blood in his veins or peerless human perfection, that constitutes his claim to uniqueness. Yet Jesus is not exclusively the Christ, as if he personally and individually constituted the entire 'Christ-event'.[3] For the New Testa-

[2] Cf. especially his books *The Gospel of Christian Atheism* and *Descent into Hell*. This is not to defend the one-sided and exegetically arbitrary form his protest seems to me to take. I have criticized his position in *Exploration into God*, ch. 2.
[3] This is the important emphasis of John Knox, especially in his book *The Church and the Reality of Christ*, Collins 1962.

ment indeed he is unrepeatable: there is no other foundation. Like God he cannot be replaced, but like God he can – and must – be represented. For just as God is to be seen, known and received in him who represents him, so Christ is to be seen, known and received in those who represent him, whether in the disciples who act in his 'name' or in his nameless brothers. For, in words attested in varying forms in the strongest possible combination of gospel sources (the Markan tradition and its parallels,[4] special Matthew,[5] special Luke[6] and John[7]), 'He who receives you (or, whom I send, or, one of these little ones) receives me, and he who receives me receives not me but him who sent me.'[8] By this identification Jesus makes himself as dependent on them as God has made himself dependent on Jesus. For this is what incarnation means: 'God' is en-manned, represented by man. And the double pattern of representation shows that this is not finished and over with, but a continuing reality.

But, as I have said, there has been a persistent tendency in popular Christianity to equate 'the Incarnation' simply with the thirty years of Jesus' life. Christ is seen as a figure deputed to tell us something and to do something and then go back, with the relationship between God and men transformed in quality but the same in structure. With his mission accomplished, the commission to act in God's name is returned. God has done something irreversible for us, but the self-emptying of God into Christ *has* been reversed. Representation is a temporary office, not an abiding pattern.

Yet in traditional Christian theology the other side has not been

---

[4] Mark 9.37 = Matt. 18.5; Luke 9.48.   [5] Matt. 10.40.
[6] Luke 10.16. Either this or the previous passage may, of course, be Q material unused by the other evangelist, but they are certainly independent of each other.
[7] John 13.20; cf. 5.23; 12.44f.; 20.21. These passages are among those of which Dodd, *Historical Tradition in the Fourth Gospel*, p.349, says: 'The conclusion may be drawn, with the highest degree of probability in such matters, that John is not dependent on the Synoptic Gospels, but is transmitting independently a special form of the common oral tradition.'
[8] For an assessment of the critical probabilities, cf. my article, 'The "Parable" of the Sheep and the Goats', *Twelve New Testament Studies*, pp.88–90; and Dodd, op. cit., pp.343–7. The poetic parallelism and rhythm of the saying may be additional evidence of its being remembered as part of the (reiterated) teaching of Jesus. We may well be hearing here what Jeremias calls the *ipsissima vox* as distinct from the *ipsissima verba* (*New Testament Theology* I, pp.14–29).

the myth goes on —

absent. It is reflected in the myth as the eternal humanity of Christ, the mediator, who ever lives to make intercession for us. Demythologized, this myth of the heavenly world stands for the fact that, spiritually speaking, the representation of God continues. The incognito by which he must be represented by man is not abrogated. God has emptied himself into Christ, and Christ into his fellow men. What the exaltation does is not to cancel the *kenōsis*: it seals the process of identification as the way of God's coming to his identity in men and men in God, which is the Kingdom. The resurrection, too, is not an isolated past event: it is the first-fruits of a continuing presence-by-representation. What Easter Day showed is that the representative of God, the Christ, is not confined to the individual body of Jesus. That indeed dies, like that of every other man (*that* is true whatever *else* one may wish to say about it), and, in the words of the myth, Jesus returns to him who sent him; for he has completed the work he personally has been given to do.[9] But his work is not finished. The Christ lives on[10] – in the lives of those who represent now the human face of God. The *prosōpon*, the face or person, of the Son is henceforth the faces of men and women. The Son of Man is not replaced but represented – as God too is not replaced but represented – by the shared life of the Spirit, which the Fourth Evangelist sees as the *alter ego* of Christ and appropriately names the 'paraclete',[11] the representative in court.[12]

But this community of Holy Spirit, or Christ in the Spirit, is not, again, to be equated simply with the church. For representation implies not interchangeable identity but identification. Never in the New Testament is the church *called* 'the community of Holy Spirit'. It exists to represent, to embody, this transcendental reality of *koinōnia*, by standing where Jesus stood, which is in the way of suffering solidarity – in the 'name' of Christ to share and articulate the anonymity of those who cannot name him but who

[9] John 17.4,13.
[10] Cf. the observations on the difference between 'objective' and 'subjective' immortality in P. N. Hamilton's essay, 'Some Proposals for a Modern Christ-ology', *Christ for Us Today*, pp.172–4; Ford, 'The Resurrection as the Emergence of the Body of Christ'.
[11] John 14.16,26; 15.26; 16.7.   [12] Cf. I John 2.1.

still represent God by their love. For '*whoever* receives . . .'[13] is the representative of God. The 'implicit Christ', the 'greater Christ', to use Sölle's terms, is much, much wider than the church. The vocation of the 'manifest' church (in Tillich's language) is what she calls 'the education of the consciousness' – to 'reflect on, promote and practise the presentation of the faith as a provisional representation of God'.[14]

This introduces the important idea of 'the provisionality of Christ'. Christian theologians have been so concerned to defend 'the finality of Christ' that they have turned this into a static, 'finished' and therefore dead reality. There is indeed a finality, as there is a uniqueness, but it relates to the beginning of the end, as the other relates to the beginning of the many. A representative is one who keeps your place *open*: if he keeps it for ever he is a replacement. The effect of much traditional substitutionary theology is to replace man by Christ who has done it all for us. The great New Testament preposition *hyper*, on behalf of,[15] is narrowed down to *anti*, instead of.[16] Equally, the effect of much radical atheistic theology is to replace God by Christ.[17] This is where Sölle seems to me to have the truth over Altizer. Both fasten, rightly, on the irreversibility of the Incarnation. But the latter sees God as finally emptied by death into Christ: transcendence is negated in total immanence. But, says Sölle, God's 'worldliness' does not mean that he is dissolved into the world:

> if only because the present condition of the world is not so 'God-tinted' as, on such an assumption, it would need to be. God is not immanent in our history, because his identity in this history remains still future.[18]

---

[13] Mark 9.37; cf. Matt. 25.31–46.
[14] Sölle, *Christ the Representative*, p.135.
[15] I Cor. 15.3; I Peter 2.21; 3.18; *et passim*.
[16] In Mark 10.45 par., the sole exception, the *anti pollōn*, is part of the metaphor of ransom; contrast the *hyper pollōn* of Mark 14.24.
[17] Cf. Ogletree, *The 'Death of God' Controversy*; Langdon Gilkey, *Naming the Whirlwind*, Bobbs-Merrill, Indianapolis and New York 1969. But this is not to say that Christ may not still function as 'ultimate' for those to whom 'God' language is dead. Cf. Mark Thomsen. 'The Lordship of Jesus and Secular Theology'. *Religion in Life* XLI, Autumn 1972, pp. 374–83.
[18] Sölle, op. cit., p.147.

Ch holds world open for God

ch + world

What Christ the representative does is to hold God's place open, to enable men to believe and hope in the unrealized transcendent possibilities. He takes responsibility, by suffering love, for the unavailable God. And this in consequence is the provisional task of the church. It is not there to take the place of the world by becoming an alternative to it. For, as Sölle says, 'the Church is not a substitute with which God' (or, we might add, the parish minister) 'consoles himself for the loss of a world slipping from his grasp'.[19] The church exists to hold the world open for God – like Christ on the cross.

This raises the question of how she understands the 'death of God' which features in the sub-title of her book and in whose wake she believes Christology has to be done today. She takes this to be an irreversible fact of our cultural consciousness, though preferring Buber's terms the 'eclipse' or 'absence' of God. The absence of God must be accepted as the *form* of his presence for us[20] – in other words, he can only be represented. The naïve theism in which God is directly present to the religious consciousness and is known by his acts in the world, is finished, though it may not have died. For there is a time-lag. Like others who speak of 'the death of God', she sees this as occurring both at 'the Incarnation' and 'in our time'.

What happened at the Incarnation, if we can so put it, is that God, the power of nature and history, the Logos or principle of the evolutionary process, began to be represented in a new way. The appearance of Jesus marked the emergence of a world 'come of age', whose ordering could no longer be understood on the model of a parent running the universe by direct rule, like 'the Lord' of the Old Testament. This had meant treating man as a minor – ruling, as it were, over his head. Yet the cry for maturity, for responsibility, for a share in the patrimony, had been ringing

[19] Ibid., p.112.
[20] Cf. Ainger on the parable of the Wicked Husbandmen, *Jesus our Contemporary*, pp.30,67: 'In this story the landowner plays a crucial part. It is the absence of the landowner which provides the setting for the whole drama. It gives meaning to the encounter between the servants and the son on the one hand, and the vine-growers on the other. Simply to remove this character from the story would be to destroy the plot.' 'Like the owner, God is neither dead nor simply present.'

in men's ears since the beginning of the species in Adam. And this, for the biblical myth, unlike the Greek myth, was no Promethean rebellion, but the call of the Father, prefigured in the vocation of Israel to the role of son of God. Yet the role was declined and the clock put back again and again. Mankind, as it were, was placed under guardians. But a minor in ward already possesses the inheritance, irrevocably; it is merely that he cannot yet exercise it.[21] But in Jesus, says the Christian gospel, mankind did come of age. For he dared to accept the role of sonship, of standing in God's stead.[22]

Jesus thereby represents a new mutation in the development of spirit, as evolution begins, not merely – as Sir Julian Huxley has expressed it – to become conscious of itself, but through personal responsibility to incarnate God. Put the other way round, henceforth 'God' is to be represented no longer simply as a personified being over man's head, but in and by man and his responsibility.[23] The Logos is personalized (rather than personified or hypostatized, as in the classic versions of Christian theology). God is thereby made dependent upon man and man's response. He can only be stood in for, not seen. His identity is no plainer than the irreplaceability of his friends. It is 'hidden in the adventure of the world's emergence'.[24]

Yet, though there is a decisive change between BC and AD, like any other new leap in the evolutionary process it was not sudden or abrupt. Long prepared for, scarcely recognized or indeed recognizable when it came, it has taken time to come to self-awareness. But the realization is fitfully dawning that 'God' now means, for us, not an invisible being with whom we can have direct communication as it were on the end of a telephone, but

---

[21] Gal. 4.1.

[22] Cf. Ainger, op. cit., pp.61–4, commenting on Mark 2.1–12: 'Throughout his ministry Jesus refused to "make room for God".' 'He stands in the dock . . . with all those . . . who have come to realize that the stewardship of the world has been placed in human hands.'

[23] Cf. Teilhard de Chardin, *Human Energy*, p.110: 'The time has passed in which God could simply impose himself on us from without, as master and owner of the estate. Henceforth the world will only kneel before the organic centre of its evolution.'

[24] Sölle, op. cit., p.147.

that by which he is represented, his surrogate[25] – the power of a love that lives and suffers for others. The heart of what makes the universe 'tick', the mechanism of evolution, is not simply natural selection, eliminating the unfit, but the identification of love redeeming the unfit. That is the way Jesus pioneered, the first representative of the 'new being'. And this henceforth is the meaning for us of living God, or of letting God live us: namely, in Bonhoeffer's phrase, 'participation in the sufferings of God in the secular life'.[26]

This realization has waited upon 'our time' (and the second half of the nineteenth century was crucial for its awareness – however twisted – in men like Hegel, Nietzsche and Blake) because modern science and technology, themselves the products of Christian civilization, have proved the indispensable solvent of the old theism. As long as men could suppose (as even Newton did in assuming that God occasionally adjusted the motions of the planets) that the universe was governed by direct action, the *deus ex machina* was not dead. As long as men could believe that God's hand was to be seen and his visitation felt in natural phenomena (and the crisis of faith provoked by the invention of the lightning conductor was symbolic – for was not this deliberately to insulate the instrument of his wrath?), then recourse to the God of religious immediacy was still available. The meaning of 'the death of God' or, better, the death of theism,[27] is that this consciousness has become impossible for more and more. If men are to believe in God, it can only be 'a-theistically',[28] that is, as he is represented – above all in the irreplaceability of men. This means believing in God politically, in the concern for 'the least of these', and in many other anonymous and indirect ways. And the meaning of

[25] Cf. Norman Pittenger, *The Christian Church as Social Process*, Epworth Press 1971, p.90: 'Whatever a man takes to be binding upon him stands for him as a surrogate or representative of "whatever-it-is" that is ultimate – and this is what we mean when we speak of God'; and id., *Love Looks Deep*, Hodder and Stoughton 1969, p.59: 'God has provided a surrogate of himself as love. That surrogate, or instrumental representative, is another of our own kind.'

[26] Bonhoeffer, *Letters and Papers from Prison*, p.361.

[27] For this distinction I would refer back to *Honest to God*, ch. 2, and *Exploration into God*, chs. 1 and 2.

[28] Cf. Dorothee Sölle, *Atheistisch an Gott glauben*, Olten 1968, ch. 1.

being a Christian is recognizing that this is not the end of faith but precisely *the difference Jesus has made*. He is unique, not for anything exclusive to himself or finished in the past, but, in Teilhard's phrase,[29] as the 'leading shoot' of the next development not only in man but in God.

The finality of Christ and the end of Christianity

I have tried so far to restate, with the help of insights from Dorothee Sölle and Teilhard de Chardin, the heart of what, it seems to me, Christian faith is claiming for the uniqueness and finality of Jesus Christ. But this is to look at things, however broadly, from the Christian centre. How can such a claim be related to taking seriously and humbly the validity of other quite different perspectives? In a pluralistic age is there still any sense in which Christ can be spoken of as the man for *all*? Many Christians, I am sure, find themselves genuinely torn at this point between not being able to deny, without betrayal of deep conviction, that Jesus Christ *for them* remains central and final, in the sense that he gives unity to their whole perspective on life, and yet not being able to assert that this must be so for all, in the sense that this is the *only* true perspective, without which, in traditional terms, men 'cannot be saved'.

We may begin by making some distinctions and clarifications. Clearly today any claim to finality for Christ cannot mean literal finality. As D. T. Niles put it, the finality of Christ means claiming 'not that everything is over, but that he encompasses everything that takes place'.[30] The first Christians – or some of them – may have believed that Jesus Christ did literally portend the end of all things. But just as we have learnt to see that Paul's language about 'the one man Adam' or 'the first Adam' does not imply a literal historical individual at the beginning of the world, so 'the one man Jesus Christ' or 'the last Adam' has different implications for our thinking today about uniqueness and finality. In an evolutionary

---

[29] Pierre Teilhard de Chardin, *The Phenomenon of Man*, Collins 1959, p.160.
[30] D. T. Niles, 'The Christian Claim for the Finality of Christ' in Dow Kirkpatrick (ed.), *The Finality of Christ*, Abingdon Press, Nashville 1966, p.18.

cosmos it is manifestly absurd to believe that there is no further development or truth after the historical character Jesus of Nazareth. In fact this is denied by the New Testament itself, which never attaches finality simply to the historical Jesus. The very point of the *parousia* myth, which exists to say 'You ain't seen nothing yet', is that the finality of Christ lies as much in the future as in the past. The Christ is being fulfilled – in everything.[31] 'The whole fullness' (*pan to plērōma*)[32] is not yet finally 'revealed'. Indeed, the word 'reveal' and the phrase 'the revelation of Jesus Christ'[33] are in the New Testament characteristically reserved[34] not for what we call 'the first coming' but for 'the second'.[35] The historical Jesus is not even the *totus Christus*, let alone the *totum Christi*, the whole of what 'the Christ' means.

Further, if Jesus Christ is *totus deus* – if, that is to say, God has wholly and not merely partially vested himself in Christ – he is, again, not *totum dei*. Jesus Christ does not represent everything of God in the sense that there is no revelation of God outside him. If he is final, it is because ultimately everything is summed up and included in him, not because he is exclusively the expression of God.[36] The Christian who asserts that for him Jesus Christ is the all-embracing principle of interpretation is asserting that there is nothing in his experience that requires any *other* explanation; for everything 'coheres' in him.[37] He makes this judgment – and calls himself a Christian – because he does not find this is true of Buddha and Mohammed, not because he does not find any truth in them. For him Christ represents the definitive revelation of God – and this is a less misleading word than final – because it is inconceivable to him that there could be any higher revelation of

[31] Eph. 1.23. Cf. J. Armitage Robinson, *St Paul's Epistle to the Ephesians*, Macmillan 1903, pp.42–5.

[32] Col. 1.19; 2.9.

[33] I Cor. 1.7; II Thess. 1.7; I Peter 1.7,13.

[34] Cf. F. Gerald Downing, *Has Christianity a Revelation?*, SCM Press 1964, where I think, however, that the thesis is overstated.

[35] The distinction in these terms goes back to Justin (*Apol.* I.52.3; *Dial.* 14.8; etc.). For the development of this polarization, as I see it, out of a single continuous presence and coming, cf. my *Jesus and his Coming*.

[36] Cf. C. F. D. Moule, 'Is Christ Unique?', in id. (ed.), *Faith, Fact and Fantasy*, Fontana Books 1964, ch.4.

[37] Col. 1.17.

God *in human terms* than 'pure, unbounded love'.[38] And he judges
that empirically it is true that no one comes – or has come – to
the *Father*, that is, to God conceived in the intimacy of '*abba*', but
by Jesus Christ.[39] Jeremias is justified in calling this one of the
distinctive marks of Christianity.[40] Certainly it is not true of
Moses or Mohammed, Buddha or Vishna, Confucius or Lao Tzu.

This involves no exaggerated historical claims that Jesus had
everything or was everything – and certainly not that there has
been nothing of truth outside him. There may be many things
that others had that he did not have – and from which Christians
may freely and gratefully learn. And there is no need to deny that
other perspectives may complete, clarify and correct[41] the Christian
one taken in isolation – and therefore distorted. Indeed, there is
every reason from recent discoveries in dialogue[42] to assert and
welcome it. We are increasingly aware of the *necessity* of listening
to the 'more' which is not contained in Jesus. In E. L. Allen's
words:

> We know the manifest Christ only in part, so that we are
> not in a position to define the outlines of the latent Christ.
> The complete Christ, it may be, includes a glory in the latent
> Christ that waits to be recognized and appropriated by those
> who know him only as manifest.[43]

[38] Charles Wesley, 'Love Divine, all loves excelling', *English Hymnal* no. 437;
cf. his 'Come, O thou Traveller unknown' (no. 378): 'Pure, Universal Love
thou art'.

[39] John 14.6.

[40] Jeremias, *The Central Message of the New Testament*, ch. 1; expanded in id.,
The Prayers of Jesus, SCM Press 1967, pp.11–65.

[41] The formula is Reinhold Niebuhr's to describe the relation of grace to
nature (*The Nature and Destiny of Man* II, pp.68,85).

[42] E.g. Klaus Klostermaier's beautiful *Hindu and Christian in Vrindaban*, SCM
Press 1969; cf., among many, Raymond Panikkar, *The Unknown Christ of Hindu-
ism*, Darton, Longman and Todd 1964; M. M. Thomas, *The Acknowledged
Christ of the Indian Renaissance*, SCM Press 1969.

[43] E. L. Allen, *Christianity among the Religions*, Allen and Unwin 1960, p.155,
quoted in Charles Davis, *Christ and the World Religions*, Hodder and Stoughton
1970, pp.131f., who also provides a valuable bibliography of this vast area. Nicholas of Cusa, cardinal, administrator and scholar-mystic, said much the same in
the Middle Ages in his dialogue *Pace Fidei*. He not only pleaded for tolerance of
other faiths but asserted that, since God is unknowable, every faith must add to
the understanding of the mystery: it is important, therefore, to see the unknowa-
bility of God through their eyes too.

But this in turn does not mean that the Christian is driven back on a reduced Christology – of a semi-final revelation of God, of an Arian *avatar* figure, one among many.[44] He can still say of Jesus 'my Lord and my God',[45] 'the way, the truth and the life'[46] for me, without denying that for other men (let alone for other planets) there may be other ways. Nor need he deny, as John V. Taylor has boldly put it,[47] that for the Muslim or Hindu the Christ may have to become a Muslim or Hindu just as he had to become 'a servant of the Jewish people'[48] in order to save Jews. And by 'save Jews' may we not understand, as Will Herberg, the Jew, has suggested, 'take them out of their exclusivism', or, in Paul's words, that 'the purpose of it all was that the blessing of Abraham should in Jesus Christ be extended to the Gentiles'?[49] Herberg quotes another Jew, Franz Rosenzweig, as saying, 'Israel can bring the world to God only through Christianity',[50] and adds:

> The Jew sees Jesus as emerging from Israel and going forth; he sees him from the rear, as it were. The Christian, on the other hand, precisely because he is a Christian, will see Christ as coming toward him, in the fulness of divine grace, to claim, to judge, and to save.[51]

The Christian and the non-Christian will inevitably view Jesus Christ differently. He can be final for one, in a way that he cannot be for the other. For the latter the path home will be by another way. But, as it proved for Gandhi, Jesus may be the way out of his

[44] Cf. Parrinder, *Avatar and Incarnation*.
[45] John 20.28.   [46] John 14.6.
[47] John V. Taylor, *The Primal Vision*, SCM Press 1963, pp.113f.
[48] Rom. 15.8; cf. Paul on his own attitude in I Cor. 9.19–23. It is equally necessary for the Christ to become a 'minister of the *uncircumcision*', if he is to save those outside religion altogether. It is a sign of what Bonhoeffer called 'the religious *a priori*' that the debate about the finality of Christ is so preoccupied with the problems of comparative religion. Cf. among the many books in this area: Fred Brown, *Secular Evangelism*, SCM Press 1970; id., *Faith without Religion*, SCM Press 1971.
[49] Gal 3.14.
[50] Nahum Glatzer (ed.), *Franz Rosenzweig: His Life and Thought*, Farrar, Straus and Young, New York 1953, p.341; quoted by Will Herberg, 'A Jew Looks at Jesus' in Kirkpatrick, *The Finality of Christ*, p.96.
[51] Herberg, op. cit., p.98.

exclusivism. When Jesus himself becomes the cause and centre of exclusivism, we are no longer dealing with Christology but with Jesuology.

The contemporary Christian who has trouble with the finality of Christ may not simply be 'selling out' or stumbling over 'the scandal of particularity'. He may be stumbling over a particular statement of that finality which we are today being forced by the Spirit to see as false. In a symposium entitled *The Finality of Christ*, from which I have already quoted, occur different statements, both, as it happens, by Methodists (here, as elsewhere, the real divisions cut through the middle of us all) of what essentially is meant by claiming finality for Christ. They may sound similar. But the first, I would suggest, is a way of putting it that we must reject (however orthodox it may have appeared – and may still appear – to Catholic and Evangelical alike). The second, if carefully weighed, is, I believe, genuinely inclusive of everything that need be intended by confessing Jesus Christ as Alpha and Omega of all life.

The first takes the form of a question by the late Carl Michalson, which it is clear that he accepts as the right one:

> What can it mean to say that faith in God is so irrevocably dependent upon Jesus of Nazareth that the wisdom communicated in this event makes all other wisdom anachronistic and obsolete, so that subsequent to this event nothing can appear that will supersede it, indeed, so that man needs to look nowhere else for God and God needs to do nothing more, and so that Jesus can be said to have the last word?[52]

The second voice is that of Dow Kirkpatrick, who summarizes the claim to finality for Christ as including the following essential elements:

1. To know Jesus Christ is to know God in a way not available in any other revelation.
2. What is available to be known in Jesus is all that man needs to know about God.

[52] Michalson, 'The Finality of Christ in an Eschatological Perspective' op. cit., pp. 169–70.

3. The whole event of Jesus Christ defines essential human nature. Any man who reaches the true goal of human existence will have done so by approximating to the humanity of Jesus.
4. The above claims are not only made valid, but made available to all men by the unique aliveness of Jesus Christ in man's experience.
5. Man's history is finally judged by its approximation to the nature of God whose nature is revealed in Jesus Christ.[53]

Or, in the words of Bishop Lesslie Newbigin, as he closes his own book of the same title:

> To claim finality for Jesus Christ is not to assert that the majority of men will some day be Christians or to assert that all others will be damned. It is to claim that commitment to him is the way in which men can become truly aligned to the ultimate end for which all things were made.[54]

These claims are high enough in all conscience, but they do not limit the mystery of the Christ to Jesus.

Yet the relation between the 'inclusive' finality of Christ and the 'exclusive' requires more thinking through and more careful statement than Christians either in the age of Christendom or in the heyday of religious imperialism have been inclined – or required – to give it. Schubert Ogden puts it like this:

> The claim 'only in Jesus Christ' must be interpreted to mean, not that God acts to redeem only in the history of Jesus and in no other history, but that the only God who redeems any history – *although he in fact redeems every history* – is the God whose redemptive action is decisively re-presented in the word that Jesus speaks and is.[55]

M. M. Thomas, the Indian Christian, quoting this, adds: 'Probably this is the only form of universalism which can ultimately be called Christian.'[56]

[53] Kirkpatrick, 'Christ and Christianity' op. cit., p.198.
[54] Lesslie Newbigin, *The Finality of Christ*, SCM Press 1969, p.115.
[55] Ogden, *The Reality of God*, p.173. Italics his.
[56] Thomas, *The Acknowledged Christ of the Indian Renaissance*, p.301.

Yet until very recently there has been a much more simplistic way of asserting 'the sovereign rights of the Redeemer' and the saving sufficiency of 'Jesus as Lord', which on the face of it stands closer to the obvious meaning of scripture. To qualify it is to invite the charge of watering down the gospel and cutting the nerve of missionary motive. Yet to claim Jesus Christ as the man for all or 'the religious ultimate'[57] today requires one to face the choice with honesty. Here again, as with the first man a hundred years ago (where the answer to the conservatives seemed so simple), I believe that fresh perspectives are requiring of Christians distinctions to which before they were not compelled.

On the face of it a passage like Acts 4.11f. seems unequivocal:

This Jesus is the stone rejected by the builders which has become the keystone. . . . There is no salvation in anyone else at all, for there is no other name under heaven granted to men, by which we may receive salvation.

Yet the situation before Christians today has parallels with that which Paul faced with regard to Judaism and Mosaic law. Because the law was the supreme embodiment of the will of God, then surely (the conservatives argued) it could never be superseded: Christians must become Jews first. But Paul distinguishes. Of the law as the expression of the revealed character and commands of God he will hear no evil: 'It is holy and just and good.'[58] Indeed he can actually say that the whole purpose of God's act in Jesus is 'that the commandment of the law may find fulfilment in us'.[59] In this sense, therefore, Christ is the end of the law as its goal;[60] and Paul refuses categorically to say that faith annuls the law.[61] Yet elsewhere he uses this very word to say of Christ that he 'annulled the law with its rules and regulations'.[62] For here he is thinking of the law not as the content of the will of God but as an

---

[57] The title of a book by D. T. Rowlingson, *Jesus the Religious Ultimate*, Macmillan, New York 1961.

[58] Rom. 7.12.   [59] Rom. 8.4.

[60] Rom. 10.4.   [61] Rom. 3.31.

[62] Eph. 2.15. I personally believe that Ephesians is Pauline, but whether or not he actually wrote this passage it is entirely in line with his position elsewhere, and it is not, as far as I know, quoted as an un-Pauline feature of the epistle.

exclusive system of salvation. And of the law so regarded he will hear no good. It cannot bring men to the life it intends and demands. Just the opposite: it leads to death.[63] In this sense, therefore, of the law as a way to being right with God, as a system of salvation, Christ is the end not as its goal but its terminus.[64]

It is frequently observed that from the beginning there was a tendency in the church to make Christ into a new law – so that he came to occupy the same position under the new covenant that the law had under the old. This is generally recognized in the field of ethics. Not only is the love commandment of Jesus seen, rightly, as summing up the whole claim of the law,[65] but his moral teaching becomes subtly transformed into a system of code-ethics of which the rubric (as before) is 'do this and live' rather than 'live and do this'.

Not so generally recognized is the way in which Christ comes to take the place of the law as religion. There is indeed a positive sense in which Jesus Christ does represent for the Christian the goal of man's spirit and the fulfilment of God's revelation. For commitment to him *is* 'to be truly aligned to the ultimate end for which all things were made'. There is no other of whom it can be said that to have seen him is to have seen the Father. Not only morally, but in terms of wholeness or salvation, to be found in him is to be found in God. That conviction the Christian cannot abandon without ceasing to be a Christian.

But this is very different from saying that Christianity as a religion is the only true path to salvation. That is to turn Christ into a new and exclusive law. It is to say that everyone has first to become a Christian, as the Judaizers whom Paul fought said that everyone had first to become a Jew.

' "Christianity" has always been a form – perhaps the true form – of "religion",' wrote Bonhoeffer.[66] For 1900 years

[63] Rom. 7.10. He says explicitly in Gal. 3.21 that 'if a law had been given which had power to bestow life, then indeed righteousness would have come from keeping the law'. The sole, but decisive, trouble was that it did not have that power.   [64] Rom. 10.4.   [65] Rom. 13.8–10.
[66] Bonhoeffer, *Letters and Papers from Prison*, p.280. He used the same analogy: 'The Pauline question whether *peritomē* [circumcision] is a condition of justification seems to me in present-day terms to be whether religion is a condition of salvation' (p.281).

Christians have not needed to distinguish, just as it was only the rise of Gentile Christianity that forced Paul to differentiate the two aspects of Judaism. But in our day we are being compelled to distinguish the truth of Christ from the 'form of religion' in which (like the Jews in the law) Christians have seen 'the very shape of knowledge and truth'.[67] For the one is in danger of becoming the enemy of the other. The sole sufficiency of the religion as a system of salvation instead of affirming the universality of Christ may precisely be *preventing* him from becoming the man for all.

If so, as Bonhoeffer warned, 'it means that the foundation is taken away from the whole of what has up to now been our "Christianity".'[68] It involves a radical reassessment of the meaning of mission and the nature of evangelism, which have tended unthinkingly to be equated with drawing men across the line from one religion to another.[69] But, as Parrinder says: 'Conversion is not necessarily changing into another religion, but it is changing into a new life, a life in Christ which is a new creation.'[70]

W. Cantwell Smith in his important book, *The Meaning and End of Religion*, makes the point that it was largely Christians (in the nineteenth century) who created titles like Hindu*ism* and Buddh*ism* and made them into 'religions' such as their devotees have not seen in them.[71] And other Christians (in the twentieth century) have then added that, whereas *these* are 'religions', Christianity is not! Whatever the truth in this (and there is an importance difference between faith and religion – in all religions), it has placed Christians in a disingenuous position. Rather, it would be more honest to say with Panikkar that,

> Christianity welcomes the 'sacrifice' that modern Hinduism

[67] Rom. 2.20.   [68] Bonhoeffer, op. cit., p.280.

[69] This is not the place for making this reassessment, but perhaps I might refer to my very brief discussion of it in *The Difference in Being a Christian Today* and quote just one sentence from it: 'The Church is missionary, not primarily because it is trying to pull people into itself (this is proselytism – whose root meaning is "come to us"), but because it is constantly reaching beyond itself – with the call "Come with us" ' (pp.55f.; cf. pp.53–7).

[70] Parrinder, op. cit., p.276.

[71] W. Cantwell Smith, *The Meaning and End of Religion*, Macmillan, New York 1962, p.61 and the whole of ch.3.

demands from every particular religion. . . . Christ does not belong to Christianity, he only belongs to God.[72]

The finality or universality of Christ is not to be identified with the finality or universality of the Christian religion. In fact it would be nearer the truth to say that Christ is the 'end' of Christianity as he is of Judaism – and that both positively and negatively.

But let me conclude this section by trying to sum up what is the distinctively Christian claim for Jesus. We may revert to our earlier distinction between the *totus Christus* and the *totum Christi*, the *totus deus* and the *totum dei*. We could say that the Christian sees in Jesus the clue to (though not the exclusive embodiment of) the Christ, who in turn is the clue to (though not the exclusive embodiment of) the nature of God *as personal* and the meaning of man's destiny *as love*. *The Christ is God with a human face.* Yet there are other faces of God and other aspects of reality. As Hick has well expressed it:

> No man cometh to the Father – that is, to God as Father – except through the Christ, in whom as Son the love of the Father is fully revealed. But millions of men and women may in Buddhism have come to God as release out of suffering into *Nirvana*; or in Islam to God as holy and sovereign will addressing the Arab peoples through Mohammed; or in Hinduism to God as many-sided source and meaning of life. And further, it may be that Christ (God as personal love) is also present in these other religions, and their several awarenesses of God likewise present to some extent in Christianity.[73]

What the *Christian* claims is that the personal is the category in which to interpret the less than personal, rather than *vice versa*, and that therefore what he sees in Jesus is the clue to the highest and most comprehensive – the light in which to see the rest. Charles Davis points out that the seemingly non-particularist tolerance of Hinduism rests on an equally dogmatic subordination

[72] Panikkar, op. cit., p.20.
[73] John Hick, 'The Reconstruction of Christian Belief', *Theology* LXXIII, September 1970, pp.404f.

of the personal and historical to the non-personal Absolute.[74] At this point we are faced with a final choice, and I call myself a Christian because I am persuaded of the ultimacy of the personal,[75] which for me finds its prism and its promise in Jesus as the Christ.

The scandal of imparticularity

But what has become familiar, in Gerhard Kittel's phrase, as 'the scandal of particularity' is not the only, nor I believe the most powerful, blockage to men seeing Jesus as the man for all. There is what I would venture to call 'the scandal of imparticularity', making it questionable how he can be the man for *any*, let alone for all. The reaction of our contemporaries is much more likely to be summed up in the question: 'But, Lord, when did we see you?'[76] It is the fact that he is not made flesh, made local, and therefore real, with any tangible immediacy that makes the 'death of Christ', even more perhaps than the 'death of God', a reality for our time – and that in a sense far removed from that of traditional Christian piety. He is dead because he is not 'represented'. And the blame for that lies chiefly in his representatives – in lives rather than language. But, since our concern here is Christology, it must be stressed that it lies also in the *logos*, the schema of thought, which should make him present but actually makes him unavailable or remote.

A symptom of this is the way in which Christian theology has come to use the definite article combined with a capital letter, in such phrases as 'the Atonement', 'the Resurrection', 'the Parousia'. This is, by intention, a way of seeking to assert universality, finality – the element of the once and for all. Yet by its very definitiveness it has the effect today of defining Christ out of universal common experience. If I am asked 'Do you believe in the Atonement?' or 'the Resurrection' or 'the Parousia', the questioner expects to elicit my attitude to something Jesus is

[74] Davis, op. cit., p.34. Cf. Panikkar, 'The Ways of West and East', in G. Devine (ed.), *New Dimensions in Religious Experience*, Alba House, New York 1972, pp.69–93, who distinguishes four 'archetypes' of the ultimate: the transcendent transcendence, the immanent transcendence, the transcendent immanence and the immanent immanence.

[75] Cf. the Prologue to my *Exploration into God*.　　　　[76] Matt. 25.31–46.

supposed to have done on the cross, something that is alleged to have happened on 'the third day' or something that may happen at the end of the world. Contrast the effect when you leave out the definite article: 'Do you believe in atonement?', 'Do you believe in resurrection?', 'Do you believe in parousia (presence, or coming)?' I am then being asked whether I take these into account as present realities or possibilities in human experience, of which for the Christian Christ is the energizing centre. There is no doubt in my mind which way of putting it more effectively universalizes the belief. The 'the' of the traditional Christian myth removes the reality of Christ from the kind of present where every eye might in fact see him[77] to the distant past or to the remote future or to 'the divine superworld' where Christ lives in a timeless realm, as unrelated to the continuing course of events as was his pre-existence to the earlier biological process.

It is difficult to state this without appearing to wish to sever the link of Christian truth with history. I hope I have made it sufficiently clear already that this is not my desire or intention. Nothing indeed has less attraction for me than the docetic, Gnostic tendency. As J. Robert Nelson has put it, 'There still abide docetism, Ebionitism and Arianism; and the worst of these is a matter of one's judgment.'[78] But I have little doubt that the most insidious and damaging today is docetism. Rather, what I am querying is the *way* in which the history is represented in the 'second' divine story, which, by giving it definition in certain once-and-for-all moments of 'sacred history', isolates it from continuous relevance to ordinary history.

Let me illustrate this of the Atonement[79] and then apply it to the rest.

There has been no more resounding affirmation of 'the man for

[77] Rev. 1.7.
[78] J. Robert Nelson, 'The Finality of Christ in Perennial Perspective', in Kirkpatrick, *The Finality of Christ*, p.111.
[79] As I explained in the Preface, I have not attempted in this book to treat at a ny length the subject of what is usually distinguished as the 'work' as opposed to the 'person' of Christ. To stress the intimate connection between the two, between incarnation and atonement, has indeed been one of the glories of Anglicanism, with its foot in both Catholic and Reformed camps (cf. the surveys in Smedes, op. cit., ch.2 and Ramsey, op. cit., ch.4). But I would mention also from the Presbyterian tradition: A. D. Galloway, *The Cosmic Christ*, Nisbet 1951;

all' than the noble words in Cranmer's consecration prayer of Christ on the cross 'who made there (by his one oblation of himself once offered) a full, perfect and sufficient sacrifice, oblation, and satisfaction, for the sins of the whole world'. Yet few words today are calculated to serve as more of a blockage to the truth they seek to communicate. Why is this so? It is not merely that the metaphors behind almost all the terms used in the course of Christian history to relate atonement to experience – justification, sanctification, sacrifice, ransom, satisfaction and the rest – are dead. It is more fundamentally, as I said earlier, that the whole notion of a transaction once accomplished for us can no longer be taken as an objective description of a happening in which men can be asked to believe as if it has changed their lives. In the same way, they cannot be expected to see the fall of Adam as describing an objective event which once decisively altered the human condition to the subsequent detriment of all our living. 'The Fall' is a profound mythological representation and interpretation of certain realities of human experience: it is not an event which in itself has changed that experience. The parallel is not exact, since the crucifixion was a historical and datable event in the sense that the Fall was not. But the cosmic myth of redemption which interprets the significance of this history is, in the same way, a profound representation of certain 'new' realities of human experience. Part of what the myth has to represent is the conviction that these realities 'broke through' historically in and as a result of the life, death and resurrection of Jesus Christ. One of its functions, therefore, is to represent the relation of these new realities to this historic event. It does this by showing, as it were, what was going on 'behind' it in the supernatural realm, as, for instance, Paul does when he says of Christ on the cross that he 'disrobed the cosmic powers and triumphed over them'.[80] But the starting-point is the transformation of human relationships – which the transaction of the myth interprets: it is not the transaction which has itself 'saved' the situation.

D. M. Baillie, op. cit., chs. 7 and 8; G. S. Hendry, *The Gospel of the Incarnation*, SCM Press 1959.
   [80] Col. 2.15.

Another way of putting this is to ask, What is the *place* of atonement? The traditional Christian answer has been to say instinctively 'the cross'. I suspect this is less and less a convincing starting-point today (any more than one can begin by ascribing all the ills of the world, including the pain of childbirth, as our grandfathers did, to 'the Fall'). People rightly ask how one man's death two thousand years ago can alter their lives today. The place of atonement is, rather, where atonement actually takes place – namely, where men and women, races, classes and nations are in fact made one, where reconciliation, release, renewal, the reunion of life with life are experienced. This, I believe, must be our starting-point. For this actually happens before men's eyes: the transformation of human relationships does take place, in all sorts of situations. The question for Christian theology is: What is the relation of all this to the Christian 'thing', to the new being in Christ? What is the distinctive or decisive Christian contribution, if any?

I think it is healthy for Christians to be made to expound their doctrine of the atonement from this end rather than from the unassailable, but for most people entirely remote, platform of the cross. What do we mean in terms of actual human experience by saying that 'in Christ' there is perfect (?) freedom, complete (?) release from fear and self, no (?) condemnation, final (?) victory over sin and death, unconditional (?) community, a new act of creation, etc., etc.? How do we make real what the dimension of transcendence adds in this realm, what openness to grace means, or to the prevenient love of God, or to the power and fellowship of the Spirit? It is from 'the power of his resurrection and the fellowship of his sufferings'[81] in the present that the Christian has to start – and then go on to speak of these in secular rather than religious terms.[82] In the process he may – or he may not – be able to refer back to the myth or theories of 'the' Atonement in such a way that men say, 'Oh, *that's* what that meant!'

And the same applies to the other realities given capital letters

[81] Phil. 3.10.
[82] For examples of this approach, cf. Rosemary Haughton, *On Trying to be Human*, Geoffrey Chapman 1966, and *The Transformation of Man*, Geoffrey Chapman 1967.

and prefixed by 'the' Christian tradition. A hundred years ago 'the Creation' was synonymous with a single divine act at the beginning of the world, just as 'the Fall' was synonymous with a single human act a little later. Soon, perhaps, we shall appreciate with Teilhard that 'like the Creation . . . the Incarnation is an act co-extensive with the duration of the world'.[83] Equally, 'the Resurrection', though it breaks through with Jesus as a new possibility of life and freedom in the spirit, is not to be confined to the 'third day' – or 'the last day':[84] the place of resurrection is not 'the place where they laid him' but 'the liberated zone',[85] wherever, in F. W. Robertson's words,[86] 'the resurrection begun makes the resurrection credible'. The Ascension is not a moment in time nor a movement in space, but the assertion of Christ's ascendancy in all the processes, personal and impersonal, conscious and unconscious, that shape the lives of groups and individuals.[87] The Parousia, too, is not a single 'second coming' at the last day, but a continuing dimension of the Incarnation. It speaks of the openness of all history to the pervasive presence, the constant coming, of Christ into every department of life *from now on*,[88] *until* he is all in all.[89]

Yet these myths or doctrines have not on the whole said this – even to Christians. The Body of Christ has not meant *wherever* the Christ takes flesh, 'love's body',[90] but the church, *whether it per-*

---

[83] Teilhard de Chardin, *Science and Christ*, Collins 1968, p.64; cf. Bethune-Baker, *The Way of Modernism*, p.85, 'The whole is Incarnation'.

[84] For a splendid elaboration of this see H. A. Williams, *True Resurrection*, Mitchell Beazley 1972; but cf. his earlier *Jesus and the Resurrection*, Longmans 1951, for the connection which the title implies.

[85] From John Pairman Brown, *The Liberated Zone*, SCM Press 1970.

[86] F. W. Robertson, *Sermons*, Second Series, p.282; quoted by John Baillie, *And the Life Everlasting*, Oxford University Press 1934, p.210.

[87] Cf. my *But that I Can't Believe!*, Fontana Books 1967, ch.16.

[88] Matt. 26.64 = Luke 22.69.

[89] Cf. my *Jesus and his Coming*; also my *Christ Comes In*, Mowbrays 1960; and my *In the End God*.

[90] From Norman O. Brown, *Love's Body*, Vintage Press, New York 1968. Blake saw 'Universal Humanity' as the 'Body of Jesus' (*Jerusalem* 36.55) in which God becomes incarnate. Cf. Sydney Carter, 'Judas and Mary', *In the Present Tense* I, Galliard 1969, p.9:

> The poor of the world
> Are my body, He said,
> To the end of the world they shall be.

forms this its role or not. Confined to the ecclesiastical, 'the extension of the Incarnation' has effectively ceased for the majority of men. This is Altizer's charge, and it is echoed by Barry Wood, when he writes: 'The Christian Church has not only failed to grasp the absolute *totality* of the incarnation; it has actually limited this "incarnating" by identifying *itself* as the body of Christ.'[91] Mooney points out in his interpretation of Teilhard de Chardin's Christology[92] that, so far from equating 'the body of Christ' with the church, he thought of it primarily in its cosmic dimensions, even when speaking of the eucharist.[93] Of course, the New Testament speaks of 'the church which is his body',[94] and I do not need to re-emphasize this here.[95] That is its essence and its glory[96] – which if it fails to be, it fails to be itself. Yet, again, this 'is' must be looked at more carefully if we are not to fall into the trap of simply reversing the proposition and saying that the body of Christ *is* the church. For this is in effect what has happened. Ignatius' formula 'Where Christ is, there is the church'[97] has been turned round to read 'Where the church is, there is Christ'. We should recall the distinction mentioned earlier, and say that the body of Christ 'subsists in' the church (unless indeed it be entirely reprobate), not that it consists of it. Otherwise we shall lose sight of an equally vital New Testament emphasis – a new humanity composed of '*all men* brought to life',[98] where 'there is no question . . . of Greek and Jew, circumcised and uncircumcised (that is, religious and irreligious) . . . but Christ is all, and is in all'.[99] Yet this is scarcely now even thought of as the great secular reality Paul proclaims. And Pentecost with its message of the outpouring

---

[91] Wood, *The Magnificent Frolic*, p.136.

[92] Mooney, op. cit., p.94. See the whole of ch.3, subtitled 'The Body of Christ as a Physical Centre for Mankind and the Material World'.

[93] Cf. Pierre Teilhard de Chardin, *Writings in Time of War*, Collins 1968, p.58: 'Mysterious and vast though the mystical body already be, it does not, accordingly, exhaust the immense and bountiful integrity of the Word made Flesh. Christ has a *cosmic* body that extends throughout the whole universe.' This insight also lay behind Luther's extravagant language about the 'ubiquity' of the body of Christ; cf. Alves, *A Theology of Human Hope*. pp.149f.

[94] Eph. 1.23.

[95] For an elaboration of this cf. my *The Body*, especially ch.3.

[96] Cf. Eph. 5.22–32.　　　　[97] *Ad Smyrn.* 8.2.

[98] I Cor. 15.22.　　　　[99] Col. 3.11.

of the Spirit on 'all mankind'[100] has been celebrated as the birthday of the church.

Still more, 'the Real Presence' has not meant real presence, like the unreserved meeting and communion of two men on a park bench of which Buber speaks:[101] it has been narrowed down not merely to the Holy Communion, but actually to the consecrated elements. The doctrines in capital letters which should have universalized and released the realities 'into all the world' have had the opposite effect. They have disincarnated the Christ from 'common flesh' and banished him from lower-case living. Their effect, though not of course their intention, has been to do the one thing the Fathers most feared: *solvere Christum*,[102] to make him a dissociated personality, with the *divinum* cut off from the *humanum*.

The human form divine

In the same letter of 30 April 1944, Bonhoeffer bequeathed to us two searching questions: 'How do we speak in a "secular" way about God?'[103] and 'Who is Christ for us today?'[104] The two, I believe, are integrally connected: for the worldliness of God is the Christ of *our* flesh. Indeed, the two questions could be rephrased as one: How do we speak of Christ in terms of *this world*? In other words, How do we interpret the cosmic Christ in terms of a Christic cosmos? How do we relate the *totus Christus* to the 'huge and *totally human* hope' of which Teilhard de Chardin spoke as the only body in which the expectation of heaven can be incarnate, and therefore alive, today,[105] to the 'never-satisfied exigency of totality' in man which, says Roger Garaudy the Marxist to Christians, is 'the flesh of your God'.[106] This, of course, is precisely what the myth, the second, divine story is meant to do – to relate this old world to a world made new in the kingdom of God, to the

---

[100] Acts 2.17, in fulfilment of Joel 2.28.
[101] Martin Buber, *Between Man and Man*, Routledge 1947, pp.3f.
[102] Based on the Latin text of I John 4.3.
[103] Bonhoeffer, op. cit., p.280.
[104] Ibid., p.279.
[105] Pierre Teilhard de Chardin, *Le Milieu Divin*, Collins 1960, p.150. Italics his.
[106] Roger Garaudy, *From Anathema to Dialogue*, Collins 1967, pp.82f.

new solidarity of humanity 'in Christ'. Its function is to clarify and interpret the present confused and ambivalent situation by reference to 'the powers of the age to come'. This second, eschatological story deliberately speaks in the unqualified terms of black and white, while history goes on in the grey. But it is still 'about' the same world that the Fall is about. It is affirming Christ not simply as Jesus according to the flesh, nor simply as a being alive in some divine superworld, but as a new corporate reality, at the level of spirit, around us and within – the Christosphere, the Christ-continuum, the divine field or *milieu* illuminated now and shot through with the knowledge that, in Archbishop Michael Ramsey's words: 'God is Christ-like and in him there is no un-Christlikeness at all.'[107]

But in the world there is much un-Christlikeness. The *kosmos* is not the *corpus Christi*. And to speak of Christ in a worldly fashion means what the New Testament describes as 'discerning the body',[108] 'distinguishing'[109] and 'testing'[110] the spirits. And the criterion for this is still the recognition or confession of 'Christ come in the flesh',[111] which, as a recent study of that passage in I John insists,[112] refers not simply to the historical Jesus but to the Christ who is now 'in the world as we are in the world'.[113] Yet he has not yet been 'manifested'.[114] There is no open vision, merely the signs of his appearing, the marks of his cross. Who Christ is for us today remains a matter for discernment, for obedient sensitivity, more for prophecy than philosophy. And above all, 'participation in the Christ', to use the strongly realistic language of the New Testament,[115] is likely today to be under the species of a broken humanity, in the breaking and sharing of our bread to what a seventeenth-century writer[116] called 'God himself in his poor members'. Our image of Christ is unlikely to be that of the *Pantocrator*, the unblinking Christ of the Byzantine dome, sitting serene above the waterfloods. His lordship will be known more in

[107] A. M. Ramsey, *God, Christ and the World*, SCM Press 1969, p.98.
[108] I Cor. 11.29. [109] I Cor. 12.10; I John 4.6.
[110] I John 4.1. [111] I John 4.2f.; cf. II John 7.
[112] Paul S. Minear, 'The Idea of Incarnation in First John', *Interpretation* XXIV, July 1970, pp.291–302.
[113] I John 4.17. [114] I John 3.2.
[115] Cf. I Cor. 1.9; 10.16–21. [116] H. L'Estrange.

the taking of the towel[117] – and by those who take the towel. In Schweitzer's haunting words, which close *The Quest of the Historical Jesus*:

> To those who obey Him, whether they be wise or simple, He will reveal Himself in the toils, the conflicts, the sufferings which they shall pass through in His fellowship, and, as an ineffable mystery, they shall learn in their own experience Who He is.[118]

The question has been posed:

> Is Jesus 'Lord' because we have found and affirmed his unique ability to shape our lives, or is it because he is 'Lord' that we cannot question his power and authority over all men whether they accept it or not?[119]

It has exercised many in the controversy that has raged since Bultmann.[120] It is a chicken-and-egg question. But in the order of knowing rather than being there is no doubt, I think, that in our day, whatever may have been true of other days, Jesus becomes Lord for us *as* we find and affirm his unique ability to shape our lives. We start from experience rather than authority. The question is more likely to ring true in the form, Can you see your humanity given its definition and vindication in Jesus Christ?, rather than, Can you believe in this individual as the Son of God? As Gabriel Moran, a modern Roman Catholic, has put it,

> What distinguishes Christianity is not the belief that a divine being appeared on earth to pronounce the final revealed truths. What Christianity claims is that the Word *has become* flesh and that man is no longer alone before God.[121]

Indeed, men ask what has *a* Christ, an individual God-man, to do with them? Messianism is the most incredible and closed world-view of all. Many, as we said at the beginning, are not looking for

---

[117] John 13.1–17.   [118] Schweitzer, op. cit., p.401.
[119] J. A. Phillips, 'Radical Christology', p.295.
[120] Cf. Schubert M. Ogden, *Christ Without Myth*, Collins 1961.
[121] Gabriel Moran, *Vision and Tactics: Towards an Adult Church*, Search Press 1969, p.48. Italics mine.

a Christ-figure at all – that is a dead category, an expired hope. The very name 'Christ' gets in the way: at its mention men switch off. For he conjures up individual, past, static exclusiveness. As someone put it to me in conversation,

> The Christian thing is not free to speak to me because it is so bogged down: all seems to depend on what I believe about this man – and if I can't, I am cut out of everything.

The way in for many is not through one man. But, as Peter Berger has insisted, the Christ is not to be equated with any one man or name; and he adds:

> If *this* exclusiveness is to be identified with the much-vaunted historical character of Christian faith, then perhaps this particular historical character will have to be left behind in favour of a more ecumenical one.[122]

Jesus is but the clue, the parable, the sign by whom it is possible to recognize the Christ in others. And it was he himself who made it clear that to men in the mass, in the 'nation',[123] the Christ normally comes *incognito*, to those who do not 'see' him and cannot 'name' him. And in the culture of our day this is the usual form of his appearing – an anonymous, elusive, yet strangely recognizable figure.

'Who is Christ for us today?' I have suggested elsewhere[124] that the gospel passages with peculiarly compelling power for our generation are those, like the Sheep and the Goats just alluded to, the walk to Emmaus[125] or the final appearance of Jesus by the lakeside,[126] which 'tell of one who comes unknown and uninvited into the human situation, disclosing himself as the gracious neighbour before he can be recognized as Master and Lord'. In this, as in other respects, our thinking today has, I am convinced, to begin 'from below' and move from immanence to transcendence, from relationships to revelation, from the Son of Man to the Son of God, rather than the other way round. Hence

---

[122] Peter Berger, *A Rumour of Angels*, Allen Lane, The Penguin Press 1970, p.115.
[123] Matt. 25.31–46.   [124] See my *The New Reformation?*, p.36.
[125] Luke 24.13–35.   [126] John 21.1–14.

the categories in which people have recently attempted to convey
the meaning of Christ[127] have been those such as the servant-
lord,[128] the way,[129] the man for others,[130] the victim,[131] the
outsider,[132] the representative,[133] the incognito,[134] even the clown
or harlequin, whose pathos and weakness and irony, as well as
whose gaiety and freedom, 'all begin to make a strange kind of
sense again'.[135] Yet *in* all these he is to be seen as the embodiment
of 'the beyond' – in the midst. Indeed, we should not forget that
Bonhoeffer's now famous phrase 'the man for others' is in answer
to the question 'Who is God?'[136] For unless the dimension of the
transcendent, the unconditional, is visible, however 'brokenly'
(and this seems almost a *sine qua non* for our generation),[137]
there is no Christ at all. Perhaps for this reason the profoundest

[127] For an instructive survey of how those have subtly changed over the
centuries, cf. Morton, *Jesus: Man for Today*.

[128] E. Schweizer, *Lordship and Discipleship*, SCM Press 1960; W. Hamilton,
ch.3; J. Vincent, *Christ and Methodism*, Epworth Press 1965, ch.2; id., *Secular
Christ: A Contemporary Interpretation of Jesus*, Lutterworth Press 1968.

[129] Hamilton, modifying his earlier position, writes to me: 'Not the only way
but the way for some of us. It works better than the idea of Lord.' A. Kee, *The
Way of Transcendence*, Penguin Books 1971, combines this category with remarkably 'absolute' statements about Jesus as its definitive revelation. His most
recent summary is: 'Jesus does not come from beyond, he points beyond.'

[130] Bonhoeffer, op. cit., p.381; Routley, *The Man for Others*.

[131] Ainger, *Jesus our Contemporary*. He also suggests 'the revolutionary', 'the
freedom fighter', 'the justified celebrant', 'the secular believer', as well as the two
next mentioned.

[132] Cf. A. Holl, *Jesus in Bad Company*, Collins 1972.

[133] Sölle, *Christ the Representative*.

[134] P. Dumitriu, *Incognito*, Collins 1964. 'The divine incognito' was, of course,
Kierkegaard's favourite category for speaking of Christ.

[135] Harvey Cox, *Feast of Fools*, Harvard University Press 1969, p.141 and ch.10
generally.

[136] Bonhoeffer, op. cit., p.281.

[137] Hamilton, op. cit., ch. 1. He observes: 'In our time, the list of novels dealing
with the weak or flawed Christ-like figure is an extensive one: Lawrence's *The
Man Who Died*; Spina in Silone's *Bread and Wine*; *Miss Lonelyhearts* by Nathaniel
West; the corporal in Faulkner's *A Fable*; and the description of Christ given by
Jean-Baptiste at the end of Camus' *The Fall*', (p.88). He would no doubt add now
Kazantzakis, *The Last Temptation*; Monterosso, *The Salt of the Earth*; and K.
Langguth, *Jesus Christs*, Harper and Row, New York 1968. Quoting Gorodetzky,
The Humiliated Christ in Modern Russian Thought, Dawe comments, op. cit.,
p.150: 'The kenotic Christologies developed in Russian thought from the end
of the nineteenth century onward spring, not as those in the West from intel-
lectual concerns, but from an ideal deep in culture. The kenotic Christologies of
Orthodoxy illustrate the comment of Nicolas Berdyaev that "Russian religious
philosophy in fact works out the subjects raised by Russian literature".'

Christological statements today are likely to be discerned hidden in fiction or art, in psychology or drama – the equivalents in our age of apocalyptic. Our 'worldly' language may be that of poetry,[138] or politics,[139] or personal relationships.[140] Yet, whether specific 'God'-talk is a help or a hindrance, it is 'transcendence *within* immanence'[141] that we have somehow to articulate and express.

The Christological mystery is centred upon what Blake called 'the human form divine'.[142] And the Christian is distinguished by the divinity he sees in man (which is very different from asserting the divinity *of* man) – the distinctive divinity that wears a human face, with a visage more marred than that of any man. Christology has to start with the flesh of God now, with his *prosōpon* in the present tense. For that is the Christ incarnate today. The clue to this is indeed the Christ who has been and the Christ who will be. For the Christian believes that the present can be understood – and changed – only by radical openness *both* to the past *and* to the future.[143] He accepts the preliminariness of all things, but believes he has already seen what Paul calls a 'preliminary sketch'; just as 'Adam prefigured the man who was to come',[144] so Jesus is the prototype[145] of the new humanity. The trouble is that the preliminary sketch has been taken as the finished portrait, and this

[138] E.g. Werner and Lotte Pelz, *God is No More*, Gollancz 1963; Sebastian Moore, *God is a New Language*, Darton, Longman and Todd 1967; id., *No Exit*, Darton, Longman and Todd 1968; id, 'The Search for the Beginning', in *Christ, Faith and History*.

[139] E.g. Harvey Cox, *The Secular City*, SCM Press 1965, ch. 11; Alves, *A Theology of Human Hope*; J. B. Metz, *Theology of the World*, Search Press 1969; and Sölle, *Atheistisch an Gott glauben*.

[140] E.g. Dumitriu, op. cit., p.432, who speaks amid so much depersonalization of 'that dense and secret undergrowth which is wholly composed of personal events'; see also the works of Rosemary Haughton (note 82 above) and H. A. Williams (note 84 above).

[141] A. C. Bouquet, 'Numinous Uneasiness', *The Modern Churchman*, NS IX, April 1966, p.206 (italics his); quoted by H. A. Williams in James Mitchell (ed.), *The God I Want*, Constable 1967, p.177. The phrase apparently goes back to a remark of Alexander Nairne.

[142] 'The Divine Image', in *Songs of Innocence*, and later *Jerusalem* 27.58. For the contributions and interpretation of Blake in this context cf. J. G. Davies, op. cit., chs. 5 and 7; T. J. J. Altizer, *The Gospel of Christian Atheism*, especially ch. 2; id., *The New Apocalypse: The Radical Christian Vision of William Blake*, Michigan State University 1967, pp.140–7.

[143] Cf. Cox, *The Feast of Fools*. [144] Rom. 5.14. [145] Heb. 6.20; cf. 2.8f.; 10.20.

portrait has been made the subject, the closed subject, of Christology. But the open subject of Christology is the humanity of
God, the glory of man. And it is when this is denied, when the
possibilities of the human scene are measured by something less
than 'the full stature of Christ',[146] that the Christian protest is to be
heard. As a friend of mine has written, 'The point at which
Christology becomes important is the point at which one is
tempted to deny the potential, the latent strength in some intractable human situation, and to write it off in favour of some more
obviously religious concern'.[147]

Christology becomes relevant *in the first instance* not (at any
rate for the vast majority of the human race) because it answers
the request, 'Sir, we should like to see Jesus'.[148] In fact, as Sydney
Carter has put it, the Jesus name-tag (or should one say, price-
tag?) has for many today just the opposite effect:

> The Jesus who
>
> keeps saying 'I am Jesus,
> look at me,
> there is no substitute'
>
> is an impostor, Do not trust
> the Christian cult of
> personality, I came
>
> to turn you on and not
> to turn you off,
> to make you free and not
>
> to tie you up.
> My yoke was easy and
> my burden light
>
> until they made
> salvation copyright, and
> all in the name of Jesus.

[146] Eph. 4.13.
[147] Peter Selby, in an unpublished manuscript 'What Would it Mean to do
Christology?'
[148] John 12.21.

So forget
my name was ever Jesus.
From now on

I am anonymous.[149]

In Barth's graphic phrase, Christology describes 'the way of the Son of God into the far country'.[150] And Christians, if they are to find themselves alongside those today who for the most part are walking *from* Jerusalem,[151] symbolically the place God chose for his 'name' to dwell,[152] must be prepared to share that anonymity.[153] We do Christology not as we are always talking about Jesus or bringing him in,[154] but as we truly respect 'the form of Christ in the world'.[155] For 'the human form divine' is the face of 'the family of man'. The suffering of a single child was for Dostoievsky the test of any theodicy.[156] It is at such a thin point of 'ultimate concern' (Tillich) or 'this-worldly transcendence' (Bonhoeffer), where the human reaches through to God and 'love comes down', that Christology has its place. The Christian indeed cannot look into man without seeing Jesus, and cannot look into Jesus without seeing God. In Bonhoeffer's early words,

Of him alone is it really true that nothing human remained alien to him. Of this man we say, 'This is God for us'.[157]

[149] Sydney Carter, 'Anonymous', *Love More or Less*, Galliard 1971.
[150] CD IV 1, pp.157–210.
[151] Luke 24.13–32.　　　　　　[152] Deut. 12.5; etc.
[153] Cf. Anita Röper, *The Anonymous Christian*, Sheed and Ward, New York 1966, interpreting the thought of Rahner.
[154] Matt. 7.21–23.
[155] Cf. John A. Phillips, *The Form of Christ in the World*.
[156] Cf. Nicolas Berdyaev, *Dostoievsky*, Sheed and Ward 1934, pp.107f.: 'The sufferings of innocent children upset him and hurt his conscience more than anything else, and the justification of their tears was for him the task of all theodicy. . . . Ivan Karamazov challenges his brother: "Suppose that you are building up a fabric of human destiny with the object of making people happy at last and giving them peace and rest, but that in order to do so it is necessary to torture a single tiny baby . . . and to found your building on its tears – would you agree to undertake the building on that condition?" "No, I wouldn't agree," answers Alyosha, and Fyodor Dostoievsky spoke through his mouth.'
[157] Bonhoeffer, *Christology*, p.107. For the complementary truth, cf. Karl Barth, *Christ and Adam: Man and Humanity in Romans 5*, Oliver and Boyd 1956, p.43: 'What is *Christian* is secretly but fundamentally identical with what is *universally*

That remains the distinctively Christian affirmation. And yet, as Bonhoeffer later went on to acknowledge ('though pietists would be shocked by such an idea, but it is true just the same'), 'we live on the next-to-last word and believe on the last, don't we?'[158] In other words, whatever may be the ultimate truth of our belief, living has to be done in the anonymity and secularity of the penultimate, where the one who is 'God for us' *is* a 'bare man', a *psilos anthrōpos*, to be served and loved for his sheer humanity. Only in such concreteness[159] is there true catholicity. Only if the copyright registered once, on behalf of all, in Jesus is not reserved can Christ be the man for all, the human face of God.

human. Nothing in true human nature can ever be alien or irrelevant to the Christian . . . Much in true human nature is unrelated to "religion", but nothing in true human nature is unrelated to the Christian faith.' (Italics his.)

[158] Bonhoeffer, *Letters and Papers from Prison*, p.157. I have here used the translation by Phillips, op. cit., p.187.

[159] Cf. Dorothee Sölle, *The Truth is Concrete*, Search Press 1969. The phrase is Lenin's.

BIBLIOGRAPHY

of principal works cited in the text

Ainger, Geoffrey, *Jesus Our Contemporary*, SCM Press 1967

Altizer, T. J. J., *The Descent into Hell*, Lippincott, Philadelphia 1970

Alves, Rubem, *A Theology of Human Hope*, Corpus Books, Washington DC 1969

Baillie, D. M., *God was in Christ*, Faber 1948

Barbour, R. S., *Traditio-Historical Criticism of the Gospels*, SPCK 1972

Barrett, C. K., *Jesus and the Gospel Tradition*, SPCK 1967

Barth, Karl, *Church Dogmatics*, T. and T. Clark 1936–69
  The Humanity of God, Collins 1961
  Protestant Theology in the Nineteenth Century, SCM Press 1972

Benoit, Pierre, *The Passion and Resurrection of Jesus Christ*, Darton, Longman and Todd 1969

Berger, Peter, *A Rumour of Angels*, Allen Lane, The Penguin Press 1970

Bethune-Baker, J. F., *An Introduction to the Early History of Christian Doctrine*, Methuen 1903

Bettenson, H. (ed.), *Documents of the Faith*, Oxford University Press 1943

Bindley, T. H., *The Oecumenical Documents of the Faith*, ed. F. W. Green, Methuen [4]1950

Bonhoeffer, Dietrich, *Christology*, Fontana Books 1971
  Letters and Papers From Prison, The Enlarged Edition, ed. Eberhard Bethge, SCM Press 1971

Brown, R. E., *Jesus, God and Man*, Geoffrey Chapman 1968

Bruce, A. B., *The Humiliation of Christ*, T. and T. Clark [2]1881

Brunner, E., *The Christian Doctrine of Creation and Redemption*, Lutterworth Press 1952

The Mediator, Lutterworth Press 1934

Buren, Paul van, *The Edges of Language*, SCM Press 1972

The Secular Meaning of the Gospel, SCM Press 1963

Theological Explorations, SCM Press 1968

Cadbury, H. J., *The Peril of Modernizing Jesus*, SPCK 1962

Clark, Neville, *Interpreting the Resurrection*, SCM Press 1967

Cobb, John B., *The Structure of Christian Existence*, Hodder and Stoughton 1968

Creed, J. M., *The Divinity of Jesus Christ*, Fontana Books 1964

Cullmann, Oscar, *The Christology of the New Testament*, SCM Press [2]1963

Dodd, C. H., *The Founder of Christianity*, Collins 1971

Dorner, J. A., *History of the Development of the Doctrine of the Person of Christ*, T. and T. Clark 1863

Downing, F. G., *A Man For Us and a God For Us*, Epworth Press 1968

Dyson, A. O., *Who is Jesus Christ?* SCM Press 1969

Evans, C. F., *Resurrection and the New Testament*, SCM Press 1970

Farrer, Austin, *Saving Belief*, Hodder and Stoughton 1964

Ferré, Nels F. S., *Christ and the Christian*, Collins 1958

Forsyth, P. T., *The Person and Place of Jesus Christ*, Independent Press 1909

Fuller, R. H., *The Foundations of New Testament Christology*, Lutterworth Press 1965

Gogarten, F., *Christ the Crisis*, SCM Press 1970

Gorodetzky, *The Humiliated Christ in Modern Russian Thought*, SPCK 1938

Grensted, L. W., *The Person of Christ*, Nisbet 1933

Grillmeier, A., *Christ in Christian Tradition*, Mowbrays 1965

Hahn, F., *The Titles of Jesus in Christology*, Lutterworth Press 1969

Hick, John, *Biology and the Soul*, Cambridge University Press 1970

'Christology at the Cross Roads', in F. G. Healey (ed.), *Prospect for Theology: Essays in Honour of H. H. Farmer*, Nisbet 1966

Hodgson, Leonard, *For Faith and Freedom*, SCM Press ²1968

Jenkins, David E., *The Glory of Man*, SCM Press 1967

Jeremias, J., *New Testament Theology*, Vol. 1, SCM Press 1971

Johnson, M. D., *The Purpose of the Biblical Genealogies*, Cambridge University Press 1969

Jüng, C. G., *Aion*, Collected Works IX 2, Routledge and Kegan Paul 1959

Kahler, M., *The So-Called Historical Jesus and the Historic, Biblical Christ*, Fortress Press, Philadelphia 1964

Käsemann, Ernst, *Jesus Means Freedom*, SCM Press 1969
The Testament of Jesus, SCM Press 1968

Kaufman, Gordon D., *Systematic Theology: A Historicist Perspective*, Scribner, New York 1968

Keck, Leander E., *A Future for the Historical Jesus*, SCM Press 1972

Kirkpatrick, Dow (ed.), *The Finality of Christ*, Abingdon Press, Nashville 1966

Knox, John, *The Church and the Reality of Christ*, Collins 1963
The Death of Christ, Collins 1959
The Humanity and Divinity of Christ, Cambridge University Press 1968
Jesus, Lord and Christ, Harper and Brothers, New York 1959

Lindars, B., and Smalley, S. S., *Christ and Spirit in the New Testament: Studies in Honour of C. F. D. Moule*, Cambridge University Press 1973

Lloyd, Raymond, 'Cross and Psychosis', *Faith and Freedom* XXIV, Autumn 1970/Spring 1971, pp. 13–29, 67–81

McArthur, H. K. (ed.), *In Search of the Historical Jesus*, SPCK 1970

McIntyre, John, *The Shape of Christology*, SCM Press 1966

Macquarrie, John, *Principles of Christian Theology*, SCM Press 1966

Martin, R. P., *Carmen Christi: Philippians 2.5–11 in Recent Interpretation and in the Setting of Early Christian Worship*, Cambridge University Press 1967

Mascall, E. L., *Christ, the Christian and the Church*, Longmans ²1955
Via Media Longmans ²1956

Matthews, W. R., *The Problem of Christ in the Twentieth Century*, Oxford University Press 1950

Moltmann, Jürgen, *Theology of Hope*, SCM Press 1967

Monod, Jacques, *Chance and Necessity*, Collins 1972

Montefiore, Hugh, *The Epistle to the Hebrews*, A. and C. Black 1964

Mooney, C. F., *Teilhard de Chardin and the Mystery of Christ*, Collins 1966

Moule, C. F. D. (ed.), *The Significance of the Message of the Resurrection for Faith in Jesus Christ*, SCM Press 1968

Newbigin, Lesslie, *The Finality of Christ*, SCM Press 1969

Norris, R. A. (ed.), *Lux in Lumine: Essays to Honor W. Norman Pittenger*, Seabury Press, New York 1966

Ogletree, T. W., *The 'Death of God' Controversy*, SCM Press 1966

Pannenberg, Wolfhart, *Jesus – God and Man*, SCM Press 1968

Parrinder, E. G., *Avatar and Incarnation*, Faber 1970

Pelikan, J. (ed.), *The Finality of Christ in an Age of Universal History*, Lutterworth Press 1965

Perry, Michael, *The Easter Enigma*, Faber 1959

Peursen, Cornelis van, 'Man and Reality—The History of Human Thought', in John Bowden and James Richmond, *A Reader in Contemporary Theology*, SCM Press ²1971

Phillips, John A., 'Radical Christology: Jesus and the Death of God', *Cross Currents* XIX, 1969

Phipps, William A., *Was Jesus Married?*, Harper and Row, New York 1970

Pittenger, W. Norman, *Christology Reconsidered*, SCM Press 1970
  The Word Incarnate, Nisbet 1959
  (ed.), *Christ for Us Today*, SCM Press 1968

Ramsey, A. M., *From Gore to Temple*, Longmans 1960
  God, Christ and the World, SCM Press 1969

Rawlinson, A. E. J., *The New Testament Doctrine of the Christ*, Longmans 1926
  (ed.), *Essays on the Trinity and the Incarnation*, Longmans 1928

Robinson, John A. T., *The Body*, SCM Press 1952
  Christian Freedom in a Permissive Society, SCM Press 1970
  The Difference in Being a Christian Today, Fontana Books 1972
  Exploration into God, SCM Press 1967
  Honest to God, SCM Press 1963

In the End, God, Fontana Books ²1970

Jesus and his Coming, SCM Press 1957

Twelve New Testament Studies, SCM Press 1962

'Was Jesus Mad?', *Faith and Freedom* XXV, Spring 1972, pp. 58–64

and David L. Edwards (eds.), *The Honest to God Debate*, SCM Press 1963

Schleiermacher, F. D. E., *The Christian Faith*, T. and T. Clark 1928

Schoonenberg, Piet, *The Christ*, Sheed and Ward 1972

Schweitzer, Albert, *The Quest of the Historical Jesus*, A. and C. Black 1910

Seeley, Sir John, *Ecce Homo*, Everyman Library, Dent 1970

Sellers, R. V., *The Council of Chalcedon*, SPCK 1953

Siggins, I. D. K., *Martin Luther's Doctrine of Christ*, Yale University Press 1970

Smedes, Louis B., *The Incarnation: Trends in Modern Anglican Thought*, Amsterdam 1953

Sölle, Dorothee, *Christ the Representative*, SCM Press 1967

Stauffer, E., *Jesus and his Story*, SCM Press 1960

Sykes, S. W. and Clayton, J. P., *Christ, Faith and History: Cambridge Studies in Christology*, Cambridge University Press 1972

Taylor, Vincent, *The Person of Christ in New Testament Teaching*, Macmillan 1958

Terry, Francis, 'Cross and Sanity', *Faith and Freedom* XXV, Autumn 1971

Tillich, Paul, *Systematic Theology*, Nisbet, I 1953, II 1957

Vidler, A. R. (ed.), *Soundings*, Cambridge University Press 1962

Weston, Frank, *The One Christ*, Longmans ²1914

Wiles, M. F., *The Making of Christian Doctrine*, Cambridge University Press 1967

Wilson, R. McL., *The Gnostic Problem*, Mowbrays 1958

Wood, Barry, *The Magnificent Frolic*, Westminster Press, Philadelphia 1970

Zahrnt, H., *The Historical Jesus*, Collins 1963

INDEXES

INDEX OF BIBLICAL REFERENCES

INDEX OF NAMES

INDEX OF SUBJECTS